ar

The Politics
of Equality

The Bobbs-Merrill Policy Analysis Series

The Politics
of Equality

Thomas R. Dye

THE BOBBS-MERRILL COMPANY, INC.
Indianapolis · New York

James A. Robinson
The Ohio State University
CONSULTING EDITOR IN POLITICAL SCIENCE

Thomas R. Dye
Florida State University
GENERAL EDITOR, *The Bobbs-Merrill Policy Analysis Series*

Preface

In 1903, the eminent black scholar W. E. B. Du Bois asserted that "the problem of the twentieth century is the problem of the color line."[1] This prophetic statement has been mirrored in the history and politics of American society ever since. *The Politics of Equality* presents an overview and analysis of the role of Negroes in the political life of the nation, and raises provocative questions concerning the capacity of the political system to accommodate black demands for legal and social equality.

In this volume, Professor Thomas R. Dye deals comprehensively with (1) the history of the development of a racially stratified society, (2) the pattern of political and social forces that maintained that society, and (3) the political role of blacks (and whites) in meeting persistent demands for changes in the relative statuses of the two races. The author draws judiciously from the literature of sociology and economics as well as from political science in presenting a balanced view of the American Negroes' long and continuing search for full equality.

Racial inequality in the United States had its origins in the eco-

[1] *The Souls of Black Folks* (New York: Fawcett Publications, 1968), p. 1.

nomic necessities of the slavery period. As Professor Dye indicates, the profitable cultivation of cotton in the pre-revolutionary South depended upon the maintenance of a pool of unpaid black labor. The ringing declaration of human freedom so loudly proclaimed by the heroes of the American Revolution soon gave way to legal and social concepts more in tune with the South's desire to hold black slaves as human chattel. The alleged biological inferiority of the Negro became the rationale for differential treatment in law and practice. Although the disintegration of the slave system in the wake of the Civil War and Reconstruction altered the legal status of blacks fundamentally, these gains were soon lost through restrictive interpretations of the Constitution by the Supreme Court followed by repressive segregation laws enacted by the Southern states. While the burden of law did not weigh as heavily against blacks who migrated to the North, they too confronted discrimination in employment, housing, education, and public accommodations.

It is against this backdrop that Professor Dye unravels the diffuse threads of the politics of race relations in the United States. In rich detail, he analyzes the organized efforts of the black community to dismantle the plethora of discriminatory laws and practices operating against it, and particularly highlights the continuing struggle over public school desegregation. Considerable attention is also given to an assessment of the political techniques employed by black political groups in seeking the fulfillment of their goals. The author carefully analyzes the role of electoral politics, litigation, nonviolent direct action, and political violence. He concludes that while lawsuits, mass protests, and bloc-voting have achieved only limited goals, they offer the best methods for the gradual achievement of equality. He deals lucidly with the "politics of rioting," locating its roots in the frustrations of the black ghetto, but adduces from the available studies that black violence generates greater hostility among whites and is, therefore, "counterproductive to success in the struggle for equality."

Black politics in its diverse forms has largely succeeded in eliminating most forms of legally sanctioned segregation and discrimination. But the attainment of legal rights has not guaranteed the Negro equality in the achievement of economic and social goals such as jobs, education, and housing. The disparity between blacks and whites in this realm has caused a refocusing of the goals of black political effort. It is now

recognized that genuine equality can come only through the con-
vergence of legal and social rights. Consequently, political activity in
the black community is aimed increasingly at a substantial redistribution of social and economic benefits so that the "life chances" of
Negroes and whites become equal. Professor Dye contends that efforts
to accomplish this goal through the political system will be infinitely
more difficult than the struggle over civil rights. For the present, at
least, there appears to be no viable political coalition interested in supporting the massive public efforts required to eliminate segregation and
social disadvantage, and establish the conditions of absolute equality
which Negroes seek.

What then lies ahead for the black man in America? Professor
Dye strikes a note of cautious optimism. He concedes that the pace
with which blacks move toward the "equalization of life chances" will
be slow. But he predicts that heightened group awareness and increased
black voting power will aid in the effort to chip away at the worst
aspects of ghetto life. While such efforts will, in his view, produce only
marginal changes in public policy, the forces of assimilation will nevertheless be at work reducing the social and economic gap between
whites and blacks. This prescription for gradual change will, undoubtedly, meet with varied responses in the black community and among
intellectual elites. Meanwhile, as the debate proceeds, every black man
in the United States will continue to wrestle with the dilemma Du Bois
perceived at the turn of the century: how to be "both a Negro and an
American . . . without having the doors of opportunity closed roughly
in his face."[2]

Paul L. Puryear
Florida State University

---

[2] *Ibid.,* p. 17.

Contents

The Politics
of Equality

chapter 1

History
in Black and White

In 1776 Thomas Jefferson presented to the Second Continental Congress a document asserting, among other things, that "all men are created equal." But when in that same document he proposed that the Continental Congress should specifically condemn slavery and the slave trade, it declined to do so. Thus, the same body of patriots who boldly proclaimed in the Declaration of Independence that all men are created equal simultaneously refused to censure the traffic in black bondage.

White Americans historically have shared the Founding Fathers' ambivalence toward black Americans: while asserting the principle that "all men are created equal," they have been noticeably reluctant to implement this principle in public policy. The evils of slavery, segregation, and racial inequality have long been recognized; yet progress toward their elimination has been slow and halting.

Gunnar Myrdal, writing in 1944, described the American racial dilemma as follows:

> The "American dilemma" . . . is the ever-raging conflict between on the one hand the valuations preserved in the general plane which we shall call the "American Creed," where the American thinks, talks, and acts under the influence of high national and Christian precepts,

and, on the other hand, the valuations on specific planes of individual and group living, where personal and local interests, economic
and social and sexual jealousies, considerations of community
prestige and conformity, group prejudices against particular persons
or types of people, all sorts of miscellaneous wants, impulses, and
habits, dominate his outlook.[1]

The long history of race relations in America has had a profound impact on current public policy.[2]

Slavery as Public Policy

Many of the Founding Fathers meeting at the Constitutional Convention in 1787 sensed an incompatibility between the institution of slavery and the precepts of a free society. Many of their contemporaries,
both in the South and in the North, regarded slave trading as a sordid
business and looked forward to its eventual abolition. However, the
Constitution of 1787 recognized, in fact sanctioned, the practice of
slavery. The Constitution specified that slaveholding states should
count three-fifths of their slaves in determining their population for the
purpose of apportioning representation in the House of Representatives. Thus, while regarding their slaves as property, slaveholders could
simultaneously count them as men for the purpose of representation.
Slavery itself was given specific constitutional protection in Article 4,
Section 2: "No person held to service or labor in one State, under the
laws thereof, escaping into another, shall, in consequence of any law

[1] Gunnar Myrdal, *An American Dilemma: The Negro Problem and Modern
Democracy*, 2 vols. (New York: McGraw-Hill, 1944), I:lxxi.

[2] For histories of black-white relations in America, see John Hope Franklin,
From Slavery to Freedom: A History of American Negroes (New York: Alfred
A. Knopf, 1956); Stanley Elkins, *Slavery* (Chicago: University of Chicago
Press, 1959); August Meier and Elliot Rudwick, *From Plantation to Ghetto*
(New York: Hill and Wang, 1966); and E. Franklin Frazier, *The Negro in the
United States* (New York: Macmillan, 1957). For excellent anthologies on the
Negro in American society, see Talcott Parsons and Kenneth B. Clark, eds.,
The Negro American (Boston: Beacon Press, 1965); and John P. Davis, ed.,
The American Negro Reference Book (Englewood Cliffs, N.J.: Prentice-Hall,
1966).

or regulation therein, be discharged from such service or labor, but shall be delivered up on claim of the party to whom such services or labor may be due." This provision (whose inclusion in the Constitution indicates that slave runaways posed a serious problem even then) constituted an invaluable protection for slaveholders.

The Constitution of 1787 provided for the abolition of the slave trade after 1808. Ironically, the strongest opponents of international slave trade were those most deeply involved in the domestic slave trade. The delegates to the Constitutional Convention from Maryland and Virginia, two states already well supplied with slaves (later they became known as "slave-raising" states), supported proposals for banning the further importation of slaves. Only the lesser-developed Southern states still in need of additional slave labor, particularly South Carolina and Georgia, held out in favor of the slave trade. Since the Southern planters were themselves divided, the framers of the Constitution ultimately compromised by prohibiting all importation of slaves subsequent to 1808, intending that those Southern states needing additional slaves might acquire them during the interim period. Though officially outlawed, transporting slaves from Africa to America continued intermittently for years after 1808.

In 1787 the Southern elites—planters, landowners, and exporters—had been prepared to envision an eventual end to slavery, but by 1820 the intensified worldwide demand for cotton had made slavery essential to the South's economy. The cotton gin, invented in 1793, had soon made cotton America's most valuable export, constituting better than half of the value of all American goods shipped abroad prior to the Civil War. A broad belt of Southern land, ranging in width from five hundred miles in the Carolinas and Georgia to seven hundred miles in the Mississippi Valley was devoted primarily to the cultivation of cotton.

Cotton could not be produced profitably without slave labor. The Border states, whose economies were not dependent upon cotton, sold great numbers of slaves to the cotton states. "Slave raising" was very profitable: a good slave-hand brought three hundred dollars at market in 1820 and more than one thousand dollars in 1860, despite the slave population's increase from a million and a half to nearly four million during the same period.

The white elites of the South, not the masses, had the greatest vested interest in the cotton and slave culture. On the eve of the Civil War no more than four hundred thousand Southern families (approximately one in four) held slaves, most of these averaging only one or two slaves apiece. Though the number of planters owning fifty or more slaves was small (probably no more than six or seven thousand), their views dominated Southern politics.

A significant number of white Americans have always believed in full citizenship for blacks. However, even when sentiment favoring emancipation was voiced, seldom was it accompanied by the conviction that blacks were the equal of whites. Northern elites, mostly merchants and manufacturers, depended upon free labor for their profit margins, and hence they had no direct interest in the abolition of slavery. Radical abolitionism never constituted a respectable social movement even in the North. Northern manufacturers making good profits from Southern trade were apt to view abolitionist activities as a pointless affront to good relations between North and South. The great abolitionist Willam Lloyd Garrison did not have to go to the South to be in danger: he was almost lynched in Boston!

But both Northern and Southern elites realized that control of the West held the key to the nation's future. Northern elites wanted a West composed of small farmers who could produce food and raw materials for the industrial and commercial East while providing a market for Eastern goods. In contrast, Southern planters were fearful of the voting power of a West composed of small farmers, and they wanted Western lands for the expansion of the cotton and slave culture. It was this conflict over the use of Western lands, in fact, that precipitated the Civil War.

Though Lincoln regarded slavery as an evil, he never attacked the institution of slavery in the South; he merely wished to halt its spread to the Western territories. Lincoln summarized his racial views in 1858 as follows:

> I will say, then, that I am not, nor ever have been, in favor of bringing about in any way the social and political equality of the white and black races: that I am not, nor ever have been, in favor of making voters or jurors of negroes, nor qualifying them to hold office, nor to intermarry with white people. . . . there must be the position of supe-

rior and inferior, and I as much as any other man am in favor of having the superior position assigned to the white race.[3]

In this statement Lincoln doubtless reflected accurately the racial views of most of his white contemporaries. Lincoln's great political skill was his determination to subordinate the issue of slavery to that of preserving the Union. Lincoln was no abolitionist. His goal in the war was simply to bring the South back into the Union, thereby restoring orderly government and establishing the principle that the states cannot resist national authority with force. Throughout the war radical Republicans attacked Lincoln as a man who had "no antislavery instincts."

As the war intensified and casualties mounted, Northerners became increasingly embittered toward Southern slave holders. Many Republicans joined the abolitionists in calling for emancipation of the slaves because they saw in this action a means of punishing "the rebels." Lincoln knew too that if he proclaimed that the war was being fought to free the slaves, there would be less danger of foreign intervention. On 22 September 1862 he issued his famous Emancipation Proclamation: "On the 1st day of January, A.D. 1863, all persons held as slaves within any State or designated part of a State the people whereof shall then be in rebellion against the United States shall be then, thenceforward, and forever free." Thus, the Emancipation Proclamation—one of the great steps forward in human freedom in this nation—was a political tactic designed to assist in preserving the Union.

The Legacy of Slavery

The experience of slavery has had a lasting impact on both blacks and whites. Stanley M. Elkins has compared the impact of slavery on the personalities of slaves to that of confinement in Nazi concentration camps on the personalities of inmates.

> The profound personality change created by Nazi internment, as independently reported by a number of psychologists and psychiatrists

[3] Quoted in Richard Hofstadter, *The American Political Tradition* (New York: Alfred A. Knopf, Vintage Edition, 1936), p. 116.

who survived, was toward childishness and total acceptance of the S.S. guards as father figures—a syndrome strikingly similar to the "Sambo" caricature of the Southern slave. Nineteenth century racists readily believe that the "Sambo" personality was simply an inborn racial type. Yet no African anthropological data have ever shown any personality type resembling Sambo; and the concentration camps molded the equivalent personality pattern in a wide variety of Caucasian prisoners. . . . Extending this line of reasoning, psychologists point out that slavery in all of its forms sharply lowered the need for achievement in slaves. . . . Negroes in bondage, stripped of their African heritage, were placed in a completely dependent role. All of their rewards came, not from individual initiative and enterprise, but from absolute obedience—a situation that severely depresses the need for achievement among all peoples.[4]

Thus, slavery rewarded obedience rather than achievement. Compliance, not individual effort, was the characteristic most valued.

Slavery also hindered the development of a strong family life. Since many slave owners separated families on the auction block, the slave household developed a matri-focal (mother-centered) pattern. Later, poverty and ghetto life strengthened the mother-centered tradition. About 25 percent of all nonwhite families, as compared to 9 percent of all white families, have female heads. The black male was the individual most humiliated by slavery and segregation. The submissiveness implied by these institutions was more destructive to the male than the female personality. Keeping the Negro "in his place" usually meant keeping the black *male* in his place.

The psychological consequences of female dominance have been acute. A low level of achievement and social responsibility, a higher level of delinquency, difficulty in distinguishing sexual roles, and inability to postpone gratification—all of these characteristics have been attributed to the instability of black families. The father's role is crucial in the socialization of boys. Overly protective mothers may precipitate overly masculine reactions from their sons, these manifesting themselves in a strong need for power in order to compensate for sexual

[4] Elkins, *Slavery*, pp. 81–82.

identity problems. Problems of this type frequently lead the young Negro toward violent antisocial behavior.[5]

Slavery also had a lasting impact upon Southern whites. De Tocqueville characterized the typical slaveholder as "a haughty and hasty man—irascible, violent, ardent in his desires, impatient of obstacles but easily discouraged if he cannot succeed upon his first attempt." Southern whites were not oblivious to the evils of slavery, and they soon developed a pronounced defensiveness about Southern culture and a suspicion of outsiders incapable of "understanding" their peculiar problem. Moreover, Southern whites felt obliged to protect themselves against the ever-present possibility of slave revolt. The specter of Nat Turner and his sixty black followers killing fifty-seven whites in two days in 1831 haunted Southern society. This fear conditioned otherwise compassionate Southern gentlemen to overlook excessive brutality practiced against blacks. But more importantly the fear of black revolt provided all white men with a common bond, a sense of mutual concern that became the basis of white unity within the South. Fear of the Negro obliged whites to set aside many of their differences in the interest of maintaining white supremacy, for they realized that petty factionalism might enable the blacks to gain an advantage over a divided white community. The basis for one-party politics and Southern unity in national affairs has its roots deeply within the slave period.

Reconstruction:
Experiment in Equality

When the radical Republicans gained control of Congress in 1867, blacks momentarily seemed destined to attain their full rights as United States citizens. Under military rule Southern states adopted new constitutions that awarded the vote and other civil liberties to Negroes. Black men were elected to state legislatures and to the U.S. Congress. In

---

[5] See Daniel P. Moynihan, *The Negro Family: The Case for National Action* (Washington, D.C.: Government Printing Office, 1965); and Lee Rainwater and William L. Yancey, *The Moynihan Report and the Politics of Controversy* (Cambridge, Mass.: MIT Press, 1967).

1865 nearly 10 percent of all federal troops were black. The literacy rate among blacks rose rapidly as hundreds of schools set up by the federal government's Freedmen's Bureau began providing education for ex-slaves.[6]

The first black actually to serve in Congress was Hiram R. Revels of Mississippi, who in 1870 took over the Senate seat previously held by Confederate President Jefferson Davis. In all, twenty-two Southern blacks—twenty Representatives and two Senators—were seated in Congress between 1870 and 1901. All were elected as Republicans; thirteen were former slaves. Many of these men made substantial contributions to Reconstruction policy. Robert B. Elliott, from South Carolina won national fame when he delivered a two-hour speech on behalf of the Civil Rights Act of 1875. The last black Congressman from the South was George H. White of North Carolina, who finally left the Congress in 1901.

The accomplishments of the Reconstruction Congress were considerable. Even before the radical Republicans gained control, the Thirteenth Amendment had become part of the Constitution:

> Neither slavery nor involuntary servitude, except as a punishment for crime whereof the party shall have been duly convicted, shall exist within the United States, or any place subject to their jurisdiction.
>
> Congress shall have power to enforce this article by appropriate legislation.

But it was the Fourteenth and Fifteenth Amendments and the important Civil Rights Act of 1875 which attempted to secure a place in America for the black man equal to that of his white neighbor. The wording of the Fourteenth Amendment was quite explicit:

> No State shall make or enforce any law which shall abridge the privileges or immunities of citizens of the United States; nor shall any State deprive any person of life, liberty, or property, without due process of law; nor deny to any person within its jurisdiction the equal protection of the laws.

The Amendment contains three important clauses: the privileges and

---

[6] For a general history of Reconstruction politics, see C. Vann Woodward's *Reunion and Reaction* (Boston: Little, Brown, 1951); and *The Strange Career of Jim Crow* (New York: Oxford University Press, 1957).

immunities clause, assuring full citizenship for Negroes; the due process clause, assuring that no "person" could be deprived of life, liberty, or property without due process of law; and the equal protection clause, guaranteeing equality before the law. It would be difficult to compose a constitutional amendment that more explicitly guaranteed blacks full equality and citizenship; yet we shall see that the meaning of each of these clauses was distorted and their collective impact nullified by a Supreme Court and a society still unprepared to accept true racial equality.

The Reconstruction Congress also passed the Civil Rights Act of 1875, which declared that all persons were entitled to the full and equal enjoyment of all public accommodations—inns, public conveniences, theaters, and other places of public amusement. Any denial of these accommodations—except for reasons applicable to citizens of every race and color—would subject the violator either to a civil suit for damages or to prosecution for a misdemeanor. In this Act Congress committed the nation to a policy of nondiscrimination in all aspects of public life. But again the Supreme Court stepped in to nullify the policies of the Reconstruction Congress.

Between 1865 and the early 1880s the success of the civil rights movement was reflected in the great prevalence of Negro voting throughout the South, the ascendance of many blacks to federal and state offices, and the almost equal treatment afforded Negroes in theaters, restaurants, hotels, and public transportation facilities. But by 1877 support for Reconstruction policies began to crumble. In what has been described as the "Compromise of 1877," the national government agreed to end military occupation of the South, thereby giving up its efforts to rearrange Southern society and lending tacit approval to white supremacy in that region. In return, the Southern states pledged their support for the Union, accepted national supremacy, and permitted the Republican candidate, Rutherford B. Hayes, to assume the Presidency following the much-disputed election of 1876 in which his opponent, Samuel Tilden, had received a majority of the popular vote.

From the standpoint of judicial process, the collapse of the Reconstruction experiment was effectuated by four Supreme Court decisions: (1) the *Slaughterhouse Cases*[7] of 1873, which nullified the

[7] *Slaughterhouse Cases*, 16 Wallace 36 (1873).

privileges and immunities clause of the Fourteenth Amendment; (2) the *Civil Rights Cases*[8] of 1883, which declared the Civil Rights Act of 1875 unconstitutional; (3) *Hurtado* v. *California,*[9] decided in 1884, which severely restricted the application of the due process clause of the Fourteenth Amendment; and (4) *Plessy* v. *Ferguson*[10] in 1896, which tacitly approved of segregation through the application of a "separate-but-equal" doctrine, thereby nullifying the equal protection clause of the Fourteenth Amendment.

Although neither the plaintiffs nor the defendants were blacks, the *Slaughterhouse Cases* of 1873 involved the privileges and immunities clause of the Fourteenth Amendment. The Louisiana legislature had granted a butchering monopoly by providing that no one could slaughter cattle except on property owned by one favored company. The excluded merchants claimed that the law abridged their privileges and immunities as citizens of the United States to engage in business in the same manner as their fellow citizens. But the Supreme Court, simply by creating an artificial distinction between national citizenship and state citizenship, effectively rendered the privileges and immunities clause a dead letter in the American Constitution. Noting that the first sentence of the Fourteenth Amendment used the phrase "citizens of the United States and of the state wherein they reside," the Court differentiated two types of citizenship—national and state. Since the succeeding sentence forbade state actions abridging the privileges and immunities of "citizens of the United States," the Court concluded that the Fourteenth Amendment did not prohibit a state from abridging the privileges and immunities of "citizens of the states." Following this rather strained interpretation, the majority opinion went on to hold that the protection of life, liberty, and property was a privilege of *state* citizenship that remained within the domain of state governmental actions. The Court very narrowly defined the privileges and immunities of "citizens of the United States" to include only such things as protection while on the high seas or within the jurisdiction of foreign governments and the right to use navigable waters within the United States. Thus, as a citizen of the United States a black could tour Europe

[8] *Civil Rights Cases*, 109 U.S. 3 (1883).

[9] *Hurtado* v. *California*, 110 U.S. 516 (1884).

[10] *Plessy* v. *Ferguson*, 163 U.S. 537 (1896).

or could operate a yacht on navigable American waters without fear of discriminatory state interference; but the state was free to legislate as it pleased concerning his rights to life, liberty, or property! The Court declared that the Fourteenth Amendment should not "radically change the whole theory of relations between the state and federal governments to each other and of both of these governments to the people" or "bring within the power of Congress the entire domain of civil rights heretofore belonging exclusively to the states." Of course, states might be limited by clauses in their own constitutions, but the privileges and immunities clause of the Fourteenth Amendment was to be no hindrance to state action. The 5–4 decision in the *Slaughterhouse Cases* has never been overruled; the "privileges and immunities" of U.S. citizenship are practically nonexistent, and the phrase has little legal significance today.

The Fourteenth Amendment gave Congress the "power to enforce, by appropriate legislation, the provisions of this article," that is, the power to enforce the various rights and privileges guaranteed to the Negro by the language in the Amendment. In 1875 the Reconstruction Congress passed a Civil Rights Act guaranteeing that

> all persons within the jurisdiction of the United States shall be entitled to the full and equal enjoyment of any of the accommodations, advantages, facilities and privileges of inns, public conveyances on land or water, theaters and other places of public amusement . . . applicable alike to citizens of every race and color, regardless of any previous condition of servitude.

The Reconstruction Congress obviously intended to prevent segregation from replacing slavery in the South. But the Supreme Court, in deciding a number of cases resulting from this legislation, declared the 1875 act unconstitutional. In the *Civil Rights Cases* of 1883 the Court held that Congress had no expressed or implied power in the Constitution to pass a law prohibiting discrimination practiced by *private individuals*—in this case, the owners and managers of these accommodations. The Court reasoned that the Fourteenth Amendment failed to give Congress the power to prevent discrimination in privately-owned accommodations because that Amendment referred only to *state* action: "No *State* shall . . . nor shall any *State*. . . ." Consequently, concluded the Court, the obligation of Congress to enforce "the provisions of this article" extended only to discrimination practiced by states, not individuals. (This holding has never been directly over-ruled, although we shall see later that in the Civil Rights Act of 1964 Congress will forbid discrimination by individual proprietors by rely-ing upon its delegated power over interstate commerce.)

In *Hurtado* v. *California,* decided in 1884, the Supreme Court held (with only Justice John Marshall Harlan dissenting) that the Fourteenth Amendment's due process clause did *not* make the Bill of Rights binding upon state governments. It is clear from the debate in the Reconstruction Congress that the Congressmen who wrote the Fourteenth Amendment definitely intended that it should operate to guarantee all individuals in America all of the freedoms of the Bill of Rights against infringement by the states. But the Supreme Court, in deciding that the Fifth Amendment's requirement for grand jury indictment in capital cases did not apply to the states, concluded that the due process clause did not apply to states' observance or non-observance of Bill-of-Rights freedoms. Forty years would pass before the Supreme Court would reverse its thinking and begin the slow, difficult, and painful restoration of the constitutional rights that it tem-porarily disavowed.

By the 1890s most of the former Confederate states had passed laws requiring segregation of the races in public facilities. Typical of these was a Louisiana statute passed in 1890 requiring all railroad companies carrying passengers in the state to "provide equal but separate accommodations for the white and colored," and command-ing that no persons be admitted to coaches other than those "assigned to them on account of the race they belong to." Homer Plessy, who was only one-eighth Negro and looked like a white man, was arrested when he refused to leave a white compartment (Louisiana law re-garded persons of even one-thirty-second Negro extraction as Negroes), and subsequently he brought suit. In 1896 the Supreme Court rejected the plaintiff's plea that segregation laws violated the equal protection clause of the Fourteenth Amendment. Segregation was given judicial approval, and, instead of insuring equality, the equal protection clause was made to bolster the practice of segregation. The majority opinion argued that the phrase "equal protection of the law" did not prevent the enforced *separation* of the races so long as each race was treated equally, an argument that became known as the "separate-but-equal" doctrine. In the words of Justice Henry B. Brown's majority opinion:

> The object of the [Fourteenth] Amendment was undoubtedly to enforce the absolute equality of the two races before the law, but in the nature of things it could not have been intended to abolish distinctions based upon color, or to enforce social, as distinguished from political, equality, or a commingling of the two races upon terms unsatisfactory to either. Laws permitting, and even requiring, their separation in places where they are liable to be brought into contact do not necessarily imply the inferiority of either race to the other. . . .
>
> We consider the underlying fallacy of the plaintiff's argument to consist in the assumption that the enforced separation of the two races stamps the colored race with a badge of inferiority. If this be so, it is not by reason of anything found in the act, but solely because the colored race chooses to put that construction upon it. . . . Legislation is powerless to eradicate racial instincts or to abolish distinctions based upon physical differences, and the attempt to do so can only result in accentuating the difficulties of the present situation. . . . If one race be inferior to the other socially, the Constitution of the United States cannot put them upon the same plane.

To no avail, Justice Harlan again dissented:

> In view of the Constitution, in the eye of the law, there is in this country no superior, dominant, ruling class of citizens. There is no caste here. Our Constitution is color-blind, and neither knows nor tolerates classes among citizens.

The Strange Career of Jim Crow

The withdrawal of federal troops from the South in 1877 did not bring about an immediate change in the status of the black man. Southern blacks voted in large numbers well into the 1880s and 1890s. White political leaders encouraged them to vote and earnestly solicited their support. Blacks held public offices, served on juries, and were represented in local councils, state legislatures, and Congress. Not until the twentieth century did the Negro disappear entirely from these forums. Black men and white men rode the railroads together without partitions separating them, ate in the same restaurants, and sat in the same theaters and waiting rooms. For years Southern states kept Reconstruction legislation forbidding discrimination on the statute books. The federal Civil Rights Act of 1875 encouraged blacks to test their rights in trains, steamboats, hotels, theaters, and other public accommodations.

Certainly we do not mean to suggest that discrimination was nonexistent during this period. On the contrary, many blacks preferred to forego rebuff or insult by deliberately refraining from testing their rights; that is, they simply avoided those hotels or restaurants where they knew they would be unwelcome. Perhaps the most debilitating of all segregation—that in the public schools—appeared immediately after the Civil War under the beneficent sanction of Reconstruction authorities. Yet, segregation in its full-blown Jim Crow form took shape only gradually, and largely as the result of political and economic conflicts that divided Southern whites.

Segregation was closely associated with the rise of Populism in the South. Typically, the Southern gentleman displayed a sense of paternalism and noblesse oblige toward the Negro that was *not* shared by the lower class white. The Southern gentleman's attitude was typified in literary form by the writings of Joel Chandler Harris: his Uncle Remus stories were certainly patronizing and overly sentimentalized, but they never contained any bitterness toward black Americans.

Interestingly, the earliest Southern Populists adopted a style of egalitarianism, and attempted to enlist blacks in a coalition of white and black poor people against their common economic oppressors. Tom Watson, the foremost leader of Southern Populism, once told the two races: "You are made to hate each other because upon that hatred is rested the keystone of the arch of financial despotism which enslaves you both. You are deceived and blinded that you may not see how this race antagonism perpetuates a monetary system which beggars you both." He argued that "the colored tenant . . . is in the same boat with the white tenant, the colored laborer with the white laborer" and that "the accident of color can make no difference in the interests of farmers, croppers, and laborers."[11]

The Populists, however, soon came to realize that their strategy of a white and black coalition of poor farmers was bound to fail since racial prejudice was greatest among the depressed lower economic

[11] Woodward, *Strange Career of Jim Crow*, p. 60.

classes to whom their appeal was directed. These were the classes most subject to deep-rooted fears of the black man. Conservatives, realizing that the Populists had erred in their strategy, were able to discredit the early Populists by fanning the flames of racial hatred, thus driving a wedge between poor blacks and poor whites. Alarmed by the Populists' successes in the 1880s and 1890s, the Conservatives soon raised the cries of "Negro domination" and "white supremacy," thereby galvanizing the racial fears of Southern whites of all classes. The planters of the rich black-belt counties needed an issue—even better, a scapegoat—to oppose the growing influence of white farmers from the mountainous counties. Soon the Populists themselves realized that they would have to disassociate themselves from blacks and adopt the white supremacy position themselves. Thus, the fragile black–poor white partnership of the early Populist days dissolved in a welter of frustration and bitterness. Many white Populists began to shout "nigger" louder than the Conservatives.

By 1906 even Tom Watson had convinced himself that Populism could achieve success only after the Negro was eliminated from Southern politics. In the Georgia gubernatorial race, he swung the Populist vote behind former Conservative Hoke Smith who was running on a platform of white supremacy. C. Vann Woodward writes: "The picture of the Georgia Populist and the reformed Georgia conservative united on a platform of Negrophobia and progressivism was strikingly symbolical of the new era in the South. The campaign made Watson the boss of Georgia politics, but it wrote off Populism as a noble experiment, and launched its leader as one of the outstanding exploiters of endemic Negrophobia."[12]

The first objective of the white supremacy movement was to disenfranchise blacks. The standard devices developed for achieving this feat were the literacy test, the poll tax, the white primary, and various forms of intimidation. In theory, literacy tests were to be applied to all would-be voters, but in practice they were required only of blacks, and few blacks were passed regardless of their degree of literacy. "No matter from what direction one looks at it," commented V. O. Key, Jr., in 1949, "the Southern literacy test is a fraud and nothing more."[13] In 1898 the Supreme Court upheld a Mississippi law requiring voters

[12] *Ibid.*, p. 72.
[13] V. O. Key, Jr., *Southern Politics* (New York: Alfred A. Knopf, 1949), p. 576.

to be able to read, "understand," and "interpret" any section of the Constitution,[14] because on the face of it the law was not discriminatory (even though, in practice, Negro applicants invariably failed to "understand" or to "interpret" the Constitution to the white officials' satisfaction). The Court struck down only the most flagrant violations of the Fifteenth Amendment. For example, an Oklahoma law imposing a literacy test for voting excepted persons whose grandfathers had been qualified voters. In *Guinn* v. *United States* in 1915 the Court held that this "grandfather clause" was an obvious effort to evade the Fifteenth Amendment and was therefore unconstitutional.[15]

While the second device, the poll tax, discouraged citizens of both races from voting, it cut most heavily against blacks. But by far the most effective device for disenfranchisement was the white primary. Prior to the Civil War most Southerners had been Democrats, and because the Republican party had prosecuted the war and had supervised the military occupation of the South, few Southerners had been converted to its ranks. In the South, winning the Democratic nomination for public office was tantamount to election, and hence the only effective political competition was confined to Democratic primaries. White supremacists argued that the Democratic party was a private association and that party elections (i.e., primaries) were private affairs not involving state action. Thus, they contended, racial discrimination in the Democratic primary did not violate the Fifteenth Amendment, which (presumably) applied only to general elections. Much constitutional litigation developed over the white primary, but not until 1944 did the Supreme Court finally outlaw it (see Chapter 2).

Finally, the white supremacy movement was accompanied by a systematic campaign of violence designed to intimidate blacks. The Ku Klux Klan had been born in Reconstruction days as a vigilante effort to curb the military occupation and carpetbagger rule. But in the 1890s the organization was revived to assist in the propagation of rigid segregationist policies. A virtual reign of terror began in the 1890s and extended to the beginning of World War I. A pioneering study of the NAACP appropriately entitled "Thirty Years of Lynching

[14] *Williams* v. *Mississippi*, 170 U.S. 218 (1898).
[15] *Guinn* v. *United States*, 238 U.S. 347 (1915).

in the United States, 1889–1918," lists the names of 3,224 lynch victims. During this period mob attacks against blacks reached their height. For example, Hoke Smith's Georgia gubernatorial victory in 1906 loosed a four-day rule of anarchy in Atlanta during which mobs swept through the city destroying black property, murdering, and lynching.

Following the disenfranchisement of blacks, the white supremacy movement established segregation and discrimination as public policy by the adoption of a large number of Jim Crow laws. Prior to 1900 the only segregation law adopted by the majority of Southern states was that applying to passengers aboard trains. But between 1900 and 1910 a wide assortment of laws were adopted by Southern state legislatures requiring segregation of the races in a variety of situations. State laws segregated the races in street cars, in hospitals, in prisons, in orphanages, in homes for the aged and indigent—even in circuses; local ordinances required separate entrances, exits, ticket windows, toilets, and water fountains for each race. A New Orleans ordinance segregated white and black prostitutes into separate districts. The courts in Atlanta even provided separate Bibles for black witnesses! In 1913 the federal government itself adopted policies that segregated the races in federal office buildings, cafeterias, and restroom facilities.

Social policy followed (indeed, exceeded) public policy. Little signs reading "white only" or "colored" appeared everywhere, with or without the sanction of law. And, of course, blacks were taught in segregated public schools to obey the little signs whether or not they had the force of law. Signs appeared in theaters and waiting rooms and on doorways, stairways, ticket windows, lavatories, water fountains, pails, cups, glasses, and dippers.

Gradually segregation replaced slavery as the social instrument by which Negroes were "kept in their place." The vast majority of blacks remained at the bottom of the social and economic structure of American society. Segregation was supported by a wide variety of social practices and institutions as well as by state law. Segregation shadowed the black man throughout his life—from birth in a segregated hospital, to education in a segregated school, to residence in a segregated neighborhood and employment in a segregated job, to burial in a segregated graveyard.

The Black Response

In 1900 nearly nine-tenths of all blacks in the United States lived in the South, and hence the policy of white supremacy and segregation pursued in the Southern states had a profound impact on black Americans. There appear to have been three distinct types of response by blacks to segregative policies: (1) accommodation and acceptance of a subordinate position in society; (2) participation in the formation of a black protest movement; (3) migration out of the South to avoid some of the consequences of white supremacy.

The foremost black advocate of accommodation to segregation was the well-known black educator Booker T. Washington. Washington enjoyed wide popularity among both white and black Americans. He was an advisor to two Presidents (Theodore Roosevelt and William Howard Taft) and was highly respected by white philanthropists and government officials. In his famous Cotton States' Exposition speech in Atlanta in 1895, Washington assured whites that blacks were prepared to accept a subordinate position in society:

> As we have proved our loyalty to you in the past, in nursing your children, watching by the sick bed of your mothers and fathers, and often following them with tear-dimmed eyes to their graves, so in the future, in our humble way, we shall stand by you. . . . In all things that are purely social we can be as separate as the fingers, yet one as the hand in all things essential to mutual progress.[16]

Booker T. Washington's hopes for black America lay in a program of self-help through education. Washington himself had attended Hampton Institute in Virginia where the curriculum emphasized practical trades for blacks. Washington obtained some white philanthropic support in establishing his own Tuskegee Institute in Tuskegee, Alabama, in 1881. His first students helped build the school. Training at Tuskegee emphasized immediately useful vocations such as farming, preaching, and blacksmithing. Washington urged his students to stay in the South, to acquire land and to build homes, thereby helping to

[16] Quoted in Henry Steele Commager, ed., *The Struggle for Racial Equality: A Documentary Record* (New York: Harper & Row, 1967), p. 19.

eliminate ignorance and poverty among their fellow blacks. One of Tuskegee's outstanding faculty members was George Washington Carver, who researched and developed new uses for Southern crops. Other privately and publicly endowed black colleges were founded that later developed into major universities, including Fisk and Howard (both started by the Freedmen's Bureau), and Atlanta, Hampton, and Southern.

While Washington was urging blacks to make the best of segregation a small band of Negro intellectuals were organizing themselves behind a platform of Negro resistance and protest that would later rewrite American public policy. The leader of this group was W. E. B. Du Bois, a brilliant historian and sociologist at Atlanta University. In 1905 Du Bois and a small group of Negro intellectuals meeting in Niagara Falls, Canada, drew up a black platform intended to "assail the ears" and sear the consciences of white Americans. In rejecting moderation and compromise, the Niagara platform proclaimed: "We refuse to allow the impression to remain that the Negro American assents to inferiority, is submissive under oppression and apologetic before insults." The platform listed the major injustices perpetrated against Negroes since Reconstruction: the loss of voting rights, the imposition of Jim Crow laws and segregated public schools, the denial of equal job opportunities, the permitting of inhumane conditions in Southern prisons, the exclusion of blacks from West Point and Annapolis, and the failure on the part of the federal government to enforce the Fourteenth and Fifteenth Amendments. Out of the Niagara meeting came the idea for a nationwide organization dedicated to fighting for fair treatment of blacks, and on 12 February 1909, the one-hundredth anniversary of Abraham Lincoln's birth, the National Association for the Advancement of Colored People (NAACP) was founded.[17]

Du Bois himself was on the original board of directors of the NAACP. But a majority of the board consisted of white liberals. In the years to follow most of the financial support and policy guidance for the NAACP was provided by whites rather than blacks. However,

[17] See W. E. B. Du Bois, *The Souls of Black Folk* (Chicago: A. C. McClung, 1903); *Black Folk: Then and Now* (New York: Henry Holt, 1939); and *Black Reconstruction* (New York: Harcourt, Brace, 1935).

Du Bois was the NAACP's first director of research and the editor of its magazine, *Crisis*. The NAACP began a long and eventually successful campaign to establish black rights through legal action. Over the years hundreds of court cases were brought at the local, state, and federal court levels on behalf of blacks denied their constitutional rights. The NAACP's first major victory occurred in 1915 when the Supreme Court declared null and void the grandfather clause in the Oklahoma Constitution. When the Ku Klux Klan was reorganized in 1915 and Klan membership increased across the nation, the NAACP attempted to mobilize public opinion against lynchings. The organization undertook the systematic recording of lynchings, floggings, and other acts of racial violence. Whenever a lynching was reported, a black flag bearing the white inscription "A Man Was Lynched Yesterday" was hung outside NAACP headquarters in New York City.

World War I provided an opportunity for restive blacks in the South to escape the worst abuses of white supremacy by migrating en masse to Northern cities. In the years 1916–18, an estimated half-million blacks moved to the North to fill the labor shortage caused by the war effort. Most migrating blacks arrived in Northern big cities only to find more poverty and segregation. But at least they could vote and attend better schools, and were not obliged to step off the sidewalk into the gutter when a white man approached.

The progressive "ghettoization" of the black American—his migration from the rural South to the urban North and his increasing concentration in central-city ghettos—had profound political as well as social implications. The ghetto provided an environment conducive to collective mass action. Later we will describe ghetto life and its implications for politics and public policy in greater detail. But it is important to note here that even as early as 1928, the black residents of Chicago were able to elect one of their own to the House of Representatives. The election of Oscar de Priest, the first Negro congressman from the North, signaled a new turn in American urban politics by announcing to white politicians that the black vote in Northern cities would have to be reckoned with. The black ghettos would soon provide an important element in a new political coalition that was about to take form, namely, the Democratic party of Franklin Delano Roosevelt.

Table 1–1   The Black Population
of the United States, 1790–1970

Year	Total U.S. Population	Negro Population	Negro Population as Percentage of U.S. Total
1970	208,600,000	23,800,000	11.4
1965	193,818,000	20,944,000	10.8
1960	179,323,175	18,871,831	10.5
1950	150,697,361	15,042,286	10.0
1940	131,669,275	12,865,518	9.8
1930	122,775,046	11,891,143	9.7
1920	105,710,620	10,463,131	9.9
1910	91,972,266	9,797,763	10.7
1900	75,944,575	8,833,994	11.6
1890	62,974,714	7,488,676	11.9
1880	50,155,783	6,580,973	13.1
1870	39,818,449	5,392,172	13.5
1860	31,443,321	4,441,830	14.1
1850	23,191,876	3,638,808	15.7
1840	17,069,453	2,873,648	16.8
1830	12,866,020	2,328,642	18.1
1820	9,638,453	1,771,656	18.4
1810	7,239,881	1,377,808	19.0
1800	5,308,483	1,002,037	18.9
1790	3,929,214	757,208	19.3

SOURCE: Computed from data from the following U.S. Bureau of the Census publications: *Historical Statistics of the United States, Colonial Times to 1957*, Series A 59–70, p. 9, and Series A 17–21, p. 8; *1960 Census of Population, Characteristics of Population, U.S. Summary*, Vol. 1, Part 1, Table 44; *Statistical Abstract of the United States, 1966*, Table 9, p. 11. The 1965 data represent estimates published in *Current Population Reports*, Series P–20, No. 155, "Negro Population: March, 1965," p. 1. The data on the Negro population for 1870 have been adjusted by the Bureau of the Census to take account of underenumeration in the Southern states.

But even while ghettoization was laying the foundations for a political coalition of blacks and whites within the Democratic party, it was also providing an environment for a new and different type of mass action—black separatism. In 1914 a self-educated Jamaican named Marcus Garvey founded The Universal Negro Improvement Association, and soon thereafter he initiated a "Back to Africa" crusade. In 1916 Garvey moved his organization to Harlem, and its membership boomed. Donning flamboyant uniforms, Garvey preached the gospel that "black is beautiful," and pledged to "take Africa, to organize it, develop it, arm it and make it the defender of Negroes the world over." Unlike Washington and Du Bois, who had appealed largely to middle-class Negro intellectuals, Garvey found his greatest support among the Negro masses. As many as four million Negroes supported Garvey's movement at its height in the early 1920s. In 1925 Garvey was convicted in federal court for mail fraud and served thirty months in federal prison. Upon his release he was deported to Jamaica, and his movement collapsed. He died in London in 1940. Gunnar Myrdal writes of the Garvey movement: "It tells of a dissatisfaction so deep that it mounts to hopelessness of ever gaining a full life in America. It suggests that the effective method of lining up the American Negroes into a mass movement is a strongly emotional race-chauvinistic protest appeal. Considering the caste conditions under which Negroes live, this is not surprising."[18]

During the 1930s W. E. B. Du Bois also began to doubt the likelihood of materially improving the black man's lot in white America. In 1934 he resigned from the NAACP and began to advocate a policy of "voluntary segregation" for Negroes. Du Bois traveled throughout the world attempting to win support for black independence. He died in 1963, angry and bitter, after having renounced his United States citizenship in favor of Ghanaian citizenship.

Cracks in the Old Regime

The Depression and the New Deal brought about a reorientation in public attitudes toward the underprivileged. With one out of four Americans unemployed and one out of six receiving relief, there was a noticeable weakening of support for Herbert Spencer's view that the poor are "themselves the causes of their own poverty." Blacks benefited economically from the various public-regarding measures of

[18] Myrdal, *An American Dilemma*, II:749.

the New Deal (i.e., provision for social security, old age pensions and relief programs, public housing projects, and minimum wage laws). Blacks also benefited politically because the public-regarding philosophy and humanitarianism of the New Deal created a more favorable climate of opinion for civil rights. The National Labor Relations Act helped blacks to secure a foothold in traditionally white unions when the Congress of Industrial Organizations (CIO) was established on an interracial basis. Black and white workers were integrated into CIO locals and received equal pay for comparable jobs. Because of the Roosevelt Administration's interest in the plight of the poor, blacks began to shift in large numbers from the Republican to the Democratic party. The New Deal, combined with the northward migration and residential segregation of blacks in large cities, stimulated black political sensibilities for the first time since Reconstruction.

Despite Washington's more favorable attitude toward civil rights, only the threat of massive direct action served to bring about the first official step toward desegregation. World War II generated a massive expansion of the defense industry, and again Southern blacks migrated to the North by the hundreds of thousands to find jobs. A. Philip Randolph, organizer of the Brotherhood of Sleeping Car Porters, requested President Roosevelt to issue an executive order barring discrimination against blacks in industries with government contracts. When FDR was slow to act, Randolph threatened to lead a massive march on Washington. Finally, FDR capitulated and on 25 June 1941 issued his famous Executive Order 8802: "There shall be no discrimination in the employment of workers in defense industries or government. . . ."

Harry Truman's commitment to civil rights was strong and uncompromising. As President, he asked Congress for a permanent fair employment practices commission that would end discrimination in private industry—but Congress was unmoved. He then appointed a President's Committee on Civil Rights which, in a hard-hitting report entitled "To Secure These Rights," recommended legislation to end segregation in voting, employment, housing, and other fields. In 1948 President Truman issued an executive order requiring "that there shall be equality of treatment and opportunity for all persons in the armed services without regard to race, color, religion or national origin." Thus, the first massive experiment in desegregation was conducted in

the armed forces. Blacks were immediately integrated at military instal-
lations throughout the country, including the huge army training camps
in the Carolinas and Georgia, the air bases in Alabama and Texas,
and the naval bases in Virginia and Florida. Thousands of black and
white Southerners were forced to reexamine their preconceptions about
each other as they lived and worked together for the first time in an
integrated setting.

At the 1948 Democratic Convention Truman supported a platform that urged the enactment of laws to ensure fair employment
practices and fair elections, the outlawing of the poll tax and a crack-
down on lynchings, the elimination of segregation in interstate transportation, and the establishment of a permanent Civil Rights Commission. Many Southern Democrats deserted their party over the 1948
platform, and in November four Southern states were won by the
"Dixiecrat" candidate, J. Strom Thurmond of South Carolina. But
Truman was elected even without the Dixiecrat vote. In fact, the black
vote in large Northern cities was rapidly becoming even more influential than the vote of Southern whites in Presidential elections. The
massive black migration to Northern big cities (see Table 1–2) had
placed black voters in a crucial position in the large "swing" states
with big blocs of electoral votes. Of course, the South still wielded
sufficient influence in Congress to prevent implementation of the
President's civil rights platform. Yet Truman's decision to put the
prestige of the Presidency behind the struggle for civil rights in itself
represented a historic turning point in civil rights politics.

Table 1–2   Distribution of the Black Population
             in the United States by Region, 1860–1965
             (Figures in percentages)

Region	1965*	1950	1940	1900	1860
Northeast	17.9	13.4	10.6	4.4	3.5
North-Central	20.2	14.8	11.0	5.6	4.1
South	53.6	68.0	77.0	89.7	92.2
West	8.2	3.8	1.3	0.3	0.1

* Data for 1965 are estimates. U.S. Bureau of Census, *Current Population Reports,*
Series P-25, No. 418.

By the 1950s a variety of historical forces were at work undermining the old regime of segregation. The status accorded to blacks had always been recognized as inconsistent with the American liberal tradition of equality of opportunity and equal rights for all. The Depression and the New Deal had made governmental elites more sensitive to the needs of the underprivileged. The massive shift of blacks from the rural South (where their voting rights were rigidly restricted) to the urban North (where their votes were actively solicited) had far-reaching political implications. The strategic location of black voters in the competitive two-party states of the North greatly increased their political leverage. Moreover, the general economic prosperity following World War II contributed to the emergence of a significantly large black middle class that made a strong bid for the respect of the white community. Meanwhile, prosperity in the South enabled that region to end its total dependence on cotton, tobacco, and other crops requiring a large force of menial laborers. Nazi warcrimes warned thinking Americans of the dangers inherent in racism. America's involvement in world affairs sensitized its leaders to outside criticism, and racial segregation was very unpopular in the new emerging nations. Finally, the growing nationalism of American life—the increasing influence of the national news media, the rising mobility of the population, and the expanding powers and functions of the federal government—made difficult the maintenance of a distinctly regional life style, namely, Southern segregation.

chapter 2

The Demise
of Jim Crow

The initial goal in the struggle for equality in America was the elimination of Jim Crow. This required the development of a national civil rights policy to eliminate direct discrimination and segregation in public and private life. First, the discrimination and segregation practiced by governments had to be prohibited, particularly in the areas of voting and public education. Only then could direct discrimination in all segments of American life—in transportation facilities, theaters, parks, stores, restaurants, places of employment, and housing facilities—come under legal attack.

At the outset we must realize that the elimination of Jim Crow, that is, the elimination of direct, lawful discrimination, does not automatically ensure equality. The civil rights policies of the national government do not affect the conditions of equality in America as directly as we might suppose. The recent civil rights gains have not dramatically affected the living conditions of the black masses in either the North or the South. The problem of racial inequality—the very real disparity between blacks and whites in income, health, housing, employment, and education—is more than a problem of direct legal discrimination. Yet certainly the first important step toward equality was the elimination of Jim Crow. And the movement to end legal discrimination laid the foundations for the politics of equality in the future.

The development of a national civil rights policy had its greatest impact on life in the Southern and Border states. In these states, direct discrimination and segregation in schools, buses, restaurants, stores, housing, and employment were expressed public policy. Frequently, even voter discrimination was an acknowledged public policy. Though segregation in Northern and Western states had some legal support, "Northern style" segregation generally resulted from government inaction rather than action. In this chapter we shall describe the development of a national civil rights policy aimed at ending direct, "Southern style" Jim Crow discrimination. We shall describe the long struggle over Southern school desegregation, the fight to end discrimination in voter registration, and the ending of segregation in public accommodations. In the next chapter we will discuss de facto segregation in Northern communities and the broader problems of racial inequality in America.

Linda Brown at the Supreme Court

In practice the Southern states never lived up to the "separate-but-equal" standard of *Plessy* v. *Ferguson:* invariably, they placed the emphasis upon "separate" rather than "equal." Black schools in segregated systems were uniformly inferior to white schools: the buildings were dilapidated and overcrowded, the books antiquated, the equipment woefully inadequate, and the teachers poorly trained. Moreover, black teachers were paid at lower salary scales than their white counterparts, and they were made to teach a curriculum that emphasized trades and commerce rather than preparation for college. Only after World War II did the Supreme Court begin to take judicial notice of these conditions. In two cases prior to 1950 the Court refused to overrule the segregationist doctrine of "separate but equal" but ordered the admission of Negroes to white law schools where comparable Negro facilities were unavailable.[1] In *Sweatt* v. *Painter*,[2] decided in

---

[1] *Missouri ex rel. Gaines* v. *Canada*, 305 U.S. 337 (1938); *Sipuel* v. *University of Oklahoma*, 332 U.S. 631 (1948).

[2] *Sweatt* v. *Painter,* 339 U.S. 629 (1950).

1950, a black student petitioned to enter the all-white University of Texas Law School even though the state had recently established a separate Negro law school. The case was brought to the Court by the NAACP under the able direction of its chief counsel, Thurgood Marshall. Marshall urged the Court specifically to repudiate the separate-but-equal doctrine as applied to public education and to declare that segregation per se violated the Fourteenth Amendment. But the Court was not yet prepared to go that far. The Court ordered the admission of black students to the University of Texas Law School, but on the grounds that Texas had not provided a truly "equal" law school under the doctrine of "separate but equal." The Court stated:

> In terms of number of the faculty, variety of courses and opportunity for specialization, size of the student body, scope of the library, availability of law review and similar activities, the University of Texas Law School is superior. What is more important, the University of Texas Law School possesses to a far greater degree those qualities which are incapable of objective measurement but which make for greatness in a law school. Such qualities, to name but a few, include reputation of the faculty, experience of the administration, position and influence of the alumni, standing in the community, traditions and prestige.

The intriguing question raised by the Court's opinion in *Sweatt* v. *Painter* was whether any segregated school system could possibly meet the Supreme Court's test of true equality, which included such factors as "the reputation of the faculty, experience of the administration, position and influence of the alumni, standing in the community, traditions and prestige." Would not the very fact of racial segregation rule out the possibility of achieving genuine equality of both black and white schools? The *Sweatt* case had a pronounced effect on Southern states and school districts, many of which immediately embarked upon a crash program to improve black schools. During the early 1950s several Southern states actually spent more on black than on white schools while equalizing black and white teacher salaries. The motive was obvious: to prevent federal courts from ordering the admission of black students to white schools because of inferior black facilities.

Leaders of the NAACP were dissatisfied with court decisions that examined the circumstances in each case to determine if separate facilities were really equal. In 1950 the NAACP decided to challenge the Plessy doctrine head-on by pressing for a ruling that, irrespective of the quality of facilities, segregation *itself* constituted inequality within the meaning of the Fourteenth Amendment. In other words, the NAACP wanted a complete reversal of the Court's separate-but-equal interpretation of the Fourteenth Amendment. It was no accident that five cases posing this single issue all found their way to the Supreme Court at approximately the same time. Although the cases had originated in different locales (Kansas, South Carolina, Virginia, Delaware, and the District of Columbia) and under different circumstances, the NAACP had assumed responsibility for the litigation of all of them. In December 1952 and again in December 1953 the five cases[3] were argued together before the Supreme Court. On 17 May 1954 the Court rendered its historic policy decision in *Brown* v. *Board of Education of Topeka*.[4]

Linda Carol Brown was a black pupil attending a segregated elementary school in Topeka, Kansas. Though a white school was located only five blocks from Linda's home, each morning thirty minutes before classes began, she would walk through a railroad yard to catch a bus to take her to the black school several miles away. The school

---

[3] In the South Carolina Case, *Briggs* v. *Elliott*, plaintiffs were Negro children residing in Clarendon County; a lower court had found that the Negro schools were inferior to the white schools and had ordered the defendants to begin immediately to equalize the facilities. But the court denied the plaintiffs admission to the white schools during the equalization program. In the Virginia case, *Davis* v. *County School Board*, the plaintiffs were Negro high school students residing in Prince Edward County. As in the South Carolina case, the lower court had found the Negro school inferior in physical plant, curriculum, and transportation facilities, and had ordered the defendants to proceed to equalize Negro and white schools. But again the lower court had denied the plaintiffs admission to white schools during the equalization program. In the Delaware case, *Gebhart* v. *Belton*, the plaintiffs were Negro children residing in New Castle County. The lower court had found that the Negro schools were inferior with respect to teacher training, pupil-teacher ratios, extracurricular activities, and physical facilities in this case, and had ordered the immediate admission of the Negro pupils to white schools. However, the court had implied that the defendant school district might obtain a reversal of this decree after the equalization of the Negro and white schools had been accomplished. See *Briggs* v. *Elliott*, 89 F. Supp. 529; *Davis* v. *County School Board*, 103 F. Supp. 337; and *Gebhart* v. *Belton*, 87 A. 2d 862.

[4] *Brown* v. *Board of Education of Topeka, Kansas*, 347 U.S. 483 (1954).

that Linda Brown attended was equal in every respect to the nearer white school. The buildings, curricula, qualifications and salaries of teachers, and other tangible factors were all comparable. Nevertheless, Linda's father, Oliver, and the parents of twelve other Negro children filed suit against the Topeka Board of Education in the United States District Court. They were soon joined in their efforts by the NAACP, which recognized that the Brown case presented an opportunity to challenge the doctrine of segregation head-on. The facts prevented the courts from ordering the admission of the Negro because tangible facilities were not equal, and forced the Court to review the doctrine of segregation itself.

In deciding the *Brown* case, the Court consciously subordinated the importance of legal precedent: "In approaching this problem, we cannot turn the clock back to 1868 when the Amendment was adopted, or even to 1896 when *Plessy* v. *Ferguson* was written. We must consider public education in the light of its full development and its present place in American life throughout the Nation. Only in this way can it be determined if segregation in public schools deprives these plaintiffs of the equal protection of the laws." Instead, the Court relied mainly upon social and psychological evidence regarding the contemporary effects of segregation upon black children.

> "Segregation of white and colored children in public schools has a detrimental effect upon the colored children. The impact is greater when it has the sanction of the law; for the policy of separating the races is usually interpreted as denoting the inferiority of the Negro group. A sense of inferiority affects the motivation of a child to learn. Segregation with the sanction of law, therefore, has a tendency to retard the educational and mental development of Negro children and to deprive them of some of the benefits they would receive in a racially integrated school system." Whatever may have been the extent of psychological knowledge at the time of Plessy v. Ferguson, this finding is amply supported by modern authority.

The Court then cited not legal precedents, but studies of sociologists and psychologists regarding the effects of prejudice and discrimination on Negro school children.[5]

[5] The exact citations given in support of this historic finding: "K. B. Clark, 'Effect of Prejudice and Discrimination on Personality Development' (Midcen-

We conclude that in the field of public education the doctrine of "separate but equal" has no place. Separate educational facilities are inherently unequal. Therefore, we hold that the plaintiffs and others similarly situated for whom the actions have been brought are, by reason of the segregation complained of, deprived of the equal protection of the laws guaranteed by the Fourteenth Amendment.[6]

While the reasoning in the historic *Brown* case centered on the effects of segregation in education, the Supreme Court thereafter moved quickly to strike down legal segregation in transportation facilities and in publicly supported parks, playgrounds, golf courses,

---

tury White House Conference on Children and Youth, 1950); Witmer and Kotinsky, 'Personality in the Making' (1952), c. VI; Deutscher and Chein, 'The Psychological Effects of Enforced Segregation: A Survey of Social Science Opinion,' 26 J. Psychol. 259 (1948); Chein, 'What are the Psychological Effects of Segregation Under Conditions of Equal Facilities?' 3 Int. J. Opinion and Attitude Res. 229 (1949); Brameld, 'Educational Costs, in Discrimination and National Welfare' (MacIver, ed., 1949), 44–48; Frazier, 'The Negro in the United States' (1949), 674–681. And see generally Myrdal, An American Dilemma (1944)."

[6] The Court felt constrained to write a separate opinion in order to strike down segregation in the public schools of the District of Columbia. Since the reasoning in the *Brown* case was based on the equal protection clause of the Fourteenth Amendment, which applies only to the states and not to Congress (which governs the District of Columbia), the Court could hardly use this clause as justification for outlawing segregation in the District. But, equally, the Court could hardly afford to ban segregation in the states while permitting it to continue in the nation's capital. Ultimately the Court based its decision to eliminate school segregation in the District of Columbia upon the due process clause of the Fifth Amendment, which applies specifically to Congress. The Court reasoned that "the concepts of equal protection and due process, both stemming from our American ideal of fairness, are not mutually exclusive. . . . . We do not imply that the two are always interchangeable phrases. But . . . liberty under law extends to the full range of conduct that the individual is free to pursue, and it cannot be restricted except for a proper governmental objective. Segregation in public education is not reasonably related to any proper governmental objective, and thus it imposes on Negro children of the District of Columbia a burden that constitutes an arbitrary deprivation of their liberty in violation of the Due Process Clause.

"In view of our decision that the Constitution prohibits the states from maintaining racially segregated public schools, it would be unthinkable that the same Constitution would impose a lesser duty on the Federal Government." *Bolling* v. *Sharpe*, 347 U.S. 497 (1954).

and bathing beaches. The *Brown* case became the precedent for declaring unconstitutional any segregation of the races enforced, maintained, or supported by state law or actions.

The full significance of the Court's decision in the *Brown* case
can hardly be overestimated. In fact, more than any other single event,
the decision inspired the social and political movement known as the
"Negro revolution." The decision raised the aspirations and expectations of black Americans. It gave legitimacy to their rejection of
second-class citizenship. It galvanized mass political action on behalf of
equality in both public and private life. When in 1896 the Court had
declined to eliminate racial segregation on railroad cars in Louisiana,
it had lent constitutional legitimacy to white supremacy, thereby en-
couraging the adoption of segregationist policies in many areas of
Southern life. In 1954, the Court was again stimulating major de-
parture in public policy. Notes Daniel M. Berman:

> The Plessy doctrine pointed the way to a racially segregated society,
> and the Brown decision to a society devoid of racial discrimination.
> . . . Accordingly, if judicial lawmaking was involved in 1954, it was
> likewise involved fifty-eight years earlier. It may follow that those who
> attack the Brown decision as an intrusion of the judiciary into the
> policy-making process either lack sufficient understanding of the
> Court's historic role or else are merely expressing their substantive
> disagreement with the school segregation decision.[7]

Resistance as Public Policy

In declaring segregation in public schools unconstitutional, the Supreme
Court had spoken forcefully. Article VI of the Constitution declares
that the words of that document are the "supreme law of the land . . .
anything in the constitution or laws of any State to the contrary not-
withstanding." Thus, from a constitutional viewpoint any state-sup-
ported segregation of the races in public schools after 1954 was prohibited; but from a political viewpoint the battle over segregation had just
begun. Though the federal courts' policy was consistently to forbid
segregation wherever it was found in the public schools, neither the

[7] Daniel M. Berman, *It Is So Ordered* (New York: W. W. Norton, 1966), p. 128.

President nor Congress spoke out in support of this policy. Segregation—however unconstitutional—would inevitably remain a part of American life until sufficient political power was mobilized to end it. Because of the American federal system's emphasis on separation of powers, the Supreme Court has little force at its disposal to implement its rulings. Congress, the President, state governors and legislatures— all of these have more powers of enforcement than the federal judiciary. Thus, the Supreme Court must rely heavily on other branches of the federal government, on the states, or on private individuals and organizations to effectuate its rulings.

In 1954 the practice of segregation was widespread and deeply ingrained in American life. Seventeen states required segregation of the races in public schools:

Alabama	North Carolina	Delaware
Arkansas	South Carolina	Kentucky
Florida	Tennessee	Maryland
Georgia	Texas	Missouri
Louisiana	Virginia	Oklahoma
Mississippi	West Virginia	

Four other states (Arizona, Kansas, New Mexico, and Wyoming) authorized segregation upon the option of local school boards. Congress itself had authorized segregation in the public schools of the District of Columbia.

Thus, in forbidding public school segregation, the Supreme Court was striking down the laws of twenty-one states and the District of Columbia. Such a far-reaching policy was bound to meet with difficulties in implementation. In 1955 the Court called the parties to the *Brown* case back to discuss "the question of relief for Brown and others similarly situated," that is, to discuss means of implementing its ruling. The NAACP strongly urged the Court to issue an order requiring immediate nationwide desegregation; attorneys for the Southern states argued for a "go slow" approach to desegregation. Attorney General Herbert Brownell and Solicitor General Simon E. Sobeloff, representing the Eisenhower Administration, supported the "go slow" approach. On 31 May 1955, more than a year after the original *Brown* ruling, the Supreme Court delivered its implementation decision:[8]

[8] *Brown* v. *Board of Education of Topeka*, 349 U.S. 294 (1955).

Full implementation of these constitutional principles may require solution of varied local school problems. School authorities have the primary responsibility for elucidating, assessing, and solving these problems; courts will have to consider whether the action of school authorities constitutes good faith implementation of the governing constitutional principles. . . .

In fashioning and effectuating the decrees, the courts will be guided by equitable principles. Traditionally, equity has been characterized by a practical flexibility in shaping its remedies and by a facility for adjusting and reconciling public and private needs. . . .

While giving weight to these public and private considerations, the courts will require that the defendants make a prompt and reasonable start toward full compliance with our May 17, 1954, ruling. Once such a start has been made, the courts may find that additional time is necessary to carry out the ruling in an effective manner. The burden rests upon the defendants to establish that such time is necessary in the public interest and is consistent with good faith compliance at the earliest practicable date. To that end, the courts may consider problems related to administration, arising from the physical condition of the school plant, the school transportation system, personnel, revision of the school districts and attendance areas into compact units to achieve a system of determining admission to the public schools on a nonracial basis, and revision of local laws and regulations which may be necessary in solving the foregoing problems. . . .

. . . the District Courts [shall] enter such orders and decrees consistent with this opinion as are necessary and proper to admit to public schools on a racially nondiscriminatory basis with all deliberate speed the parties to these cases.

This decision represented a serious setback for the NAACP, which had urged immediate and complete desegregation. The Court had assigned the responsibility for implementation to the local school authorities, which were to be supervised by the federal district courts. The local authorities were required only to make a "prompt and reasonable start toward full compliance." Once a "start" had been made, delays in desegregation were authorized if "necessary in the public interest and . . . consistent with good faith compliance at the earliest practicable date." In determining what was "practicable," federal courts were advised to consider a variety of "problems." Finally, in summarizing its decision, the Court employed the phrase "with all deliberate speed," creating something of a paradox: as an adjective modifying "speed," "deliberate" connoted slowness.[9]

The Supreme Court's 1955 implementation decision paved the way for more than a decade's successful resistance to desegregation in the South. Perhaps the Court believed that gradual enforcement would make desegregation more acceptable to a hostile white population. But the effect of the implementation decree was to encourage rather than to discourage resistance. The way was opened for extensive litigation, obstruction, and delay by states choosing to resist desegregation. However, we should note that neither the President nor Congress made the Court's task any easier: the Court was sailing alone on an uncharted and stormy sea.

In the ten years following the *Brown* case, not only did Congressmen refrain from supporting the Court's ruling, but, in fact, Southern Congressmen spearheaded the campaign of resistance. President Eisenhower, too, declined to place the prestige of his office behind desegregation efforts; in fact, he frequently made statements about how difficult it was for the law to change the minds of men.

Despite the legislative and executive branches' lack of enthusiasm for desegregation efforts, the six Border states with segregated school systems (Delaware, Kentucky, Maryland, Missouri, Oklahoma, and West Virginia), along with the segregated school districts in Kansas, Arizona, and New Mexico, chose *not* to resist the Court's decree. In 1955 the District of Columbia also desegregated its public schools. Table 2–1 shows the progress in desegregation in Border states; by 1964 almost three-fifths of the black children in these states were attending integrated schools.

Resistance to school desegregation was the policy choice of the eleven states of the Old Confederacy. The means for implementing the policy of resistance varied from violence and intimidation to complex litigation over subtle legal points. On the whole the policy of resist-

---

[9] It has been suggested that Justice Felix Frankfurter contributed this phrase, one originally coined by his idol, Oliver Wendell Holmes. In a 1911 opinion Holmes had written, "A state cannot be expected to move with the celerity of a private businessman; it is enough if it proceeds, in the language of the English chancery, with all deliberate speed." *Virginia* v. *West Virginia*, 222 U.S. 17 (1911).

Table 2–1   Desegregation Speed-Up, 1964–67

	Blacks in School with Whites, As a Percentage of Total Black Enrollment	
	1964	1967
Alabama	0.03	4.4
Arkansas	0.8	15.1
Florida	2.6	22.3
Georgia	0.4	8.8
Louisiana	1.1	3.4
Mississippi	0.02	2.5
North Carolina	1.4	15.4
South Carolina	0.1	5.6
Tennessee	5.3	28.6
Texas	7.3	44.9
Virginia	5.1	25.3
Southern states	2.1	15.9
Delaware	57.8	100.0
Kentucky	62.5	90.1
Maryland	51.7	65.3
Missouri	44.1	77.7
Oklahoma	31.7	50.8
West Virginia	88.1	93.4
Border states	59.2	75.7

ance was surprisingly successful during the ten-year period 1955–64. Table 2–1 indicates that in 1964 only 2 percent of the black school-children in eleven Southern states were attending integrated schools. Only 604 of the 2220 Southern school districts encompassing black students had been officially desegregated, and most of these had experienced only token desegregation. The effectiveness of state and local governments in resisting policies of the federal courts prior to 1965 is an important commentary on the powers of states and communities in our federal system.

The most common form of resistance was a school district's declining to take any action toward desegregation until confronted with a federal court injunction. Federal courts initially did not prod the local school districts to act; instead, they waited for black plaintiffs and their representatives to file desegregation suits. In hundreds of school districts it took time for blacks to find the resources to initiate suits against the local school officials. Typically, a group of concerned Negro parents would ask the NAACP's regional or national office to send a legal aide to their next meeting to explain the legal steps necessary to achieve desegregation. The legal aide would often bring printed forms to these meetings authorizing the NAACP's attorneys to act on behalf of the black parents in initiating legal proceedings. The NAACP would then take the case to a federal district court. Of course, the social, economic, and sometimes physical intimidation exerted on black parents who were parties to these suits was considerable. Federal court dockets were crowded, and often long delays were endured before the suits were heard. When federal district courts finally took up the cases, school authorities would inevitably press for postponements and then belatedly submit plans for limited or only "token" desegregation.

Segregationists also pressed for state laws that would create an endless chain of litigation in each of the two thousand Southern school districts, hoping that integration efforts would drown in a sea of protracted court controversy. Some states amended compulsory attendance laws to provide that no child could be required to attend an integrated school; other laws required schools faced with desegregation orders to cease operation; still others provided for state payment of private school tuition in lieu of providing for public schools. Prince Edward County in Virginia even closed down its public schools rather than desegregate. State officials attempted to prevent desegregation on the grounds that it would endanger public safety; they even resurrected John C. Calhoun's old philosophy and attempted to "interpose" state authority and to "nullify" federal authority within their states. Southern legislators were aware that these laws were unconstitutional even as they fashioned them, and they realized that eventually these laws would be invalidated by the federal courts. Yet each law made possible another round of motions, briefs, hearings, rulings, and appeals. "As long as we can legislate, we can segregate," one segregationist was quoted as saying. Eventually the Supreme Court did strike down all of these attempts to evade the Fourteenth Amendment, but not without a great deal of delay.

Another strategy of the segregationists was to attack the NAACP itself, since that organization was responsible for almost all of the desegregation action then taking place. Without the financial help, moral encouragement, and legal know-how of the NAACP, few blacks would have had the money, the knowledge, or the courage to seek desegregation in their school districts. One strategy was to require the NAACP to disclose the names of all its members. Segregationists knew that if the organization's local membership were made known, employers might deny those members jobs, and bankers and white merchants might deny them credit. After a lengthy period of litigation, the Supreme Court upheld the right of the NAACP to refuse to disclose its membership.[10] In several states the NAACP was attacked for committing "barratry," that is, the unprofessional practice of law or the unnecessary instigation of lawsuits. In Arkansas and South Carolina the legislatures even when so far as to make membership in the NAACP cause for dismissal of public school teachers. Eventually the NAACP won most of its cases against anti-NAACP laws, but the laws succeeded in diverting the time, energy, and resources of the organization away from the desegregation fight.

Of all delaying tactics, the most successful was the pupil placement law. Under this law each child was guaranteed "freedom of choice" in the selection of his school. Prior to the fall term all pupils, black and white, filled out a form indicating their choice of schools. School authorities then assigned pupils to the schools of their choice provided that space was available and that no other "problems" interfered. School authorities relied on the fact that most blacks and most whites selected the schools they previously attended, that is, segregated schools. A pupil requesting a transfer usually encountered overcrowding at the school of his choice since pupils previously attending that school were given preference. Transfers were denied for a wide variety of administrative reasons. Of course, race was carefully avoided as the reason for denying any transfer, and sometimes it was difficult to prove that race affected a pupil assignment decision. Since pupil placement laws and freedom of choice plans were at face value nondiscriminatory the Supreme Court held them to be constitutional so long as there was no proof of discrimination in their administration. But by 1968 most federal district courts had come to realize that little

---

[10] See *NAACP* v. *Alabama*, 357 U.S. 449 (1958); *NAACP* v. *Alabama*, 377 U.S. 288 (1964); and *NAACP* v. *Button*, 371 U.S. 415 (1963).

desegregation was occuring under freedom of choice plans. Increasingly federal courts declined to accept such plans from local school authorities as "good faith" implementation of desegregation. Gradually freedom of choice plans have dissappeared in favor of unitary school districts with pupil assignment by school officials.

Finally, resistance has taken the form of violence. The best-known incidents of violent resistance to court-ordered desegregation occurred in Clinton, Tennessee, in 1956; in Little Rock, Arkansas, in 1957; in New Orleans, Louisiana, in 1960; and at the University of Mississippi at Oxford in 1962.

A major showdown between state power and federal court policy transpired in 1957 when Governor Orval Faubus of Arkansas used the Arkansas National Guard to prevent a federal district court from desegregating Central High School in Little Rock.[11] Violent mobs—themselves a byproduct of inflammatory statements by Governor Faubus—had prevented federal marshals from securing the black students' admission, and Faubus had ordered his National Guard to the high school ostensibly to prevent violence. Yet the Guard itself was under orders to prevent federal marshals from bringing blacks into the school. Though the President constitutionally is required to enforce the law of the land, President Eisenhower's noncommittal views on school desegregation[12] had led many segregationists to believe that he might allow state armed force to prevail against the federal court's decree. But Little Rock was soon making headlines throughout the world, and

---

[11] See Jack W. Peltason, *58 Lonely Men* (New York: Harcourt, Brace, 1961), for an excellent description of the Little Rock crisis.

[12] When queried at a 1958 press conference about reports that he had disagreed with the original desegregation decision and had opposed its early implementation, President Eisenhower responded: "I might have said something about 'slower,' but I do believe that we should—because I do say, as I did yesterday or last week, we have got to have reason and sense and education, and a lot of other developments that go hand in hand as this process—if this process is going to have any real acceptance in the United States." Dwight D. Eisenhower, press conference of August 27, 1958; also cited in Berman, *It Is So Ordered*, p. 127.

A year later, speaking before a conference of state advisory committees of the U.S. Commission on Civil Rights, Eisenhower admitted that his hopes for improvements in the field of race relations were based on "moral law rather than statutory law because I [have] very little faith in the ability of statutory law to change the human heart or to eliminate prejudice." *Facts on File*, 4–10 June 1959, p. 184.

Eisenhower was forced to intervene on behalf of national authority. The direct challenge to federal supremacy was too much for even Eisenhower to ignore. After tolerating several days of disturbances, the President ordered United States Army troops to Central High School to enforce the federal court's desegregation order. Later the Supreme Court, convening in special session to deal with the Little Rock crisis, held that the threat of white mob violence was not sufficient cause for the refusal to desegregate. The Court minced no words in accusing Faubus and the Arkansas legislature of inciting the disorder at Central High. "The constitutional rights of respondents," said the Court, "are not to be sacrificed or yielded to violence and disorder which have followed upon the actions of the governor and legislature. . . . Law and order are not here to be preserved by depriving the Negro children of their constitutional rights."[13] The use of federal troops to enforce desegregation dashed the hopes of many segregationists that federal policy could be obstructed through violence. Again in 1962 President Kennedy used army troops to enforce federal court orders to desegregate the University of Mississippi, following several hours of rioting in which three people were killed.

The "Guidelines" Approach

In the Civil Rights Act of 1964 Congress finally entered the civil rights arena in support of judicial efforts to achieve desegregation. Among other things, the Civil Rights Act of 1964 required that federal departments and agencies take action to end segregation in all programs or activities receiving federal financial assistance. Title VI specified that this action was to include the termination of financial assistance to states and communities that refused to comply with federal desegregation orders; in addition, administrative orders, or "guidelines," from various federal agencies threatened the loss of federal funds for those governments not complying with desegregation requirements. Acting under the authority of Title VI, the U.S. Office of Education ordered all school districts in the seventeen formerly segregated states to submit desegregation plans as a condition of continued federal financial assistance. "Guidelines" governing the acceptability of these plans were

13 *Cooper* v. *Aaron*, 358 U.S. 1 (1958).

frequently unclear, often conflicting, and always subject to change; yet they were quite effective in accelerating the pace of desegregation.

The threat of monetary loss did more to bring about desegregation than all of the previous actions of the federal courts. Table 2–1 indicates the U.S. Office of Education's dramatic success in speeding up desegregation: after only three years of guidelines, the percentage of Southern blacks attending school with whites had increased from 2 percent to 16 percent—an eight-fold leap.

The first set of guidelines from the Office of Education stipulated that a public school district would be deemed to have satisfied the requirements of Title VI if (1) it were under a U.S. court order for desegregation and had provided assurance that it would comply with the order, or (2) it had submitted a desegregation plan that would be approved by the Commissioner of Education. These first guidelines stated only that school systems must "begin" desegregation and provide a "substantial good faith start." The Office of Education also announced that it would accept "freedom of choice" plans in satisfaction of the desegregation requirements of Title VI.

In 1966 the Office of Education issued a new set of guidelines that required the desegregation of all twelve grades in all school systems by 1967 and the complete desegregation of teacher staffs. More importantly, these guidelines employed a percentage guide for student transfers to measure the "effectiveness" of free choice desegregation plans. For example, the new guidelines provided that if a significant percentage of students (8 or 9 percent) transferred from segregated schools in 1965, at least twice that percentage of transfers would be expected in 1966. In this way the Office of Education hoped to employ percentage guidelines to measure the extent of desegregation. However, since the 1964 Civil Rights Act specifically barred the use of quotas to achieve racial balance, these new guidelines came under attack. The Office of Education denied that it was using a quota system, contending that it was merely measuring the success of freedom of choice plans. Despite heavy Congressional criticism, the Office of Education continued to employ its percentage guidelines.

In 1968 the Office of Education began to scrutinize Northern as well as Southern schools. While not requiring the correction of racial imbalances resulting from private housing patterns (a requirement that would violate the 1964 Civil Rights Act), the new guidelines did prohibit school systems from denying a minority-group student the education "generally obtained" by other students in the school system. The forms of discrimination cited by the guidelines included poorer facilities and equipment, lower per-pupil expenditures, fewer (and more unqualified) teachers, and less adequate curricula.

The last vestige of legal justification for delay in implementing school desegregation collapsed in 1969 when the Supreme Court rejected a request by Mississippi school officials and Robert H. Finch, Secretary of Health, Education, and Welfare, for a delay in implementing school desegregation plans in that state. School officials, with the support of the Nixon Administration, contended that immediate desegregation in several southern Mississippi counties would encounter "administrative and legislative difficulties." The Supreme Court stated that no delay could be granted because "continued operation of segregated schools under a standard of allowing 'all deliberate speed' for desegregation is no longer constitutionally permissible."[14] The Court declared that every school district was obligated to end dual school systems "at once" and "now and hereafter" to operate only unitary schools. The effect of the decision—fifteen years after the original *Brown* case—was to eliminate any further legal justification for the continuation of segregation in public schools.

Bussing and Neighborhood Schools

As we have noted, Southern school officials face both federal court orders and U.S. Office of Education guidelines to end segregated schools and establish unitary school systems. On the surface, this mandate seems clear enough, but is it really? Are Southern school districts permitted to operate predominantly black schools in black neighborhoods and predominantly white schools in white neighborhoods? In other words, in establishing unitary school districts, can Southern school officials draw school boundaries along neighborhood lines similar to the practice in Northern school districts, if the resulting neighborhood schools are racially imbalanced? Or are Southern school officials required to bus black and white children out of their neighborhoods in order to achieve a racial balance in each school equivalent to the racial composition of the district at large?

It has been argued that because of past legal segregation Southern

---

[14] *Alexander* v. *Holmes County Board of Education*, 396 U.S. 19 (1969).

school officials have a special constitutional obligation to eliminate the last vestiges of segregation. This means eliminating *all* predominantly black schools even in black neighborhoods where extensive bussing would be required to do so. This position has been set forth by some, but not all, federal district courts. Although bussing and the break-up of the neighborhood school pattern is not constitutionally required of Northern school districts (See Chapter 3, " 'De Facto' School Segregation in Cities"), it is contended that Southern school districts come under a special constitutional duty to racially balance their schools because of past segregation.

In contrast, many Southern school officials have argued that the elimination of segregation and the establishment of unitary school districts should not mean "forced bussing" where neighborhood residential patterns result in some predominantly black and some predominantly white schools. Southern Congressmen and Governors argue that Southern school districts should be given "equal" treatment with Northern school districts, and not be required to bus students out of their neighborhoods to achieve racial balancing. In 1970, President Richard Nixon announced his support of the neighborhood school concept. The Office of Education and the Justice Department would not require the elimination of predominantly black neighborhood schools if the color composition of the schools was solely a product of residential patterns and could not be altered by any feasible neighborhood school assignment plan. But the fight is likely to continue in the federal courts, in school boards throughout the nation, and in the national news media.

By 1970 southern school desegregation had proceeded to the point where more black pupils were attending integrated schools in the South than in the North. The Department of Health, Education, and Welfare reported that 58.3 percent of black pupils in the *South* were attending school with whites (up from 15.9 percent in 1967), whereas only 42.6 percent of black pupils in the *North* were attending integrated schools. This is an important comparison between the *diminishing* impact of segregation by law in the South and the *continuing* impact of de facto segregation in the North. If the issue is posed as one of "racial isolation," then by 1970 the efforts to eliminate segregation by law had reduced racial isolation in the South to the point where it was less than racial isolation in the North. In Chapter 3 we will explore the problem of de facto school segregation in Northern cities in greater detail.

Southern School Desegregation:
A Comparative View

The decision of the eleven Southern states to resist school desegregation was, of course, a product of the cultural history of that region.
However, progress in desegregation was uneven throughout the Southern states, and therefore we can employ comparative analyses to identify those factors that most influenced public policy in desegregation.
We can contrast the characteristics of those states and counties in the
South where progress toward desegregation was slow and painful with
the characteristics of states and counties where desegregation was accomplished faster and easier. For example, desegregation has been
especially difficult to achieve in Mississippi, Alabama, and South Carolina, while in Texas, Tennessee, and Florida the changes have been
more readily accepted. What accounts for the differences among these
Southern states in their degree of resistance to desegregation?

One hypothesis that might be examined is that desegregation is
significantly affected by the proportion of black population. The available evidence suggests that a large black population, instead of assist-
ing the movement toward integration, strengthens the determination
of segregationists to resist. Table 2–2 lists the Southern states in order
of their proportion of black population. We can clearly see that as black
population proportions decline, progress in desegregation improves.
(The rank-order correlation coefficient for the relationship between
black population percentages and progress in school desegregation is
a highly significant $-.87$).

Though large black population percentages appear to stimulate
resistance to desegregation, wealth and urbanization seem to have the
opposite effect. (The rank-order correlation coefficients for relationships with school desegregation in the eleven states are .64 for urbanization and .76 for median family income.) These variables are not as
significant as black population percentages in explaining progress
toward desegregation. However, the high degree of ruralism and the
prevalence of poverty in Mississippi, Alabama, and South Carolina do
help to explain these states' resistance. Progress in desegregation is
also related to black voter participation. (The rank-order correlation
coefficient between school desegregation and the percentage of blacks

Table 2–2   Southern States: Black Populations,
             School Desegregation, and Voter Registration
             (*Rankings by Black Population Percentages, 1960*)

		Black Population Percentage, 1960	Percentage of Blacks in School with Whites, 1967	Percentage of Blacks Registered to Vote, 1964
1.	Mississippi	42.3	2.5	6.7
2.	South Carolina	35.0	5.6	38.8
3.	Louisiana	32.1	3.4	32.0
4.	Alabama	30.1	4.4	23.0
5.	Georgia	28.6	8.8	44.0
6.	North Carolina	25.4	15.4	46.8
7.	Arkansas	21.9	15.1	54.4
8.	Virginia	20.8	25.3	45.7
9.	Florida	18.0	22.3	63.7
10.	Tennessee	16.6	28.6	69.4
11.	Texas	12.6	44.9	57.7

registered to vote in 1964 is .72.) However, rather than concluding that black voting provides a stimulus to desegregation, we should more logically infer that higher levels of school desegregation and black voter registration are by-products of the same socioeconomic conditions—a smaller black population, urbanism, and economic development.

An examination of desegregation at the county level confirms our analysis of statewide figures. Donald B. Matthews and James W. Prothro systematically examined the socioeconomic and political factors associated with desegregation policy in 997 Southern counties.[15] Their dependent variable was simply the presence or absence of some school desegregation in each county in 1960. The socioeconomic variables that correlated most closely with this rough measure of desegregation were in order of strength:

[15] Donald B. Matthews and James W. Prothro, "Stateways versus Folkways: Critical Factors in Southern Reactions to *Brown* v. *Board of Education*," in *Essays on the American Constitution*, ed. Gottfried Dietze (Englewood Cliffs, N.J.: Prentice-Hall, 1964), pp. 139–58.

1. percentage of population urban
2. nonwhite median income
3. nonwhite median school years completed
4. white median income
5. percentage of population Negro
6. percentage of population increase, 1940–50
7. percentage of Church members Roman Catholic
8. percentage of Church members Baptist
9. percentage of nonwhite labor force in white collar jobs
10. percentage of labor force in agriculture

Matthews and Prothro concluded that desegregation was most likely to occur in an urban environment in which blacks and whites receive relatively high incomes and blacks are relatively well-educated. In addition, they found that a large black population was a distinct barrier to desegregation. Apparently the presence of large numbers of Negroes in a county stimulates white resistance to desegregation rather than engendering positive support for it.

Matthews and Prothro discovered that political variables were much less influential in accounting for school desegregation policy than socioeconomic variables. Their political variables were the following:

1. percentage, States Rights Party Presidential vote in 1948
2. percentage, Republican Presidential vote in 1960
3. highest percentage Republican in race for statewide office, 1950–59
4. presence-absence of Negro race organization
5. presence-absence of white race organization
6. percentage of voting age Negroes registered to vote

Further analysis by Matthews and Prothro disclosed that most of the correlation between these political variables and school desegregation policy was accounted for by environmental variables. In other words, socioeconomic factors tended to mold the political orientation of Southern counties as well as their policies toward desegregation.

The Politics of Southern School Desegregation

By the 1960s most administrators in Southern school districts had come to the realization that desegregation was inevitable. Not that they welcomed integration, but most school board members (and most parents) appeared to prefer limited integration to closing of the schools. And the vast majority wanted to avoid the violence that had characterized desegregation efforts in Little Rock, Arkansas, and Clinton, Tennessee. Robert L. Crain accurately portrays the typical reaction of Southern school boards to desegregation initiatives:

> Their first and least difficult problem was to find ways to put off desegregation as long as possible. The best solution was simply to find the most capable lawyer and let him use all the legal tricks he could borrow or invent. The second problem was to mobilize whatever resources were necessary to develop a favorable climate for desegregation and to minimize demonstrations, violence, or bad publicity. Third, the school board members had to decide whether they were willing to be labeled integrationists; if they were not, they had to decide how they could protect themselves by expressing public disapproval of integration and at the same time not give aid and comfort to the citizens' councils and the potential troublemakers. Finally, the school board had to decide how to prevent the intervention of the state legislature or the governor.[16]

Crain examined school desegregation in seven Southern cities. Actually, desegregation in most large Southern cities was accomplished with relatively little difficulty. In Crain's study only New Orleans experienced conflict and violence over desegregation. The reaction of extremists to desegregation in New Orleans in 1960 was so intense and so prolonged that the city suffered serious dislocations as a result. At one point thousands of whites rampaged through the downtown business district hurling bricks and bottles. For an entire year white children boycotted the two schools selected for integration, and—in full view of national television network cameras—unruly crowds cursed, stoned, and spat upon the few white children who continued to attend the two schools. School board members who had desegregated the schools under federal court order were ostracized by their friends, harrassed and threatened, and eventually removed from office by the state legislature. Teachers and school administrators went unpaid for many months as the legislature held up school funds and local banks refused to cash school checks. Despite New Orleans' reputation as one of

[16] Robert L. Crain, *The Politics of School Desegregation* (Chicago: Aldine, 1968), pp. 232–34.

America's most cosmopolitan cities—heterogenous, cultured, and civilized—it provided the battleground for one of the nation's most chaotic and violent desegregation confrontations.

In contrast, desegregation in Atlanta proved to be almost the model for civic action. Atlanta was the first city to desegregate in the Deep South states of Mississippi, Alabama, Georgia, and South Carolina. It desegregated quietly despite the unreceptive mood of the state legislature and a governor, Ernest Vandiver, who had earlier campaigned on the pledge that "no, not one" black would be admitted to white schools during his administration. As Crain reports, Atlanta's business leaders constituted a self-conscious "power structure" that exercised its influence responsibly to achieve desegregation in a peaceful and orderly manner. Mayor William B. Hartsfield, himself a prominent Atlanta businessman, kept in close contact with business leaders throughout the desegregation effort, which began in 1961. First, the business community persuaded the governor to appoint a special commission headed by an Atlanta banker. The commission held hearings throughout the state and then recommended passage of a local option law on desegregation that would effectively prevent the state from interfering in Atlanta's school system. Once this law had been passed, Atlanta citizens organized a save-the-schools committee, which soon launched an extensive educational campaign. Businessmen, members of the Chamber of Commerce, clergymen, and policemen all committed themselves publicly to preserving the peace. The prevailing attitude in Atlanta reflected the business community's view that good race relations were necessary in order to attract new industry. Thus, as a result of careful preparation and education, Atlanta desegregated peacefully, establishing in the process a reputation as the leader of the "New South."

How do we explain the difference in desegregation policies in two cities as similar in size and socioeconomic character as Atlanta and New Orleans? Crain contends that the difference can be explained by the attitudes and the sense of responsibility demonstrated by each city's business and civic elite. School board members and elected officials are too insecure in their positions and too accessible to the opinions of the white masses to be able to assume leadership roles in desegregation efforts. In contrast, members of the business and civic elite collectively have sufficient power to direct the course of events, and yet these indi-

viduals are much more insulated from public opinion than elected officials. The power of the business and civic elite takes several forms.
These individuals have the money to influence political campaigns and
to influence public opinion, and they enjoy positions of high prestige,
especially in a Southern city. They have personal influence over many
leaders in the community. Moreover, whereas elected officials can be
defeated at the polls, ministers abruptly transferred, and employees
fired, business leaders are relatively invulnerable to attacks from "red-
necks"—those lower class whites possessing the most intense racial
animosity. Crain concludes that "the ideology of the civic elite is the
dominant factor in determining whether the city will acquiesce peacefully to the desegregation order, and that the composition of the school
board is less important."[17]

According to Crain, the civic elite of New Orleans (very much in
keeping with the traditional aloofness of that city's old-line elite) had
withdrawn from politics and had assumed no responsibility in the desegregation proceedings. Unlike Atlanta's business elite, which took a
strong interest in their city's economic development and its national
reputation (the mayor hired a management consultant firm to produce
a report, widely circulated among Atlanta's elite, that traced the slow-
down in Little Rock's industrial growth to its earlier desegregation disorders), New Orleans' elite was not strongly committed to attracting
new industry. In New Orleans the elite is truly Southern: its members
disdain economic development efforts as brash, money-grubbing
schemes of the *nouveaux riches*. Money and achieved status determine
elite membership in Atlanta, but in New Orleans being a native and
coming from a "good family" are more important determinants. Comments Crain:

> New Orleans is thus an anachronism—a traditionalist society in mid-
> twentieth-century America. We find attitudes in New Orleans which
> were prevalent in the traditionalist societies of the nineteenth-
> century South, the most obvious of which is a resistance to new ideas
> and new values. Since new values are brought in by new wealth and
> by outsiders, the economic elite in New Orleans is predictably not as
> hospitable to new industry as the elites in other southern cities.[18]

[17] *Ibid.*, p. 325.
[18] *Ibid.*, p. 303.

Success in desegregating Southern cities appears then to be directly related to the progressivism and cosmopolitanism of the individual cities and to the willingness of their business and civic elites to shoulder unpopular responsibilities. These elites, relatively insulated from public opinion, have the freedom, security, prestige, and power to achieve a political objective—desegregation—that is clearly at variance with the preferences of the masses.

Securing the Right to Vote

The fight to end discrimination in voting predates the struggle over school segregation. The white primary was frequently the object of federal court litigation before World War II. When the Texas legislature flatly prohibited Negroes from voting in that state's Democratic primaries, the Supreme Court invalidated the statute as a "direct and obvious infringement" of the equal protection clause of the Fourteenth Amendment.[19] Later, when the Texas legislature responded with a law authorizing the executive committees of state parties to prescribe voting qualifications for primaries, the Court held that these committees were acting as agents of the state, and therefore their action in barring Negroes from primaries was unconstitutional as a denial of equal protection.[20] Undaunted, the Texas legislature then dropped all references to voter qualifications in primary elections from its statute books; the Texas Democratic party declared itself a private club, and then proceeded to restrict membership in the "club" and voting in the "club's" elections to white citizens. By unanimous vote the Supreme Court in *Grovey* v. *Townsend*[21] concluded that the terms of the Fourteenth and Fifteenth Amendments had not been infringed since action was taken by the party as a private organization rather than by the state.

Thus, for a time the Supreme Court endorsed the view that political parties were private clubs unencumbered by constitutional restraints on state action and that primary elections were not part of the election process. Both of these propositions were so obviously contrary

---

[19] *Nixon* v. *Herndon*, 279 U.S. 536 (1927).

[20] *Nixon* v. *Condon*, 286 U.S. 73 (1932).

[21] *Grovey* v. *Townsend*, 295 U.S. 45 (1935).

to the facts that they were easy targets for additional court action. Consequently, a new test case from Texas was begun, which ultimately resulted in the reversal of *Grovey* v. *Townsend* and a ruling that party primaries were "an integral part of the election machinery" and that discrimination against Negroes in party primaries was "state action within the meaning of the Fifteenth Amendment." Decided in 1944, *Smith* v. *Allwright*[22] marked the beginning of the long road toward Negro voting in the South under the protection of the national government.

The poll tax lasted longer than the white primary, but eventually it too was recognized as a discriminatory device. In 1962 Congress passed the Twenty-Fourth Amendment to the Constitution of the United States declaring that "the right of citizens of the United States to vote in any primary or other election . . . shall not be denied or abridged by the United States or any State by reason of failure to pay any poll tax or other tax." This Amendment was ratified by the states in 1964. The Twenty-Fourth Amendment applied only to federal elections, but in 1966 the Supreme Court declared that the poll tax was inherently discriminatory, adding that "wealth, like race, creed, or color, is not germane to one's ability to participate intelligently in the electoral process." The Court therefore held that poll taxes in any election —federal, state, or local—violated the equal protection clause of the Fourteenth Amendment.[23] This ruling, together with the Twenty-Fourth Amendment, brought an end to poll taxes in American politics.

In contrast to their action on the poll tax, federal courts proved unwilling to strike down the literacy test as a discriminatory device for assuring that those participating in elections be able to understand the purpose and importance of their vote. Literacy tests normally require the prospective voter to demonstrate to voting officials that he can read, write, and understand the general terms either of his state constitution or of the U.S. Constitution. Of course, the practice in many parts of the South was to administer the literacy test in a discriminatory fashion. The literacy test was rarely administered to whites, yet the standard of literacy required of blacks was so high that few, regardless of their educational attainments, were ever able to pass the test. In

[22] *Smith* v. *Allwright*, 285 U.S. 355 (1944).
[23] *Harper* v. *Virginia State Board of Elections*, 383 U.S. 663 (1966).

recognition of the discriminatory administration of literacy tests, Congress, in Title I of the Civil Rights Act of 1964, made it unlawful "in determining whether any individual is qualified under State law or laws to vote in any Federal election, [to] apply any standard, practice, or procedure different from the standards, practices, or procedures applied under such law or laws to other individuals within the same county." The Act further required that all literacy tests be given in writing and stipulated that any person who had completed a sixth-grade education in an English-speaking school should be presumed literate enough to vote unless proven otherwise.

Despite this legislation, many local registrars in the South succeeded in barring blacks by means of an endless variety of obstacles, delays, and frustrations. Application forms for registration were lengthy and complicated; even a minor error (for example, underlining instead of circling in the "Mr.—Mrs.—Miss" set of choices as instructed) would lead to rejection. Often registration boards "misplaced" or lost Negro registration records; or altered their meeting times and places without notice; or opened their rolls only one or two hours a month; or limited the processing of new (Negro) voters to one or two a month. Occasionally, registrars deliberately resigned unexpectedly so that the delay in appointing a replacement might prevent the registration of new voters. In Selma, Alabama, in early 1965, civil rights organizations protested that local registrars were effectively keeping large numbers of blacks off the voting rolls by using such tactics. Led by Martin Luther King, Jr., president of the Southern Christian Leadership Conference, Negroes marched from Selma to the capital in Montgomery to dramatize that local registrars were still refusing to enforce voting laws equitably.

The Selma marchers convinced Congress that its earlier legislation[24] was inadequate to the task of securely guaranteeing the right to

---

[24] In the Civil Rights Act of 1957 Congress had established a U.S. Commission on Civil Rights to investigate civil rights violations and to suggest corrective legislation. It had also created a special civil rights section in the Justice Department to secure civil rights enforcement and had authorized federal judges to enforce voting rights through the use of court injunctions against election officials. An election official under federal court injunction to refrain from discriminating in voting registration would be subject to "contempt of court" proceedings if he continued to discriminate. Obviously, this enforcement procedure

vote for all Americans. In response to the march, Congress enacted the Voting Rights Act of 1965, which threatened federal intervention in local voting matters to a degree never before attempted. The Act had a "triggering" formula which applied its provisions specifically to those states or counties where (1) a literacy test or similar qualifying device was enforced as of 1 November 1964 and where (2) fewer than 50 percent of the voting-age residents either were registered or had cast ballots in the 1964 Presidential election. In these areas the Attorney General, upon evidence of voter discrimination, was empowered to replace local registrars with federal examiners, who were authorized to abolish literacy tests, to waive poll taxes, and to register voters under simplified federal procedures. Opponents of the new law argued that it interfered with the historic right of states to determine "voter qualifications." Article I of the Constitution declares that "the electors in each State shall have the qualifications requisite for electors of the most numerous branch of the State legislature." However, a constitutional amendment takes precedence over earlier language in the U.S. Constitution, and the Fifteenth Amendment specifically prohibited racial discrimination in voting, simultaneously giving to Congress the "power to enforce this article by appropriate legislation." In 1966 the Supreme Court took note of the long history of discrimination by Southern voting registrars and upheld the Voting Rights Act of 1965 as "appropriate legislation" in the fight against voter discrimination.[25]

The impact of the Voting Rights Act of 1965 and earlier national legislation is revealed in black voter registration figures in the South. From an estimated 5 percent of voting-age blacks registered to vote in

---

was a clumsy one involving expensive court litigation and delay. Some improvement in voting rights enforcement was made in the Civil Rights Act of 1960, which authorized federal attorneys to bring suit to protect an individual Negro's right to vote. If the court found that a general pattern of discrimination prevailed in the area, the court was authorized to register Negroes provided they met general state voting requirements and had exhausted remedies available to them under local law. Again, the provisions of the 1960 Act were cumbersome and time-consuming; requiring Negro complainants to avail themselves of all remedies under local law invited lengthy litigation and evasion by local authorities. In spite of the enactment of these two Acts, blacks remained conspicuously absent from the voting rolls of Selma, Alabama, and hundreds of other Southern communities.

[25] *South Carolina* v. *Katzenbach*, 383 U.S. 301 (1964).

eleven Southern states in 1940, black registration rose to an estimated 20 percent in 1952, 25 percent in 1956, 28 percent in 1960, 45 percent in 1964 and 57 percent in 1968. Not only did black registration increase, but blacks throughout the South were also being elected to public office. In 1968 blacks sat in the state legislatures of Tennessee, Kentucky, Texas, Georgia, Virginia, and even Mississippi. We shall examine the political impact of black voting at some length in Chapter 6.

The New Emancipation—
The Civil Rights Act of 1964

The initial objective of the civil rights movement was to prevent discrimination and segregation practiced by or supported by *governments,* particularly states, municipalities, and school districts. But even while important victories for the civil rights movement were being recorded in the governmental arena, the movement began to broaden its objectives to include the elimination of discrimination in all segments of American life, private as well as public.

As long as the civil rights movement was combating *governmental* discrimination, it could employ the U.S. Constitution as a weapon in its arsenal. Since the Supreme Court and the federal judiciary were charged with the responsibility of interpreting the Constitution, the civil rights movement could concentrate on judicial action to accomplish its objective of preventing governmental discrimination. But the Constitution has considerably less bearing upon the activities of private individuals than do the laws of Congress and of the various states. Thus, when the civil rights movement turned its attention to combating private discrimination, it had to carry its fight into the legislative branch of government. The federal courts could help to restrict discrimination by state and local governments and school authorities, but only Congress could restrict discrimination practiced by private owners of restaurants, hotels, and motels, private employers, and other individuals who were not government officials.

Congress, after attempting to prevent private discrimination by passing the Civil Rights Act of 1875, had been content to let other agencies, including the President and the courts, struggle with the problem of civil rights. But by 1964 Congress could no longer ignore the nation's most pressing domestic issue. The civil rights movement had stepped up its protests and demonstrations and was attracting world-wide attention with organized sit-ins, freedom rides, picketing campaigns, boycotts, and mass marches (see Chapter 5). The mass media vividly portrayed the animosity of segregationists and helped to convince millions of Americans of the need for national legislation. After the massive "March on Washington" in August 1963, President Kennedy asked Congress for the most comprehensive civil rights legislation it had ever considered. After Kennedy's assassination, President Johnson brought heavy pressure upon Congress to pass the bill as a tribute to the late President. Senator Everett M. Dirksen of Illinois, Republican leader in the Senate, provided Johnson with the bipartisan support needed to overcome a Southern filibuster. The Civil Rights Act of 1964 finally passed both houses of Congress by better than a two-thirds vote and with the overwhelming support of both Republican and Democratic Congressmen (see Chapter 5). It can be ranked with the Emancipation Proclamation, the Fourteenth Amendment, and *Brown* v. *Topeka* as one of the most important steps toward full equality for the Negro in America.

The Act provides that:

1. It is unlawful to apply unequal standards in voter registration procedures or to deny registration for irrelevant errors or omissions on records or applications. Literacy tests must be in writing and a sixth-grade education is a presumption of literacy.

2. It is unlawful to discriminate or segregate persons on the grounds of race, color, religion, or natural origin in any place of public accommodation, including hotels, motels, restaurants, movies, theaters, sports arenas, entertainment houses, and other places offering to serve the public. This prohibition extends to all establishments whose operations affect interstate commerce or whose discriminatory practices are supported by state action. Private clubs are specifically exempted.

3. The Attorney General shall undertake civil action on behalf of any person denied equal access to a public accommodation. If the proprietor continues to discriminate, he may be held in contempt of court and subjected to peremptory fines or imprisonment without trial by jury. (This mode of enforcement gave proprietors an

opportunity to adjust to the new law without being punished, and it also avoided the possibility that Southern juries would refuse to convict violators of the Act.)

4. The Attorney General shall undertake civil actions on behalf of persons attempting the orderly desegregation of public schools.

5. The U.S. Commission on Civil Rights, first established by the Civil Rights Act of 1957, shall be empowered (1) to investigate deprivations of the right to vote, (2) to collect and to study information regarding discrimination in America, and (3) to make reports to the President and Congress as necessary.

6. Each federal department and agency shall take appropriate action to end discrimination in all programs or activities receiving federal financial assistance in any form. These actions may include the termination of assistance.

7. After 1967 it shall be unlawful for any firm or labor union employing or representing twenty-five or more persons to discriminate against any individual in any fashion because of his race, color, religion, sex, or natural origins; an Equal Employment Opportunity Commission shall be established to enforce this provision by investigation, conference, conciliation, or civil action in federal court.

Opponents of the Civil Rights Act of 1964 argued that Congress unconstitutionally exceeded its delegated powers when it prohibited discrimination and segregation practiced in *privately-owned* public accommodations and by *private* employers. Nowhere among the delegated powers of Congress enumerated in Article I of the Constitution or even in the Fourteenth or Fifteenth Amendments is Congress specifically given the authority to prohibit discrimination practiced by private individuals. In reply, supporters of the Act argued that Congress has the power to regulate interstate commerce and that discrimination in public accommodations and employment affects interstate commerce. In unanimous opinions in *Heart of Atlanta Motel* v. *United States* and *Katzenbach* v. *McClung* in December 1964, the Supreme Court upheld the constitutionality of the Civil Rights Act.[26] The Court

[26] *Heart of Atlanta Motel* v. *United States*, 379 U.S. 241 (1964); *Katzenbach* v. *McClung*, 379 U.S. 294 (1964).

held that Congress, by virtue of its power over interstate commerce, could prohibit discrimination in any establishment that serves or offers to serve interstate travelers or that sells food or goods previously moved in interstate commerce. This power over commerce extended not only to major establishments like the Heart of Atlanta Motel but also to the family-owned Ollie's Barbecue, which served only a local clientele.

The Civil Rights Act of 1964 was truly a new emancipation for Southern blacks. Enforcement proved to be no real difficulty. Southern businessmen seemed almost to welcome the excuse of a federal directive to open their facilities to black customers. A few isolated communities attempted to evade the law by turning their theaters and public swimming pools into "private clubs." Atlanta restaurant owner Lester Maddox closed his restaurant in the face of federal contempt charges arising out of his highly publicized refusal to obey the new law; his defiance won him sufficient popularity among Georgia's segregationists to propel him to the governor's chair in that state in 1966. But Maddox was a highly publicized exception. The prevailing attitude of the white South was to accept, albeit begrudgingly, the end of Jim Crow.

chapter 3

The Persistence
of De Facto Segregation

The demise of Jim Crow does not ensure equality in America. Despite the success of the civil rights movement in ending legal discrimination and segregation, blacks and whites in America still remain largely segregated. Most black adults continue to live in predominantly black neighborhoods, and most black children continue to attend predominantly black schools. Though the segregation of blacks in Southern communities was generally recognized as the product of political systems (i.e., "de jure segregation"), it is sometimes contended that "racial isolation" in Northern communities is unrelated to public policy. After all, blacks are not legally *required* to live in ghettos, and their children are assigned to neighborhood schools rather than to schools segregated by law. Yet, the existence of racial ghettos and predominantly black schools (i.e., "de facto segregation") in big cities does testify to the absence of any effective public policy to eliminate segregation. Thus, public policy reflects "nondecisions" in behalf of segregated housing and segregated public schools.

The Making of Ghettos

The two outstanding trends in black population migration in America have been the outflow of blacks from the South and their movement from rural to urban areas. Census figures show, for example, that while 87 percent of the nation's blacks lived in the South in 1900, only about 50 percent live there today. In leaving the rural South, blacks tended to concentrate heavily in the central cities of large metropolitan areas rather than in small towns or in suburbs. While blacks constitute only 11 percent of the total population of the United States, they make up a disproportionate share of the population of many of the nations largest cities. Black Americans already constitute a majority of the population of Washington, D.C. They make up more than 40 percent of the population of Detroit, Baltimore, St. Louis, New Orleans, Atlanta, Newark, Oakland, Birmingham, and Gary. They comprise nearly one-third of the population of Chicago, Philadelphia, Cleveland, Memphis, Columbus, and Cincinnati. These population trends are bound to have an impact on politics and public policy in these cities.

The concentration of blacks in large central cities is a product of (1) the availability of low priced rental units in older run-down sections of central cities, (2) the heavy out-migration of whites from the central city to the suburbs, and (3) the discriminatory practices of public and private real estate owners and developers. Of course, underlying the concentration of blacks in low priced run-down sectors of the central city is their lack of sufficient income to purchase housing in the suburbs or in better city neighborhoods. This poverty is in turn the product of inadequate training and education, job discrimination, low levels of aspiration, and often a lack of motivation. And problems in education, in employment, and in motivation are themselves frequently related to a breakdown in family life or to delinquency and crime. Thus, the "ghetto" is a product of a whole series of interrelated problems: discrimination, poverty, insufficient education, lack of job skills, family problems, lack of motivation, delinquency, and crime. One cannot discuss the ghetto meaningfully without taking into account all of these interrelated difficulties.

In recent years the migration of blacks into the cities has been accompanied by a sizable out-migration of whites headed for the suburbs. Whites flee to the suburbs for many reasons: the promise of better education for their children, more space for gardening and recreation, a belief that their taxes will be lower, the avoidance of city noise and dirt, an attraction to the middle class style of suburban life, and, of course, a desire to place physical distance between themselves and the black ghettos. The population totals in many central cities have remained stagnant in recent years or have even declined slightly; black population percentages have increased because white out-migration has been accompanied by black in-migration (see Table 3–1). For example, the white population of New York declined by 7 percent between 1950 and 1960, that of Philadelphia by 13 percent, Boston by 17 percent, Newark by 27 percent, Chicago by 13 percent, Detroit by 24 percent, and Cleveland by 19 percent. In contrast, the nonwhite population increased in that same ten-year period by 47 percent in New York, 41 percent in Philadelphia, 60 percent in Boston, 84 percent in Newark, 64 percent in Chicago, 60 percent in Detroit, and 69 percent in Cleveland. Negro birth rates in urban areas have also tended to be slightly higher than those of whites. In summary, while the population totals in the nation's largest cities have not changed materially in recent years, the color composition of those cities has changed dramatically.

Housing in America is becoming not less but more segregated. Not only are blacks being concentrated in central cities while whites flee to the suburbs, but even *within* central cities black housing is highly segregated. (Figure 3–1, showing the distribution of the Negro population in St. Louis in 1960, typifies the residential patterns of most large cities.) All major American cities are characterized by a high degree of residential segregation. Karl E. Tauber and Alma F. Tauber report that the average "segregation index" for American cities is 86.2, meaning that 86.2 percent of all Negroes would have to change their place of residence in order to create an unsegregated population distribution.[1] The segregation index of Chicago, for example, was 92.6; New York, 79.3; Los Angeles, 81.8; Detroit, 84.5; and Philadelphia, 87.1. These figures are *not* decreasing but rather increasing with time. Moreover, comparative analysis fails to reveal any significant forces or conditions tending to reduce residential segregation. Tauber and Tauber conclude:

> In the United States there is a very high degree of segregation of the residences of whites and Negroes. This is true for cities in all regions of the country and for all types of cities—large and small, industrial

[1] Karl E. Tauber and Alma F. Tauber, *Negroes in Cities* (Chicago: Aldine, 1965).

Table 3–1   Black Population of Nation's Largest Cities

	Black Population Percentage				Population Change, 1950–60, in Percentage	
	1940	1950	1960	1970 (estimated)	White	Nonwhite
New York	6	9	14	19	− 6.7	47.2
Chicago	8	14	23	32	−12.8	64.4
Los Angeles	4	9	14	23	17.2	97.2
Philadelphia	13	14	26	32	−13.3	41.2
Detroit	9	16	29	47	−23.5	60.4
Houston	22	21	23	27	8.1	42.1
Baltimore	19	24	35	47	−15.6	45.3
Cleveland	10	16	29	38	−18.6	69.3
Washington, D.C.	28	38	54	68	−33.3	47.3
Milwaukee	2	3	9	18	−10.1	185.5
Dallas	17	13	19	25	4.9	59.2
San Francisco	1	6	10	17	−12.9	66.8
St. Louis	13	18	29	46	−24.0	39.9
Boston	3	5	9	13	−17.1	59.9
New Orleans	30	32	37	45	1.2	28.6
San Antonio	7	7	7	10	8.9	20.0
San Diego	2	4	6	10	46.9	135.1
Pittsburgh	9	12	17	21	−15.3	22.3
Seattle	1	3	5	9	− 3.5	69.5
Memphis	41	37	37	39	− 1.2	24.1
Buffalo	3	6	13	22	−15.3	94.7
Phoenix	6	5	5	10	− 2.3	34.6
Atlanta	38	37	38	39	−19.6	21.2
Denver	2	4	6	10	5.8	91.8
Columbus, Ohio	12	13	16	32	− 2.4	58.8
Indianapolis	13	15	21	29	− 9.1	53.9
Kansas City, Mo.	11	12	17	24	−12.7	49.9
Cincinnati	12	15	22	31	− 9.4	39.4
Minneapolis	1	1	2	5	− 9.0	84.2
Newark	11	17	34	46	−26.8	84.2

Table 3–1 *(continued)*

	Black Population Percentage				Population Change, 1950–60, in Percentage	
	1940	1950	1960	1970 (estimated)	White	Nonwhite
Fort Worth	14	13	16	20	2.4	40.0
Louisville	15	16	18	24	−17.1	21.6
Long Beach	1	2	3	7	10.7	121.7
Portland, Ore.	1	3	4	7	− 5.4	57.6
Oklahoma City	9	9	12	18	− 0.9	54.9
Oakland	3	12	23	39	−17.7	73.9
Birmingham	41	40	40	40	− 1.5	3.8
Norfolk	32	29	26	23	− 2.3	11.8
Miami	22	16	22	28	8.2	62.2
Omaha	5	6	8	12	0.4	54.7

SOURCE: *Revolution in Civil Rights* (Washington, D.C.: Congressional Quarterly Service, June 1968), p. 117.

and commercial, metropolitan and suburban. It is true whether there are hundreds of thousands of Negro residents or only a few thousand. Residential segregation prevails regardless of the relative economic status of the white and Negro residents. It occurs regardless of the character of local law and policies, and regardless of the extent of other forms of segregation or discrimination.[2]

The separation of racial groups between cities and suburbs and within cities is encouraged by the practices of the private housing industry—builders, mortgage lenders, landlords, and real estate brokers. The typical housing development concentrates homes in a single price bracket not varying more than two or three thousand dollars. Real estate developers contend that the alternative pattern of building high and low priced houses in the same neighborhood does not appeal to prospective customers. The result of this practice of building neigh-

[2] *Ibid.*, pp. 35–36.

Figure 3-1

DISTRIBUTION OF NEGRO POPULATION IN ST. LOUIS BY CENSUS TRACT, 1960

LEGEND:

0-19% ☐
20-49% ▨
over 50% ■

SOURCE: U. S. Commission on Civil Rights, *Racial Isolation in the Public Schools,* I (Washington, D.C.: Government Printing Office, 1967), 33.

borhoods with uniformly priced homes is the creation of social class homogeneity within neighborhoods. This homogeneity means that whites at lower income levels must live in less fashionable neighborhoods and it also means that less affluent Negroes are concentrated in areas where low priced housing is available. Thus does the social class segregation of neighborhoods lead directly to the de facto segregation of Negroes within central city ghettos.

In addition to economically imposed, de facto, housing segregation, Negroes must also contend with direct discrimination in the sale and rental of housing. Until recently a significant proportion of private housing in America carried racially restrictive covenants in deeds, an example of which reads as follows:

> No part of the land hereby conveyed shall ever be used or occupied by or sold, demised, transferred, conveyed unto, or in trust for, leased, or rented or given to Negroes, or any other person or persons

of Negro blood or extraction, or to any person of the Semitic race, blood, or origin which racial description shall be deemed to include Armenians, Jews, Hebrews, Persians and Syrians.[3]

Not until 1948 was the judicial enforcement of such covenants held unconstitutional.[4] Although racially restrictive covenants are no longer judicially enforceable, they are still used today on an informal basis; more importantly, the pattern they helped to create persists.

Government policies have also contributed to housing segregation in America. By insuring more than $150 billion in mortgage loans for some fifteen million housing units, the Federal Housing Administration and the Veterans Administration made possible the flight of the white middle class to the suburbs by making home ownership easily available to the middle class. In addition, the FHA and VA condoned direct discrimination by encouraging restrictive covenants under the "homogeneous neighborhood" policies then in effect. The result was to create many all-white suburbs around major urban centers, such as the various Levittowns (in New York, Pennsylvania, and New Jersey), Lakewood (near Los Angeles), and Forest Park (outside of Chicago), which systematically barred Negroes. Equally important, federal housing programs have made no investment in the housing needs of lower income families comparable to the FHA and VA investment in middle income housing. Since Negroes make up a disproportionate share of low income housing clientele, they have not had nearly the same opportunity as whites to acquire homes under government-insured programs.

Low rent public housing has been an important source of housing for Negroes, but public housing has been confined almost entirely to central cities. Of the nation's twenty-four largest cities, only one, Cincinnati, has ever permitted its public housing authority to build new units outside of the central city. Public housing programs, therefore, have generally intensified the concentration of the poor and the black in central cities. Even *within* central cities, public housing authorities have usually preferred to locate their projects in large blocks of the

[3] Cited in U.S. Commission on Civil Rights, *Civil Rights U.S.A.: Housing in Washington, D.C.* (Washington, D.C.: Government Printing Office, 1962), p. 58.
[4] *Shelley* v. *Kraemer*, 334 U.S. 1 (1948).

ghetto districts (i.e., where the concentration of Negroes is already greatest) rather than to scatter them on smaller sites throughout the city.

National "Fair Housing" Policy

For many years "fair housing" was considered the most sensitive area of civil rights legislation. Discrimination in the sale and rental of housing was the last major civil rights problem to confront Congress. Discrimination in housing had been mentioned in no previous national legislation—not even in the comprehensive Civil Rights Act of 1964. Not until 1966 did the President formally request Congress to pass open housing legislation; even then, fair housing bills died in both the 1966 and 1967 sessions. Prohibiting discrimination in the sale or rental of housing affected the constituencies of Northern members of Congress more than any of the earlier, Southern-oriented legislation. The real estate industry in America was squarely opposed to the fair housing concept. The National Association of Real Estate Boards published a "Property Owners Bill of Rights" asserting the "right" of the individual American property owner "to determine the acceptability and desirability of any prospective buyer or tenant of his property . . . to choose who, in his opinion, are congenial tenants in any property he owns—to maintain the stability and security of his income . . . to enjoy the freedom to accept, reject, negotiate or not negotiate with, others."[5] Moreover, there was reason to believe that a majority of white Americans agreed with the housing industry and opposed laws prohibiting discrimination in the sale or rental of housing. When the California legislature passed a fair housing law, the state's voters responded by overwhelmingly supporting (by a margin of almost two to one) a state constitutional amendment (known as Proposition 14) that prohibited the legislature from abridging the rights of citizens to sell, lease, or rent properties to persons of their choice. (Later the Cali-

[5] National Association of Real Estate Boards, "Property Owners Bill of Rights," 4 June 1963; reprinted in Thomas R. Dye and Brett W. Hawkins, eds., *Politics in the Metropolis* (Columbus, Ohio: Charles E. Merrill, 1965), pp. 119–20.

fornia Supreme Court held Proposition 14 to be in violation of the Fourteenth Amendment, deciding, in effect, to throw out the results of the referendum; but nonetheless the popular margin of victory was itself clear evidence of the widespread opposition to fair housing.) Finally, major urban riots in 1967 appeared to harden the attitudes of whites toward further civil rights legislation.

Thus, the prospects for enacting a national fair housing law were unpromising at the beginning of 1968. With the assassination of Martin Luther King, Jr., on 4 April, however, the mood of the nation and of Congress changed dramatically. Many people came to feel that Congress should pass a fair housing law as a tribute to the slain civil rights leader. Moreover, the final version of the Civil Rights Bill of 1968 included amendments making it a crime for persons to travel in interstate commerce with the intent to incite or to take part in a riot or to manufacture or transport firearms or explosives for use in a civil disorder. These "antiriot" provisions won crucial support for the bill.

The Civil Rights Act of 1968 prohibited the following forms of discrimination:

> Refusal to sell or to rent a dwelling to any person because of his race, color, religion, or national origin.

> Discrimination against a person in the terms, conditions, or privileges of the sale or rental of a dwelling.

> Indicating a preference or discriminating on the basis of race, color, religion, or national origin in advertising the sale or rental of a dwelling.

> Inducing persons to sell or to rent a dwelling by referring to the entry into the neighborhood of persons of a particular race, religion, or national origin (the "block-busting" technique of real estate selling).

The Act applied to all apartments and houses rented or sold by real estate developers or private individuals utilizing the services of real estate agents. It specifically exempted homes sold by their owners without the services of a real estate agent (provided the owners did not indicate any preference or discrimination in advertising) and apartments of less than five units in cases where the landlord maintained his own residence in the building. The enforcement provisions allowed a person who believed he had been discriminated against to

file a complaint with the Secretary of Housing and Urban Development, who would then investigate and attempt to conciliate the matter;
if conciliation failed, the individual could sue in a federal court for in-
junctive relief. But where state and local remedies were available, the
individual was required first to seek these local remedies before initiating federal court action. Thus, the enforcement procedure was quite
troublesome for the individuals discriminated against.

It is still too early to assess the impact of the 1968 Act's fair housing provisions on housing practices in America. One can with good reason doubt that fair housing laws—whether federal, state, or local—will
ever succeed in breaking up America's ghettos. A crucial problem is
the enforcement of the laws. Eliminating overt discrimination may be
possible, but detecting discrimination in the seller or agent who chooses
to disguise his prejudice will be very difficult. For the present, an even
more important obstacle to the success of fair housing legislation is
the economic inability of most blacks to take advantage of it and to
purchase homes in affluent neighborhoods. Until the income levels of
blacks are raised sufficiently to enable them to buy suburban homes,
fair housing legislation will remain largely a symbolic commitment.

"De Facto" School Segregation in Cities

In *Brown* v. *Board of Education of Topeka*, the Supreme Court quoted
approvingly the view that segregation had "a tendency to retard the
educational and mental development of Negro children and to deprive
them of some of the benefits they would receive in a racially integrated
school system." In 1967 the U.S. Commission on Civil Rights reported
that even when the segregation was *de facto*, that is, the product of
segregated housing patterns and neighborhood schools rather than direct discrimination, the adverse effects on black students were still significant.[6] In Northern urban school districts the Commission found
that predominantly black schools were less likely to have good libraries
or advanced courses in the sciences and in languages than predominantly white schools; moreover, the former were more likely to have

[6] U.S. Commission on Civil Rights, *Racial Isolation in the Public Schools* (Washington, D.C.: Government Printing Office, 1967).

overcrowded classrooms, poorly trained teachers, and teachers who were dissatisfied with their school assignments. Black students attending predominantly black schools had lower achievement scores and lower levels of aspiration than blacks with comparable socioeconomic backgrounds who attended predominantly white schools. When a group of black students attending school with a majority of advantaged whites was compared to a group of blacks attending school with a majority of disadvantaged blacks, the average difference in levels of achievement amounted to more than two grade levels. On the other hand, the Commission found that the achievement levels of white students in classes roughly half-white in composition were not substantially different from those of white students in all-white schools. This finding comprises perhaps the best single argument for ending de facto segregation in Northern urban systems.[7]

Racial segregation of public school pupils is widespread throughout the nation (see Table 3–2). The U.S. Commission on Civil Rights reported that in the 1965–66 school year 75 percent of the black elementary school pupils in seventy-five large cities attended predominantly black schools (those with 90 percent or more black enrollment).[8] However, ending de facto segregation would require drastic changes in the prevailing concept of "neighborhood schools." Schools would no longer be a part of the neighborhood or the local community but rather part of a larger city-wide or area-wide school system. Students would have to be bussed into and out of the ghettos on a massive scale. In several large cities where blacks comprise the overwhelming majority of public school students, desegregation would require city students to be bussed to the suburbs and suburban students to be bussed to the core city. Such a program would require the cooperation of independent suburban school districts, which seems very unlikely. Many suburbanites moved out of the central city in order to get their

[7] The Commission relied heavily on a report to the U.S. Office of Education by James S. Coleman, Equality of Educational Opportunities (Washington, D.C.: Government Printing Office, 1966). This important study has been the object of considerable comment and controversy. See, for example, Christopher Jencks, "Education: The Racial Gap," The New Republic 55 (October 1966): 21–26; and James K. Kent, "The Coleman Report: Opening Pandora's Box," Phi Delta Kappa 49 (January 1968): 242–45.

[8] U.S. Commission on Civil Rights, Racial Isolation in Public Schools, p. 3.

Table 3–2   Segregation in Public Elementary Schools
of Large Cities, 1965–66

	Negro Students as a Percentage of Total Students	Percentage of Negro Students in Schools 90-100% Negro	Percentage of Negro Teachers in Schools 90-100% Negro
New York	31.0	20.7	56.8
Chicago	52.8	89.2	88.8
Los Angeles	19.2	39.5	94.7
Philadelphia	58.6	72.0	57.7
Detroit	55.3	72.3	65.0
Baltimore	64.3	84.2	67.0
Houston	33.9	93.0	97.3
Cleveland	53.9	82.3	80.2
Washington	90.9	90.4	34.3
St. Louis	63.3	90.9	66.0
Milwaukee	26.4	72.4	86.3
San Francisco	28.8	21.1	65.1
Boston	28.9	35.4	76.5
Dallas	27.5	82.6	90.1
New Orleans	65.5	95.9	83.8
Pittsburgh	39.4	49.5	62.3
San Antonio	14.3	65.9	89.4
San Diego	11.6	13.9	88.7
Seattle	10.5	9.9	89.8
Buffalo	34.6	77.0	81.1

SOURCE: U.S. Commission on Civil Rights, *Racial Isolation in the Public Schools* (Washington, D.C.: Government Printing Office, 1967).

children out of city schools, and these persons are highly unlikely to favor any proposal to bus their children back into the ghettos. Finally, the ending of de facto segregation would require school districts to classify students on the basis of race and to use racial categories as a basis for school placement. Although this would be a supposedly benign form of racial classification, nevertheless it would represent a return to both government-sponsored racial classification and the differential application of laws to the separate races (in contrast to the notion that the law should be "color-blind").

The Congress of the United States neither encourages nor discourages school segregation outside of the Southern and Border states. In other words, federal policy to date constitutes a "nondecision" in support of de facto segregation in Northern cities. Title VI of the Civil Rights Act of 1964, which authorizes the withholding of federal funds from programs operated in a racially discriminatory manner and which has been the most effective instrument in desegregating Southern states, specifically excludes de facto segregation from its purview. The word "desegregation" is defined in the Act to mean "the assignment of students to public schools and within such schools without regard to race, color, religion or natural origin, but . . . shall not be construed to mean the assignment of students to public schools in order to overcome racial imbalance." The Act also provides that "nothing herein shall empower any official or court of the United States to issue any order seeking to achieve a racial balance in any school by requiring the transportation of pupils or students from one school to another or one school district to another in order to achieve such racial balance." Thus, Congress in effect has forbidden the U.S. Office of Education to withhold federal funds because of *de facto* segregation.

While the Supreme Court has shown its distaste for racial classification under the Constitution, those classifications declared unconstitutional by the Court have all been harmful to the minority race. It is very unlikely that the Supreme Court would hold that racial classification and "bussing" for the purpose of achieving integration are unconstitutional, since such a racial classification scheme would be aimed at helping rather than harming the minority race. Federal district courts have rejected the arguments of white parents that consciously assigning children to schools and classes on the basis of race in order to eliminate de facto segregation violates the equal protection clause of the Fourteenth Amendment. The courts have held that "a local Board of Education is not constitutionally prohibited from taking race into account in drawing or re-drawing school attendance lines for the purpose of reducing or eliminating de facto segregation in its public schools."[9] The argument that race may never be taken into account in pupil placement has relied upon Mr. Justice Harlan's famous dissent in *Plessy* v. *Ferguson* to the effect that "our Constitution is color-blind, and neither knows nor tolerates classes among citizens." But this was a dissenting view, not a majority opinion, and, rightly or wrongly, the Supreme Court has never completely adopted "color-blind" as a constitutional standard. Thus, there is no constitutional barrier to a policy of "bussing."

To date federal courts have *not* held that there is any affirmative duty to correct de facto racial imbalances in Northern schools. In other words, as yet there is no constitutional *duty* to eliminate de facto segregation, so long as school attendance lines are drawn with no real intention of segregating the races. Several U.S. circuit courts have held that the equal protection clause of the Fourteenth Amendment does not create an affirmative duty for school districts to correct imbalances resulting from neighborhood school plans not consciously devised to segregate the races.[10]

"De Facto" Segregation: A Comparative View

Though racial segregation in public schools is widespread, there are marked differences among states and cities in the degree of school segregation.[11] For example, among Northern cities in 1966 New York City had only 21 percent of its black pupils attending predominantly black schools whereas the comparable figure for Buffalo was 77 percent. Among representative Southern cities, the figures ranged from

[9] *Fuller* v. *Volk*, 230 F. Supp. 25 (1964); see also the "Legal Appendix" in U.S. Commission on Civil Rights, *Racial Isolation in Public Schools*.

[10] In the leading case of *Bell* v. *School City of Gary,* the Supreme Court denied certiorari where a lower federal court had upheld Gary's neighborhood school plan in the context of a racially segregated housing pattern resulting in racial imbalance in the public schools. *Bell* v. *School City of Gary*, 213 F. Supp. 819 (1963), 324 F. 2d 209 (1963); *cert. denied*, 377 U.S. 924 (1964).

[11] See Thomas R. Dye, "Urban School Segregation: A Comparative Analysis," *Urban Affairs Quarterly* 4 (December 1968): 141–66.

31 percent in Corpus Christi, Texas, to 99 percent in Tuscaloosa, Alabama. These different patterns of school segregation present both an opportunity and a challenge for comparative policy research.

As recently as 1966, Northern and Southern cities differed markedly in the extent of pupil and teacher segregation in their public schools (see Table 3–3). Southern cities in our sample had an average of 87 percent of their Negro pupils in schools that were 90-100 percent Negro in composition, while for Northern cities the comparable figure was only 46 percent.

However, segregation in Southern cities is steadily *decreasing*. Even though pupil and teacher segregation indexes are still higher for Southern than for Northern cities, they do represent a sizeable decrease from the nearly total segregation prevailing in 1954. In contrast, the available evidence indicates that school segregation in Northern cities is slowly *increasing*. While complete data are not available for many cities, the data compiled by the U.S. Commission on Civil Rights suggests that larger percentages of Negro pupils were attending predominantly Negro schools in 1965 than in previous years (see Table 3–4).

A commonly accepted hypothesis is that school segregation varies directly with the proportion of blacks enrolled in public schools. Comparative analysis reveals that indeed black pupil percentages *are* the single most important determinant of pupil and teacher segregation in both Northern and Southern cities. Table 3–5 presents simple and partial correlation coefficients for a series of urban environmental variables and black pupil and teacher segregation measures for both Northern and Southern cities. Simple coefficients indicate that black pupil and teacher segregation are more closely related to black pupil percentages than to any other environmental variable. The strong partial coefficients indicate that this relationship is an independent one; that is, it does not depend upon the intervening effect of some other environmental variable. These findings suggest that cities with large black enrollments have the greatest difficulty in creating an effective policy of desegregation.

Figure 3–2 permits us to observe which cities segregate more or less of their Negro pupils than would be predicted from their Negro enrollment. The figure is a scatter-diagram of the relationship between the proportion of Negro pupils enrolled and the percentage of Negro

Table 3–3   Averages for Northern and Southern* Cities
              on Pupil and Teacher Segregation Measures

	Southern Cities	Northern Cities
Negro pupils as percentage of total	31.5	32.5
Negro teachers as percentage of total	27.3	19.8
Negro pupil segregation	86.7	45.5
Negro teacher segregation	94.5	45.0

* Southern and Northern cities are same as those used in Figure 3-2.

students assigned to predominantly Negro schools. Each city is represented by a dot (Northern cities) or an X (Southern cities) placed
upon the graph, with the city's percentage of Negro enrollment and the
Negro pupil segregation figure as coordinates. Line A represents the
line of regression for Northern cities and line B the line of regression
for Southern cities. The closer a Northern or Southern city lies to its
respective line of regression, the more it conforms to the proposition
that segregation is a function of Negro enrollment. These lines represent predictions of the extent of school segregation based upon Negro
enrollment percentages. Cities that segregate more than expected on
the basis of Negro enrollment lie above the line of regression; cities
that segregate less than expected lie below the line of regression.

   Among Northern cities, Milwaukee and Buffalo are much more
segregated than one would expect on the basis of their Negro enrollments. They segregate a larger percentage of their Negro pupils than
cities such as Pittsburgh, Cincinnati, Rochester, and Akron, which
have roughly the same proportion of Negro students. In contrast, New
York City, Wilmington, and especially Hartford are more integrated
than one would predict on the basis of their Negro enrollments.[12]
Whatever else may be said about New York City schools, clearly they
have achieved a remarkable degree of desegregation in comparison
with other cities' schools.[13]

[12] See Connecticut State Department of Education, *Project Concern*, 20 September 1966; and U.S. Commission on Civil Rights, *Racial Isolation in Public
Schools*, p. 153.

[13] See New York State Education Commissioner's Advisory Committee on Human Relations, "Desegregating the Public Schools of New York City," 12 May
1964.

Table 3–4 Changes in Pupil Segregation in Selected Cities

City	Year	Number of Negro Students in Schools 90-100% Negro	Percentage of Total Negro Students in Schools 90-100% Negro	Year	Number of Negro Students in Schools 90-100% Negro	Percentage of Total Negro Students in Schools 90-100% Negro
Cincinnati	1950	3,981	43.7	1965	11,155	49.4
Milwaukee	1950	1,316	51.2	1965	14,344	72.4
Philadelphia	1950	29,555	63.2	1965	66,052	72.0
Pittsburgh	1950	3,226	30.4	1965	9,226	49.5
Indianapolis	1951	7,637	83.2	1965	15,426	70.5
Cleveland	1952	12,369	57.4	1965	41,034	82.3
Oakland	1959	1,110	7.7	1965	9,043	48.7
Detroit	1960	62,391	66.9	1965	77,654	72.3
Buffalo	1961	9,199	80.5	1965	13,106	77.0
San Francisco	1962	1,579	11.6	1965	3,031	21.1
Harrisburg	1963	2,103	58.1	1965	2,075	54.0
Springfield	1963	0	0.0	1965	567	15.4
New Haven	1963	1,196	22.5	1965	2,171	36.8

Table 3–5 Environmental Variables and Public School Segregation in Northern and Southern Cities

Environmental Variables	Segregation Measures							
	Northern Cities				Southern Cities			
	Negro Pupils		Negro Teachers		Negro Pupils		Negro Teachers	
	Simple	Partial	Simple	Partial	Simple	Partial	Simple	Partial
Negro pupils as percentage of total population	.76*	.60*	.79	.67	.46	.66	.35	.36
Status characteristics of city population								
Adult education	−.46*	−.34*	−.51	−.42	.20	.52*	−.03	.63*
White collar employment	−.56*	−.44*	−.57	−.51	.12	.32*	−.08	.58
Family income	−.04	−.25	−.15	−.25	.06	.05	−.10	.29
Status characteristics of Negro population								
Adult education	−.42*	−.20	−.46*	−.12	.05	.11	−.07	.20
White collar employment	−.14	.19	−.13	.27	.33*	.46*	.16	.27
Family income	−.05	.13	−.19	.05	.02	.10	.19	.05
Ethnicity	−.31*	−.21	−.39*	−.39*	−.24	−.40*	−.43*	−.62*
Size of city	.49*	.37*	.43*	.38*	.16	.21	.06	.24
Age of city	.54*	.32*	.53*	.38*	.12	−.11	−.10	−.44*
Private school enrollment	.25	.17	.22	.02	.35	.28	.17	.59

NOTE: Figures are simple and partial correlation coefficients for the relationships between pupil and teacher segregation measures and environmental variables for Northern and Southern cities respectively; partial coefficients show the influence of each environmental variable while controlling for *all* other environmental variables including Negro pupil percentages; an asterisk indicates a significant relationship.

Figure 3–2

DISTRIBUTION OF NORTHERN AND SOUTHERN CITIES BY
NEGRO ENROLLMENT AND PUPIL SEGREGATION PERCENTAGES

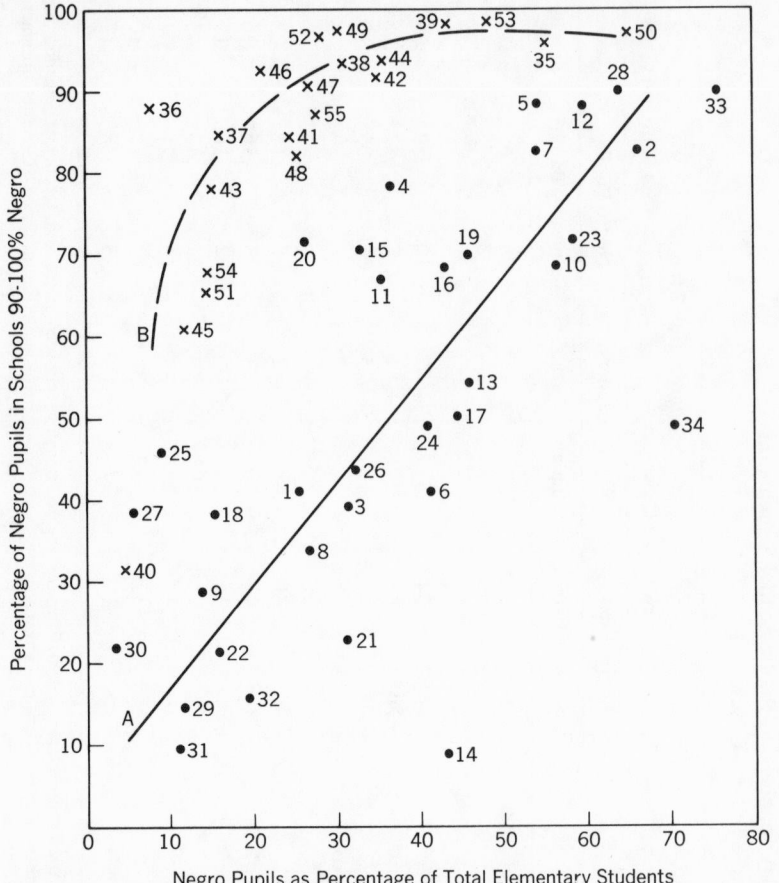

Negro Pupils as Percentage of Total Elementary Students

NORTHERN CITIES: (1) Akron (2) Baltimore (3) Boston (4) Buffalo (5) Chicago (6) Cincinnati (7) Cleveland (8) Columbus, O. (9) Denver (10) Detroit (11) Flint (12) Gary (13) Harrisburg (14) Hartford (15) Indianapolis (16) Kansas City (17) Lexington (18) Los Angeles (19) Louisville (20) Milwaukee (21) New York (22) Peoria (23) Philadelphia (24) Pittsburgh (25) Portland (26) Rochester (27) St. Joseph (28) St. Louis (29) San Diego (30) San Francisco (31) Seattle (32) Springfield, Mass. (33) Washington, D. C. (34) Wilmington

SOUTHERN CITIES: (35) Atlanta (36) Amarillo (37) Austin (38) Charleston (39) Columbia (40) Corpus Christi (41) Dallas (42) Houston (43) Knoxville (44) Little Rock (45) Lubbock (46) Oklahoma City (47) Miami (48) Nashville (49) Raleigh (50) Richmond (51) San Antonio (52) Texarkana (53) Tuscaloosa (54) Wichita Falls (55) Winston-Salem

What other variables, aside from Negro pupil percentages, might be expected to affect school desegregation policy? Among Northern cities, the extent of racial segregation in public schools is significantly correlated with the educational and the occupational levels (though not the income levels) of the urban population. Increases in adult education and in white collar employment are associated with decreases in Negro pupil and teacher segregation. Ethnicity also appears to have some independent relationship to desegregation policy even when other variables are controlled, cities with larger ethnic populations tending to be less segregated.

Comparative analysis reveals that among Northern cities both the size and the age of the community are independently associated with segregation policy. Large and old cities tend to have more pupil and teacher segregation than small and new ones. The partial coefficients in Table 3–5 indicate that these associations exist separately from the influence of Negro enrollment percentages (which, of course, are greatest in large and old cities). In contrast to Northern cities, neither the size nor the age of the community is associated with segregation policy in Southern cities: small and new Southern cities are just as segregated as large and old ones.

In summary, the comparative analysis of aggregate figures on school segregation in large cities reveals several interesting correlates of de facto public school segregation in both Northern and Southern cities. Of course, these correlations do not tell us exactly how demands regarding school policy develop out of the environmental conditions, nor how these demands are communicated, nor how school systems adapt themselves to these demands, nor exactly how governmental structures and political variables modify these demands. Nor are these correlations necessarily proof of cause and effect relationships. But they do direct our attention to the underlying environmental conditions and the political variables that are linked to urban school segregation policy.

The Politics of Northern School Desegregation

How do big city school systems respond to demands to reduce de facto segregation? How are these demands expressed, and how do school officials react to them? What factors shape the outcome of desegre-

gation issues? Sociologist Robert L. Crain studied desegregation controversies in eight Northern cities, and in the process conducted extensive interviews with school officials, school board members, civil
rights leaders, and community influentials.[14] One of his most important
findings was that school desegregation is a substantially different problem in the North than in the South.

According to Crain, desegregation controversies in Northern
cities usually begin with the presentation of charges or demands to
local school administrators by civil rights groups. These may range
from concrete requests for school boundary changes, to charges of
favoritism toward white schools, to demands for the closing of predominantly black schools and the bussing of black pupils to white
schools, to pleas for a clear-cut policy statement on desegregation.
Civil rights leaders often pursue "symbolic" more than "welfare" goals,
sometimes stressing the moral or ideological principle of desegregation
as much as the individual Negro child's education. Interestingly, the
intensity of the group's demands often has little to do with the actual
extent of de facto segregation. For example, some of the most intense
civil rights activity has occurred in relatively well-integrated cities like
San Francisco and Pittsburgh. Since the integrationists' demands are
usually oriented as much toward symbolism as substance, naturally
the *tone* or the *style* of the community's response is often more important to them than the actual number of Negroes assigned to integrated
classrooms.

In Northern desegregation controversies the initial charges or
complaints of the civil rights group are frequently denied by school
administrators. The most frequent response of school administrators is

> (a) an insistence that the only morally correct position is strict non-
> discrimination (color-blindness) and that efforts to intentionally in-
> tegrate schools are improper for this reason; (b) an insistence on a
> narrow definition of the function of the school which stresses "edu-
> cational" rather than "social" values and hence sees integration as
> outside the school's province; and (c) an unwillingness to engage in
> serious discussion of the issue with lay persons, and an extreme de-
> fensiveness in the face of criticism.[15]

[14] Robert L. Crain, *The Politics of School Desegregation* (Chicago: Aldine,
1968).
[15] *Ibid.*, p. 136.

School superintendents and civil rights leaders generally do not share the same values, attitudes, or social backgrounds, and therefore attaining even the semblance of communication between these two sets of actors is sometimes difficult. Crain writes that "the interaction between civil rights leaders and school superintendents has the preconditions for conflict. They literally do not speak the same language. In addition, both live in a world hostile to them and are unlikely to be very patient in dealing with each other. In six of the eight cities, school integration quickly became a conflict between the movement and the superintendent."[16]

After their initial encounter with school administrators, civil rights leaders next proceed to bring the issue to the attention of the school board. In most cases this step entails real or threatened demonstrations. The school boycott or strike constitutes the heaviest artillery in the civil rights arsenal. A successful school boycott, more than any other demonstration, can seriously embarrass the school board while simultaneously demonstrating massive support within the black community for the civil rights demands. Since school boycotts violate truancy laws, however, civil rights leaders must carefully consider the possible consequences before instigating one. Then, too, the leaders realize that if they call for a boycott and most black students continue to attend the school, the net effect is merely to undermine their own bargaining position. Hence, civil rights leaders must exercise extreme caution in the use of this direct action tactic. As an alternative to school boycotts, the filing of court suits generally works to the disadvantage of the civil rights leaders. As was earlier noted, the courts have not yet taken a clear position on de facto segregation, and once a suit has begun the school can delay action on the demands by claiming that it is awaiting the outcome of the suit.

It is during the initial encounter between the civil rights leaders and the school board that the latter makes the "key" response that sets the tone for almost all subsequent actions. The board supplants the school administrator as the primary decision maker, and actions at this juncture are generally more favorable toward the group's demands than any previous action. The first question members of the board must face is: "Should this body intentionally attempt to integrate schools, or should we insist that they continue to operate in a color-blind

16 *Ibid.*, p. 123.

fashion?" In all eight Northern cities that Crain studied, the school boards were asked to state publicly (1) their recognition of the existence of segregated schools and (2) their promise to do something about it. "Such a statement meets some of the more symbolic goals of the Civil Rights movement," notes Crain; "it puts a governmental body on record as opposed to discrimination, not only in the schools but in effect in housing as well, and commits it to making a demonstration of its belief in racial equality."[17] Normally the board has a great deal of flexibility in meeting both the symbolic and the concrete demands of local civil rights leaders, since generally white parents are not nearly as organized or cohesive or as vocal in their demands as the civil rights groups. As Crain points out, "white parents will not protest integration as long as (1) the school their children are to attend is not predominantly black; (2) white students are not transferred out of their present schools; (3) white students are not forced to attend schools located in the ghetto; and (4) neighborhood racial stability is not threatened."[18] The board is usually free to take action within broad limits: it can bus blacks out of ghetto schools, adopt an open enrollment policy allowing blacks to select whichever schools they wish to attend, redraw school boundaries to achieve better racial balance, or close black schools, redistributing Negro students among other schools.

The board's action usually results in a compromise, frequently one that achieves greater racial balance without actually admitting that the actions were prompted by racial considerations. If the board decides to acquiesce to the demands made of it, the local civil rights leaders may be satisfied to drop the issue, or alternatively, the school board can publicize its concessions, attempting thereby to cut off the leaders' grass-roots support. If the board rejects the civil rights demands, it is likely to be faced with intensified demonstrations. But, as Crain reports, the intensification of demonstrations will seldom change the board's attitude once it has committed itself to a particular policy.

Perhaps the most interesting finding presented by Crain is that the ideological orientations of the school board members are the most important factor in determining how a community will respond to

[17] *Ibid.*, p. 129.
[18] *Ibid.*, p. 128.

demands for changes in racial patterns in the schools. Crain ranked his cities according to their acquiescence to civil rights demands and then searched for community factors that appeared to influence the degree of acquiescence.[19] Certainly intense civil rights activity did not necessarily lead to acquiescence; in fact, the relationship was just the opposite: the most intense activity took place in cities that proved to be nonacquiescent.

While the cities with the largest black populations were most likely to have acquiescent school boards, the correlation was not as good as one might expect ($r = .53$). Apparently the potential black vote was *not* a very strong influence on school board policy making. Perhaps one reason the percentage of black population correlated poorly with the acquiescence to black demands is that cities with the largest black populations are characterized by greater anti-Negro sentiment among whites. But, in an apparent paradox, Crain also discovered that the status characteristics of white populations (particularly high educational level) that might be expected to correlate with acquiescence to black demands apparently did not influence board policy. Thus, Crain concluded that neither the characteristics of the community nor the activities of the civil rights leaders (except for their initial presentation of the issue) had much influence on board policy.

The most important factor influencing desegregation policy was the civil rights attitudes of school board members. Figure 3–3 plots the median civil rights liberalism of the boards (obtained by analyzing responses to questionnaires filled out by board members) against the degree of acquiescence by the school board. Though the overall correlation (.65) is not very high, the pattern does reveal an important

---

[19] Crain ranked the cities, from most acquiescent to least acquiescent, as follows: (1) Pittsburgh: adoption of open enrollment after hearing parents' testimony (November 1965); (1—tie) Baltimore: decision by ad hoc committee to eliminate districting (June 1963); (3) San Francisco: decision to close Central Junior High School (August 1962); (4) Newark: adoption of open enrollment to settle suit (January 1962); (5) St. Louis: receipt and adoption in general terms of Maher committee report (June 1963); (6) Lawndale: refusal to change Woodside boundaries (January 1961); (7) Bay City: fruitless discussion of de facto segregation prior to the first boycott (June 1963); and (8) Buffalo: designation of Woodlawn School boundaries (March 1963). *Ibid.,* pp. 145–46.

Figure 3–3

**CIVIL RIGHTS LIBERALISM OF SCHOOL BOARDS
AND ACQUIESCENCE IN DESEGREGATION
IN NORTHERN CITIES**

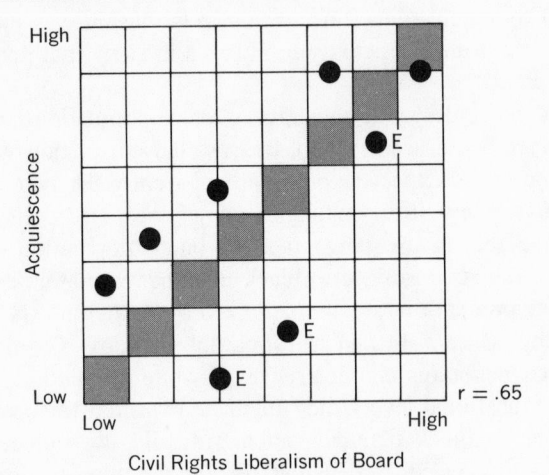

NOTE: E indicates an elected board; r, among appointed
board = .97; r, among elected board = 1.00.

SOURCE: Robert L. Crain, *The Politics of School Desegregation* (Chicago: Aldine, 1968),
p. 161. Copyright © 1968 by National Opinion Research Center. Reprinted by
permission.

difference: the three cities falling below the line of regression (i.e.,
those less acquiescent than we would expect from the liberalism score
of the members) were all *elected* boards whereas the other five were
all appointed boards. Since elected board members with the same liberalism scores as appointed board members were less acquiescent in the
demands of civil rights groups, we may conclude that their desire to be
reelected probably tempered the expression of liberal personal views.

Restyling Ghetto Education

Such recent works as Bel Kaufman's *Up the Down Staircase*[20] and

[20] Bel Kaufman, *Up the Down Staircase* (Englewood Cliffs, N.J.: Prentice-Hall,
1964).

Jonathan Kozol's *Death at an Early Age*[21] have helped to familiarize the public with the plight of the nation's ghetto schools. Disadvantaged black pupils score lower than whites on standard achievement tests in the primary grades, and they fall progressively further behind as they pass from one grade to the next. By the twelfth grade, the average black pupil is more than two years behind the average white student on standardized tests of achievement; the black drop-out rate is more than double the white rate, and the black pupils' self-esteem is considerably lower. Though the validity of achievement and intelligence tests can be disputed, there seems little doubt that most ghetto blacks are educationally ill-prepared for college, post–high school training, or the job market. Indeed, the question of "equality of educational opportunity" is a serious one not only for urban schools but for the entire nation.

To date, public policies relating to equality of educational opportunity have emphasized compensatory programs for disadvantaged children. Compensatory educational programs generally assume that environmental problems create in the disadvantaged pupil certain learning difficulties—whether caused by verbal retardation, lack of motivation, or experiential and sensory deprivation—that can be corrected in part by special attention and treatment. In addition to special remedial programs grafted onto the regular school curriculum, compensatory efforts have also been attempted at the preschool level.

The major thrust for the compensatory education movement came in Title I of the Elementary and Secondary Education Act of 1965, which provided more than $1 billion a year for "poverty impacted" schools, thereby stimulating public schools throughout the nation to upgrade their remedial programs for the poor. In addition, the Economic Opportunity Act of 1964 encouraged community action agencies throughout the nation to initiate preschool remedial programs for disadvantaged children under the rubric "Project Head Start." The popular Head Start program was later transferred to the public schools for administration with funds and assistance from the Office of Economic Opportunity.

But in 1967 the compensatory education approach was seriously

---

[21] Jonathan Kozol, *Death at an Early Age: The Destruction of the Hearts and Minds of Negro Children in the Boston Public Schools* (Boston: Houghton Mifflin, 1967).

challenged in an influential report written by Professor James S. Coleman of Johns Hopkins University and entitled *Equality of Educational Opportunity*.[22] The Coleman Report took eighteen months to complete, cost $2 million to produce, and included data on 600,000 children, 60,000 teachers, and 4,000 schools. Its conclusions included the astounding observation that formal educational inputs, such as per pupil expenditures, teacher training programs, teacher-pupil ratios, library funds, laboratory equipment, and special programs and materials really make relatively *little* difference in pupils' achievement levels and motivation. However, Coleman found that children from disadvantaged backgrounds (regardless of race) do benefit from integration with advantaged children (also, regardless of race). Moreover, advantaged children are not harmed by integration, particularly if the disadvantaged constitute only a minority in the classroom. The startling implication of the Coleman Report was that schools are in essence merely places where kids learn from one another and that, therefore, money spent improving ghetto schools is unlikely to produce any meaningful results. Later the U.S. Commission on Civil Rights, in its report *Racial Isolation in the Public Schools,* used the Coleman data as ammunition to support its contention that integration, not compensatory education, is the key to the problem of equal educational opportunity.

Earlier we discussed the feasibility (especially the political feasibility) of ending de facto segregation. Neither Congress, nor the federal courts, nor most urban school districts are enthusiastic about enforced racial balancing or bussing to overcome de facto segregation. The prospects for widespread urban school integration are therefore very dim. It is unlikely that many school boards in Northern cities will require that all their schools maintain a black quota equivalent to the black percentage of the city-wide school population. First of all, this would require extensive bussing of students away from their neighborhood schools and their dispersal throughout the city, with a

---

22 See note 7. As one might expect, Coleman's explosive findings have been challenged. See Samuel Bowles and Henry M. Levin, "The Determinants of Scholastic Achievement—An Appraisal of Some Recent Evidence," *Journal of Human Resources* III (Winter 1968): 3–24; Peter Schrag, "Why Our Schools Have Failed," *Commentary* 45 (March 1968): 31–38.

resulting increase in time and cost. Moreover, in some cities, achieving racially balanced public schools would require bussing of students out of city school districts to independent suburban school districts, and perhaps bussing of students from independent suburbs into city ghettos. It is doubtful if independent suburban school districts would agree to do this, and state governments are not likely to force them to do so. Finally, ghetto residents themselves have frequently shown concern for their own neighborhood schools, and they may not wish to see their children bussed long distances to white sections of the city or to white suburbs. These problems, together with the finding of the Coleman Report that compensatory education has little value, have stimulated the search for some other approach to equality of educational opportunity.

Decentralization of big city school systems leading to "community control" of local schools as an approach to equality in urban education has recently produced a great deal of controversy. Proponents of community control have suggested that ghetto residents should be given control over ghetto schools (1) to achieve a shift from professional and administrative "dominance" of the schools to "a meaningful parental and community role in the education process"; (2) to deemphasize students' acquisition of achievement skills (reading, writing, and arithmetic) in favor of "a humanistically-oriented curriculum modifying the skill-performance standard by which educational quality is primarily measured"; and (3) to bring personnel into the schools who have "broader talents than the conventionally prepared career educator." Support for the community control concept is common among black power advocates and racial separatists as well as educational reformers. Black militants have attacked desegregation for its implication that black pupils can learn well only by sitting next to white pupils. They want educational programs emphasizing black identity and self-awareness, and they reject programs designed to make black pupils "like" white pupils (see the "black power" discussion in Chapter 4). More importantly, they want black political control of educational resources in the ghetto. As Professor Marilyn Gittell explains:

Community control implies a redistribution of power within the educational subsystem. It is directed toward achieving a modern mechanism for participatory democracy. It attempts to answer the political failure in education systems, and, as regards the educational failure, community control is intended to create an environment in which more meaningful educational policies can be developed and a wide variety of alternative solutions and techniques can be tested. It seems plausible to assume a school system devoted to community needs and serving as an agent of community interests will provide an environment more conducive to learning.[23]

New York's unhappy experience with community control illustrates some of the problems involved in this concept.[24] In 1967 the Ford Foundation sponsored demonstration projects in community control in New York City, including a project in a ghetto area known as Ocean Hill–Brownsville. At the same time Mayor John V. Lindsay created an Advisory Panel on Decentralization of New York City Schools headed by Ford Foundation President McGeorge Bundy, which recommended a city-wide program of school decentralization (the Bundy Plan).[25] An Ocean Hill–Brownsville local governing board was established and proceeded to act with considerable autonomy from the New York City Board of Education. When schools opened in September 1967, the local governing board appointed as principals five persons who were not on the civil service list, thereby alienating the Council of Supervisory Associations, which represented local school administrators. During a city-wide teachers' strike over pay increases and smaller classes, the local board kept Ocean Hill–Brownsville schools open, thereby earning the dislike of the United Federation of Teachers, which represented New York City teachers. Throughout the 1967–68 school year increasingly hostile rhetoric was exchanged between white teachers and administrators on the one hand and the Ocean Hill–Brownsville governing board on the other. The board charged that certain white teachers were uncooperative and failed to understand ghetto problems; the teachers replied that the Board was

23 Marilyn Gittell and Alan G. Hevesi, eds., *The Politics of Urban Education* (New York: Praeger, 1969), pp. 365–66.

24 *Ibid.*, Section V, pp. 305–77.

25 Mayor's Advisory Panel on Decentralization of the New York City Schools, *Reconnection for Learning: A Community School System for New York City* (1967); reprinted in Marilyn Gittell and Alan G. Hevesi, eds., *The Politics of Urban Education* (New York: Praeger, 1969), pp. 261–76.

infected with black racism and even anti-Semitism (a large share of New York City's teachers and administrators are Jewish). In May 1968 the board dismissed nineteen white teachers without prior notice or hearings seven weeks before the end of the term because they were "out of tune with the political atmosphere in the community." The United Federation of Teachers protested the dismissals as violations of civil service regulations and due process of law and in September called for a city-wide strike. The strike seriously curtailed education in New York City during the 1968–69 school year. The issues of the strike were eventually mediated, but not without tragically increasing the distrust and suspicion between the races both in the school system and in the city at large.

Opponents of community control—particularly white teachers, the leaders of teachers' unions, and administrators—argue that decentralization creates administrative duplication, inefficiencies, and increased overhead costs. They contend that community control results in wasted educational dollars, the destruction of the merit system, and the introduction of political and racial considerations into educational policies, and that ultimately it promotes racial separatism and black militancy. Though decentralization suffered a setback in New York City as a result of the Ocean Hill–Brownsville experience (the state legislature subsequently rejected the Bundy Plan), it may eventually emerge again in that city and elsewhere as an approach to improving ghetto education.

In summary, the existence of black ghetto neighborhoods and predominantly black public schools remains a persistent political issue in the nation's cities. Several approaches to the problem of de facto school segregation have been suggested, including special compensatory education programs for ghetto schools, the integration of black and white pupils through racial balancing in school assignments, and the decentralization of school administration to encourage the development of black-controlled educational programs. But all of these approaches involve serious political problems, and none appears to offer an early solution to the problem of upgrading ghetto schools.

chapter 4

The Struggle
for Equality

White Americans can understand the unfairness of legal discrimination, and the majority agree that such discrimination is inconsistent
with the norms of a democratic society. Yet, though the *legal* foundations of segregation have collapsed, the *actual* disparity between blacks
and whites in terms of income, education, employment, housing and
other conditions of life have not changed greatly. Though the victories
of the civil rights movement were immensely important, they are primarily *symbolic* gains rather than *real* changes in the conditions under
which most blacks live in America. Racial politics today revolve
around the actual inequalities existing between blacks and whites in
incomes, jobs, housing, health, education, and the other conditions
of life.

The "Life Chances" of Blacks and Whites

The problem of inequality is posed as one of differences in the "life
chances" of blacks and whites. Figures can only suggest the bare outline
of a black's "life chances" in American society (see Table 4–1). The
income of the average black family is only half that of the average white

Table 4–1   Economic Characteristics of Black
            and White Populations in the United States, 1960

	Black	White
Median family income	$2,520	$5,088
Percentage of families with annual incomes less than $3,000	39.6	18.6
Median school years completed by adults	8.2	10.9
Fertility rate (per 1,000 females of child-bearing age)	2,002	1,712
Percentage of families headed by females	22.4	8.7
Male occupations in percentages		
Professional workers	3.9	11.0
Managers	2.3	11.5
Clerical workers	5.0	7.1
Salesmen	1.5	7.4
Farmers	4.4	5.6
Craftsmen	10.2	20.5
Operatives	23.5	19.5
Service personnel	13.7	5.2
Farm laborers	7.1	2.3
Manual laborers	19.4	5.6
Not reported	8.4	4.2
Infant mortality rate (per 1,000 live births)	43.2	22.9
Percentage owning homes	38.4	61.6
Median size of family	4.34	3.64

family. Two-fifths of all black families have annual incomes of less than $3,000, the government's oft-cited "poverty line." Proportionately twice as many blacks live in substandard housing as whites. The black unemployment rate is twice as high as that among whites. The average black acquires 2.7 years less education than the average white. Blacks are far less likely than whites to hold prestigious white collar jobs in professional, managerial, clerical, or sales work. They hold few skilled craft jobs in industry, but are concentrated rather in operative, service, and laboring positions. Black women not only have more children but also have them earlier than white women, and bearing too many children too early usually complicates the parents' lives, making it difficult for them to finish school or to save money. Thus, a cycle is at work in the ghettos: low education levels produce low income levels, which prevent parents from moving out of the ghettos, which deprive children of educational opportunities, and so repeats the cycle.

Changes over time offer little encouragement. Though the average black's income has risen substantially in the postwar years, the ratio between his and the average white's income has remained stable at one to two. While the number of blacks acquiring white collar jobs as managers, officials, and proprietors has increased by nearly half in ten years, the corresponding percentage figure is quite small. The problem of black unemployment is particularly serious: during the past forty years the black unemployment rate, once on a par with the white figure, has steadily degenerated to the point where today it is consistently more than twice the rate for whites (see Table 4–2). This change is related to the massive migration of blacks from farms to cities. Unlike earlier immigrants, blacks are arriving in the nation's cities at a time when the demand for unskilled labor is lessening and when the premium is on educational and occupational skills.

Inequality *among* blacks is much greater than that *among* whites. The black social class structure resembles a pyramid with the great majority of blacks at the bottom and only a small number at the top. The white social class structure, on the other hand, is diamond-shaped, with few whites at either top or bottom and most in the middle. Blacks at the top of their social pyramid are at approximately the same position in society as middle class whites. The black upper class includes professionals—especially doctors, dentists, and lawyers—public administrators, civic leaders, educators, politicians, and a few businessmen.

The ghetto is peopled primarily by lower class black masses. Individual blacks who have attained middle class status are generally more acceptable to whites than are blacks living in the ghettos. Whites feel that they can communicate with the black middle class, but not with the black masses. They regard blacks at the top of the social pyramid as living examples of what the determined or talented Negro can accomplish in a democratic capitalist society.

In addition to poverty, family disorganization, and inequality, the ghetto also harbors various social pathologies. Crime and delinquency, mental illness, and drug addiction haunt America's ghettos.

Table 4–2   Unemployment Rates for Blacks and Whites, 1930–69

	1930	1940	1950	1960	1964	1967	1969
White (%)	6.6	14.1	4.5	5.0	4.6	3.4	3.1
Black (%)	6.1	16.9	7.9	10.2	9.8	7.4	6.1
Ratio	.92	1.20	1.76	2.04	2.13	2.15	2.0

By and large the victims of these social pathologies are the ghetto residents themselves. Blacks are the principal victims of lawlessness in America: they are 78 percent more likely than whites to be victimized by criminals. Hence, the suppression of crime would benefit blacks comparatively more than it would whites.

According to FBI crime statistics, blacks (which comprise 11 percent of the population) account for 28 percent of all criminal arrests. In all major categories of offenses, the rate of arrests for black people is higher than that for white persons. Assuming that arrests are a rough indicator of the number of crimes committed, the black crime rate is apparently more than twice their proportion of the total population.

Blacks comprise about 40 percent of all persons confined in state prisons, a proportion significantly higher than the black arrest rate. The discrepancy between the arrest rate and the percentage of prisoner population suggests that among those arrested, blacks are more likely to draw prison sentences than whites and less likely to be the beneficiaries of pardon or parole policies.

Blacks also constitute a disproportionate share of the drug addicts in the United States. In 1965 the Federal Bureau of Narcotics reported that 51.6 percent of all narcotics addicts in the United States were blacks. Drug addiction is primarily an urban phenomenon, with more than a half of the nation's addicts living in New York City—and a large proportion of these in central Harlem. Narcotics addiction is an expensive habit for a ghetto resident to maintain, and many addicts must eventually resort to theft to support their habits.

Sociologist Alphonso Pinkney summarizes the reasons that social deviance is disproportionately common among blacks:

(1) In the United States black people occupy a separate and subordinate economic and social position which leads to frustration. Their frustrations are usually displaced in acts of aggression against fellow

Negroes, thus leading to a higher proportion of intraracial criminal acts. (2) As Myrdal has demonstrated, the caste system under which black people live operates in such a way as to prevent them from identifying with the society and the law. The very legal system itself is manipulated to discriminate against black people. (3) Black persons, far more than white persons, are forced to live in deteriorated sections of cities. These areas are characterized by widespread social disorganization and organization in terms of criminal values, as well as poverty, poor housing, restrictions on settlement, and limited outlets for recreation and employment. "Out of these and similar conditions arise elements conducive to greater criminality, as well as other forms of pathology, among the Negro population." (4) The high crime rate among black people is partially a function of their reaction to having their means to success blocked by discriminatory behavior. "Crime may thus be utilized as a means of escape, ego enhancement, expression of aggression, or upward mobility." . . . (5) Black people are overrepresented in the lower class, and recorded crime tends to be concentrated in this class.[1]

Daniel P. Moynihan has argued persuasively that one of the worst effects of slavery and segregation has been their impact on Negro family life.[2] As earlier noted in Chapter 1, the black male was most humiliated by segregationist practices. Segregation, with its implications of inferiority and submissiveness, damaged the male more than the female personality: the black female was a threat to no one. Not surprisingly, the female-headed black family emerges as one of the striking features of life in the ghetto. Almost 25 percent of all black families are headed by women. For the young black male brought up in a matriarchal setting in the ghetto, the future is often depressing, with defeat and frustration repeating themselves throughout his life. He may drop out of school in the ninth grade as a protest of his lack of success. If he fails his armed forces qualification test (and a majority of young men from the ghetto do fail it), he may never again have an

[1] Alphonso Pinkney, *Black Americans* (Englewood Cliffs, N.J.: Prentice-Hall, 1969), pp. 124–25. For the two quotations, Pinkney cites, respectively, Earl R. Moses, "Differentials in Crime Rates Between Negroes and Whites Based on Comparisons of Four Socio-Economically Equated Areas," *American Sociological Review* 12 (August 1947): 420; and Thomas F. Pettigrew, *A Profile of the Negro American* (Princeton, N.J.: Van Nostrand, 1964), p. 156.

[2] Daniel P. Moynihan, *The Negro Family: The Case for National Action* (Washington, D.C.: Government Printing Office, 1965).

opportunity for further education or job training. Lacking parental supervision and with little to do, he may soon get into trouble with the police. A police record will further hurt his chances of getting a job. The ghetto male with limited job skills enters the job market seriously handicapped. His pay is usually not enough to support a family, and he has little hope of advancement. He may tie up much of his income in installment payments for a car, a television set, or the other conveniences that he sees in widespread use among middle class Americans. Because of his low credit rating, he will be forced to pay excessive interest rates, and sooner or later his creditors will garnishee his salary. If he marries, he is likely to have five or more children, and he and his family will live in overcrowded substandard housing. As pressures and frustrations mount, he may decide to leave his family, either because he has found his inability to support his wife and children humiliating or because only in this way will his wife and children be eligible for welfare payments. Thus, welfare policy also strengthens the role of the female in the black family because she can get the family on welfare (particularly Aid to Families with Dependent Children) while the male cannot. In fact, his remaining with his family is often an obstacle to its receiving welfare payments.

The feeling of powerlessness that black ghetto residents possess is reflected in a comparison of ghettos with the "colonies" of an earlier era. Ghetto residents feel they have little control over the institutions in their own communities: businesses, schools, welfare agencies, the police, and most other important agencies are all controlled from the outside. Often the agents of these institutions—the store managers, clerks, teachers, welfare workers, and policemen—are whites who live outside of the ghetto. Thus, the important institutions of the ghetto are staffed and controlled almost entirely by outsiders—and hence the analogy with colonialism. Sociologist Kenneth Clark writes:

> The dark ghetto's invisible walls have been erected by the white society, by those who have power, both to confine those who have *no* power and to perpetuate their powerlessness. The dark ghettos are social, political, educational, and—above all—economic colonies. Their inhabitants are subject peoples, victims of the greed, cruelty, insensitivity, guilt, and fear of their masters.[3]

[3] Kenneth Clark, *Dark Ghetto: Dilemmas of Social Power* (New York: Harper & Row, 1965), p. 11.

In analyzing urban riots, the National Advisory Commission on Civil Disorders also referred to powerlessness, this time as a contributing cause to both urban social disorders and the rise of militant mass movements:

> Many Negroes have come to believe that they are being exploited politically and economically by the white "power structure." Negroes, like people in poverty everywhere, in fact lack the channels of communication, influence and appeal that traditionally have been available to ethnic minorities within the city and which enabled them—unburdened by color—to scale the walls of the white ghettos in an earlier era. The frustrations of powerlessness have led some to the conviction that there is no effective alternative to violence as a means of expression and redress, as a way of "moving the system." More generally, the result is alienation and hostility toward the institutions of law and government and the white society which controls them. This is reflected in the reach toward radical consciousness and solidarity reflected in the slogan "Black Power."[4]

Thus, the ghetto provides an environment that encourages appeals to racial consciousness, black solidarity, and black power. Feelings of powerlessness, alienation, and hostility toward white society can easily be exploited by political movements that reject traditional democratic methods and integrationist goals while asserting the coming of "black power" and black separatism (see Chapter 5).

Public Policy and Black-White "Life Chances"

The civil rights movement opened up new opportunities for black Americans. But equality of *opportunity* is not the same as *absolute* equality. In a significant speech to the graduating class of Howard University in 1965, President Lyndon B. Johnson identified the fundamental problem of equality in America today:

> You do not take a person who for years has been hobbled by chains and liberate him, bring him up to the starting line of a race, and then say, "you are free to compete with all the others," and still justly believe that you have been completely fair.

[4] National Advisory Commission on Civil Disorders, *Report* (Washington, D.C.: Government Printing Office, 1968), p. 205.

Thus it is not enough to open the gates of opportunity. All our citizens must have the ability to walk through those gates.

This is the next and more profound stage of the battle for civil rights. . . . The task is to give twenty million Negroes the same choice as every other American to learn to work and share in society, to develop their abilities—physical, mental, and spiritual—and to pursue their individual happiness.[5]

But the complexity of this task is enormous. The problems are many-fold—how to overcome the interlocking effects of deprivation in education, job training, health, housing, and employment, excessive crime and delinquency, and lack of human motivation. Can deprivations resulting from the unequal treatment of blacks in the past be eliminated without preferential treatment for present-day victims? And if preferential programs are begun, how will we know when blacks have been brought up to "the starting line"? What about the blacks who do succeed in joining the affluent American middle class: will they suffer from feelings of guilt in leaving most of their black brothers behind in the ghetto? Will the integration of middle class blacks result in "skimming off the cream" of potential leadership of the Negro masses?

Let us pose another problem. Successful "integration" assumes that individual blacks will acquire the skills, education, jobs, and income requisite for maintaining a secure position in the affluent middle class, and moreover that most blacks will regard the traditional American values and institutions as legitimate and desirable. Blacks in the past have had little part in shaping these institutions or in determining these values, and the most they can expect in the future is a greater share in their *joint* determination. Given these conditions, can we rightly assume that blacks will voluntarily choose to join affluent white America? Once their right to choose has been firmly established, will the blacks choose integration or instead opt for separation?

It is far beyond our intentions to review here all of the proposed or existing public programs that may contribute to reducing inequality in American society. But we can discuss at some length the Economic Opportunity Act of 1964, the moving force of the widely heralded

---

[5] President Lyndon B. Johnson in a speech at Howard University, 4 June 1965; quoted in Henry Steele Commager, ed., *The Struggle for Racial Equality: A Documentary Record* (New York: Harper & Row, 1967), p. 246.

"War on Poverty," which constituted the national government's most direct attempt to cope with the complex problems of poverty and inequality. The experience of the economic opportunity program demonstrates the variety of political issues involved in public efforts aimed at equalizing "life chances."

The Economic Opportunity Act of 1964 was not an attempt to remove *legal* inequalities so much as an attempt to make equality of opportunity a meaningful concept by giving the poor, particularly blacks, the tools to take advantage of the new opportunities that had been opened to them in recent years. The Economic Opportunity Act did not undertake to ameliorate poverty by increasing public assistance payments or creating government jobs but sought rather to deal with the *causes* of poverty. The focus was on case poverty, and the objective was to help the poor and unemployed become self-supporting and capable of earning adequate incomes by bringing about changes in the individuals themselves or in their environment. The Act placed emphasis on education, vocational training, and work experience, particularly for young people. It undertook to organize the poor in community action agencies so that they could act to improve conditions in their own communities. Originally, the Act relied upon local initiatives and community cooperation in planning and implementing antipoverty schemes. A new agency, the Office of Economic Opportunity (OEO), was created to encourage innovation and experimentation in policies and programs and to avoid the traditionalism of older governmental agencies.

The heart of the Economic Opportunity Act was a grass-roots "community action program" to be carried on at the community level by nonprofit corporations with 90 percent federal financial assistance. Communities were urged to form these "community action agencies," composed of representatives of government, private organizations, and—most importantly—the poor themselves. It was originally intended that OEO would support any reasonable antipoverty program devised by the local community action agency. Projects might include (but were not limited to) literacy training, health services, homemaker services, legal aid for the poor, neighborhood service centers, manpower vocational training, and childhood development activities. The Act also envisioned that a community action agency would help to organize the poor so that they could become participating members of the communities, avail themselves of many public programs already in existence, and effectively petition private and public agencies for a redress of their grievances.

But to date the war on poverty has had little success. The Office of Economic Opportunity has been the scene of great confusion. New and untried programs have been organized at breakneck speed. There has been delay and confusion in releasing funds to local community action agencies. There has been an excess of scandal and corruption, particularly at the local level. Community action agencies with young and inexperienced personnel have frequently offended experienced governmental administrators as well as local political figures. Congressional action has been uncertain: the agency's life has been extended for only a year at a time, and its appropriations have been delayed and poorly defined. But most damaging of all, even where these programs have been put in operation, they have had little success in achieving their objectives, namely, the elimination of the causes of poverty.

Daniel P. Moynihan summarized the community action experiences as follows:

> Over and again the attempts by official and quasi-official agencies (such as the Ford Foundation) to organize poor communities led first to the radicalization of the middle-class persons who began the effort; next to a certain amount of stirring among the poor, but accompanied by heightened radical antagonism *on the part of the poor* if they happened to be black; next to retaliation from the larger white community; whereupon it would emerge that the community action agency, which had talked so much in the way of change in the fundamentals of things, was powerless. A creature of a Washington bureaucracy, subject to discontinuation without notice. Finally, much bitterness all around.[6]

The Democratic Administration under President Johnson had never intended to finance a conflict between poor blacks and Democratic big-city mayors and party organizations. It had no wish to stir up antagonisms in cities between blacks and lower income white, labor, and ethnic groups that have made up the winning Democratic party coalition since the days of FDR. Local power structures are not

[6] Daniel P. Moynihan, *Maximum Feasible Misunderstanding: Community Action in the War on Poverty* (New York: Free Press, 1969), pp. 134–35.

without influence in Washington: in the present case, they were capable of striking at the financial roots of the program in Washington without risking direct confrontation at the local level. Even before Johnson left office, the War on Poverty had been substantially downgraded in policy priorities. The Nixon Administration began a gradual dismantling of OEO. Although the final verdict on the War on Poverty is not yet in, the interim report is exceedingly negative.

The War on Poverty illustrates the difficulties and complexities of dealing meaningfully with the problem of equality. In short, there is no guarantee that equality can be achieved *even if* the government embarks upon a multibillion dollar effort to do so.

The equalization of life chances of blacks and whites in America would most certainly involve a massive public effort in redistributing income, education, jobs, and other resources. Even at the present time there appears to be no real national commitment to this effort. In the wake of a series of urban riots the National Advisory Commission on Civil Disorders recommended "a commitment to national action on an unprecedented scale" requiring "unprecedented levels of funding and performance." Among other things, the Commission called for two million new jobs, including one million government jobs; substantial federal aid to eliminate de facto segregation; a uniform national welfare program with assistance set at least as high as $3,335 annually per urban family of four; and six million federally financed units of low and moderate income housing (see Chapter 7). But the Commission's report was not favorably received in many political quarters, and consequently no real effort has been made to implement the Commission's recommendations. The war in Vietnam doubtlessly had something to do with the federal government's failure to respond to the Commission's recommendations. But it may be equally true that even in the absence of the Vietnam war there would be insufficient commitment by the American people to undertake a massive public effort to achieve absolute equality between blacks and whites.

Inequality:
A Comparative Analysis

The American states provide an opportunity to examine inequality in a comparative, systematic fashion, that is, to observe the environmental correlates and political consequences of inequality in fifty political systems.[7] Economists have already provided us with a way of measuring income distributions within political systems. Income distributions may be observed by means of a Lorenz curve, which shows the cumulative proportions of aggregate income (on the vertical or y axis) accruing to cumulative proportions of the population ranging in order from the lowest to highest income earners (on the horizontal or x axis). The total area on a diagram that lies between the Lorenz curve, representing the actual income distribution, and the straight diagonal line, representing perfect income equality, expresses the extent of income inequality within a political system (see Figure 4–1). This area is measured by a Gini (general inequality) index, which ranges from a plus 1.00 (theoretical perfect inequality) to 0.00 (theoretical perfect equality). Gini indices for the fifty states reveal that income inequality is greatest in Mississippi and least in Utah.

Black-white differentials in the states can be measured by observing the ratios between black and white incomes, white collar occupation percentages, and educational attainment figures. Unlike the Gini index, which measures *general* income inequality in the population, these measures focus on *racial* inequality. They deal with inequality between whites and blacks in the acquisition of valued resources—income, jobs, high status occupations, and education.

While black-white ratios in valued resources measure inequality, they do not necessarily measure direct discrimination. Operationally we have defined "discrimination" to mean inequalities of income between blacks and whites holding the same categories of jobs. Specifically, we have examined ratios of black and white incomes in "professional" jobs, as defined by the Census Bureau, and in "craftsmen" jobs. Thus we have one measure of "discrimination" at the professional level and one measure at the blue collar level.

Table 4–3 shows (1) Gini indices; (2) black-white ratios in income, unemployment percentages, white collar occupation percentages, and educational attainment; and (3) income discrimination ratios in professional and craftsmen jobs; figures are given for each of the fifty states. There are substantial differences among the states in

[7] See Thomas R. Dye, "Income Inequality and American State Politics," *American Political Science Review* 63 (March 1969): 157–62, on which the following material is based.

Figure 4–1

MEASURING INCOME INEQUALITY

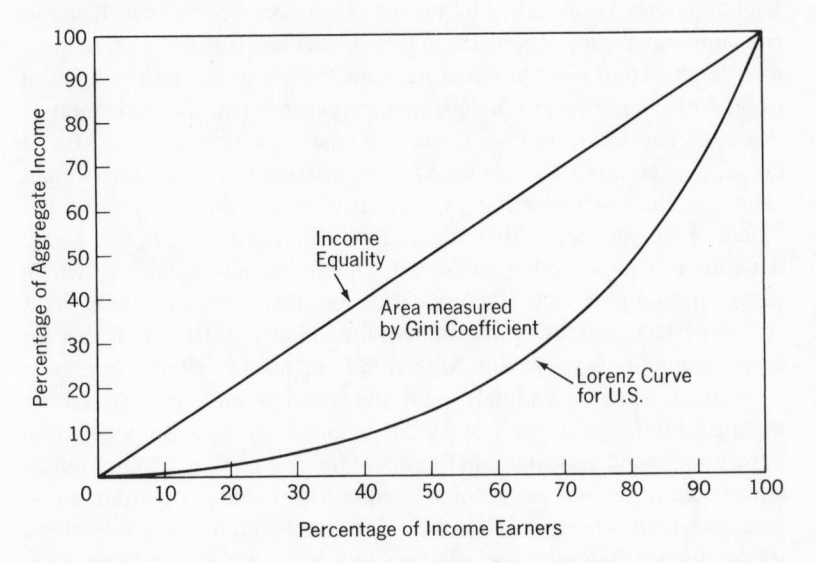

all of these measures of inequality. Predictably, the most unequal state in the nation is Mississippi. General income inequality (Gini) in Mississippi is 50 percent greater than in Utah, the state with the most equal income distribution. In general, racial inequality is also the greatest in Mississippi, followed by the other Southern states. In contrast, racial inequalities are practically nonexistent in Hawaii.

The environment of inequality is economic underdevelopment together with large black population concentrations (see Table 4–4). Overall, the most important environmental factors explaining interstate variations in inequality are median family income and nonwhite population percentage. As income increases, inequality declines. As the nonwhite population percentage increases, inequality increases. Inequality is also associated with lower adult educational levels, ruralism, and agricultural employment, in descending order of importance. (Black-white differentials relating to white collar employment were not associated with any environmental variables in the states; this finding may reflect the fact that segregation in the underdeveloped

Southern and Border states has long provided white collar job opportunities for blacks).

Black-white income "discrimination" was more closely related to adult educational levels in the states than to income levels. This is an interesting finding; it suggests that direct discrimination is more closely associated with adult educational levels, while inequality is more closely associated with income levels. We might speculate that direct discrimination is a product of inadequate education while inequality is more a product of economic underdevelopment.

Inequality and Civil Rights Policy

What is the impact of inequality on politics and public policy? Does inequality affect voter participation and party competition? What are the relationships between inequality and civil rights policies in the states?

Again the fifty American states provide an opportunity to employ comparative analysis to examine these questions.[8] First of all, we can observe some interesting relationships between inequality and party competition and voter participation. Among the fifty states an increase in inequality is associated with a reduction in party competition and a decline in voter participation (see Table 4–5).

Even more noteworthy is the fact that inequality (particularly income inequality) is *more* closely related to lower party competition and voter participation than are environmental variables such as income, urbanization, industrialization, and education. In the past, political scientists had been aware of the relationships between low levels of economic development and reduced party competition and voter participation. These calculations suggest that reduced party competition and voter participation are more closely related to *inequalities* in the distribution of social and economic resources than to the absolute *levels* of social and economic resources. These findings, together with the findings reported in Table 4–4 about the relationships between levels of economic development and inequality, suggest the fol-

[8] See Thomas R. Dye, "Inequality and Civil Rights Policy in the States," *Journal of Politics* 31 (November 1969): 1080–97.

Table 4–3 Rankings of the States—Inequality

	Gini Index		Income		White-Nonwhite Differences						Income Discrimination Ratios			
					Education		Occupation		Unemployment		Professional jobs		Craftsmen jobs	
1.	Miss.	.510	Miss.	.343	Alaska	.532	Fla.	.177	S.D.	.16	Alaska	.473	S.C.	.523
2.	Ark.	.486	S.C.	.347	Del.	.545	Del.	.206	N. Dak.	.21	Miss.	.563	Ark.	.528
3.	Ala.	.478	Alaska	.414	Miss.	.571	Nebr.	.240	S.C.	.26	S.C.	.594	Miss.	.535
4.	Tenn.	.478	Ala.	.421	La.	.572	Mont.	.272	Ky.	.32	N. Dak.	.598	N. Dak.	.540
5.	La.	.477	La.	.423	S.C.	.592	Wis.	.273	Ga.	.33	Ky.	.600	S. Dak.	.540
6.	S.C.	.474	Ariz.	.424	Ga.	.598	Ill.	.278	Ill.	.33	Ga.	.605	La.	.545
7.	Ky.	.474	N.C.	.434	Ind.	.637	Iowa	.288	Ala.	.33	Ala.	.615	Ala.	.553
8.	Ga.	.469	Ga.	.435	Kans.	.617	Ariz.	.294	Iowa	.33	La.	.618	Tex.	.569
9.	Okla.	.465	Ark.	.444	Conn.	.666	Maine	.298	Ariz.	.36	Ariz.	.623	Ga.	.573
10.	N.C.	.465	Va.	.448	N.J.	.684	Mich.	.311	Va.	.36	Tex.	.623	Tenn.	.604
11.	Tex.	.464	Ky.	.461	Nev.	.714	Minn.	.314	Tex.	.36	Tenn.	.623	Ky.	.605
12.	Fla.	.462	Okla.	.492	Md.	.721	Nev.	.321	Maine	.36	Ky.	.624	N.C.	.606
13.	Va.	.461	Nev.	.494	Mo.	.724	Md.	.321	Mich.	.37	N. Mex.	.632	Fla.	.614
14.	Mo.	.459	Del.	.502	Ky.	.736	Kans.	.325	Minn.	.39	Ark.	.642	Alaska	.630
15.	S. Dak.	.456	Tex.	.503	Mich.	.743	N. Mex.	.325	Nebr.	.39	Fla.	.653	N. Mex.	.647
16.	Alaska	.456	Md.	.528	Iowa	.750	Md.	.327	Ark.	.40	Del.	.660	Va.	.647
17.	W. Va.	.451	S. Dak.	.541	Va.	.768	Iowa	.330	Kans.	.40	Va.	.676	W. Va.	.652
18.	Hawaii	.446	Mont.	.552	Hawaii	.798	Va.	.334	N. Mex.	.40	W. Va.	.682	Del.	.669
19.	Ariz.	.445	Wyo.	.560	Ohio	.803	Ark.	.337	Md.	.40	Del.	.685	Okla.	.673
20.	N. Mex.	.440	Pa.	.585	Okla.	.804	Ohio	.363	Del.	.41	Okla.	.686	Md.	.689
21.	Nebr.	.440	N. Dak.	.591	W. Va.	.813	Mo.	.366	Alaska	.41	Wis.	.697	Mo.	.690
22.	Kans.	.439	Kans.	.592	Ala.	.813	N.J.	.369	Ind.	.47	Mo.	.701	Ariz.	.702
23.	Iowa	.439	Fla.	.618	Tenn.	.814	Okla.	.371	N.C.	.47	Conn.	.704	N.J.	.707
24.	Del.	.434	W. Va.	.619	Alaska	.819	Alaska	.388	Wash.	.48	N.C.	.712	Kans.	.741
25.	Vt.	.434	Mo.	.648	Ill.	.819	Ill.	.399	Conn.	.49	Minn.	.713	N.Y.	.746

Table 4–3 (continued)

	Gini Index	Income	White-Nonwhite Differences			Income Discrimination Ratios	
			Education	Occupation	Unemployment	Professional jobs	Craftsmen jobs
26.	Minn. .431	Maine .651	Nebr. .820	Pa. .408	La. .49	S. Dak. .713	Nebr. .747
27.	N. Dak. .430	Conn. .653	Ind. .825	Maine .409	N.C. .49	Maine .724	Ohio .760
28.	N.Y. .429	N.J. .657	Utah .827	Ariz. .424	Va. .49	Mass. .724	Ill. .763
29.	Calif. .427	Idaho .659	Ohio .827	N. Mex. .431	Pa. .51	N.H. .724	Maine .765
30.	Colo. .425	Nev. .673	Mich. .827	S.C. .439	R.I. .52	R.I. .724	Mass. .765
31.	Md. .424	N.Y. .678	Tenn. .833	La. .454	Wyo. .52	Vt. .724	N.H. .765
32.	Ill. .423	Ill. .679	Miss. .838	Wyo. .468	Mass. .53	Ill. .726	R.I. .765
33.	R.I. .418	Fla. .689	Oreg. .838	Mass. .470	Ill. .58	Mich. .731	Vt. .765
34.	Mont. .415	Mass. .694	Fla. .838	N.C. .470	Calif. .58	Oreg. .731	Conn. .771
35.	Ind. .414	Iowa .695	Iowa .840	Calif. .473	Ark. .58	Kans. .732	Mich. .782
36.	Nev. .414	Ohio .701	Ill. .841	Nev. .485	Mich. .58	Iowa .742	Ind. .787
37.	Mass. .414	Kans. .709	Wis. .865	S. Dak. .487	Oreg. .58	Ind. .747	Minn. .789
38.	Wash. .413	Pa. .711	Wash. .867	Wyo. .509	Colo. .59	Ohio .751	Oreg. .801
39.	Pa. .412	Utah .716	Calif. .867	Colo. .519	Ohio .60	Mo. .760	Calif. .802
40.	Wis. .412	Calif. .724	N.Y. .870	Ga. .563	Nebr. .60	Ind. .769	Wis. .809
41.	Maine .412	Ind. .742	Mo. .887	Vt. .598	Mo. .60	Pa. .792	Iowa .821
42.	Oreg. .411	Minn. .743	Mass. .887	Oreg. .601	Ind. .60	Calif. .810	Wash. .830
43.	Mich. .409	Wash. .750	N. Dak. .903	Miss. .602	Oreg. .62	Colo. .862	Pa. .839
44.	Ohio .408	Colo. .776	Minn. .916	Hawaii .607	Calif. .63	Idaho .862	Colo. .853
45.	N.H. .407	Oreg. .779	Colo. .925	Fla. .608	Miss. .63	Mont. .862	Idaho .853
46.	Conn. .404	Wis. .782	Ky. .942	Idaho .612	Fla. .65	Nev. .862	Mont. .853
47.	N.J. .403	Vt. .801	R.I. .950	Utah .640	Colo. .65	Utah .862	Nev. .853
48.	Idaho .402	Nebr. .815	Wis. .954	Wash. .645	Idaho .65	Wash. .862	Utah .853
49.	Wyo. .399	Iowa .847	Maine .972	Tenn. .747	N.Y. .66	Wash. .885	Wyo. .885
50.	Utah .394	Hawaii 1.057	N.H. 1.073	Hawaii .796	Hawaii 1.20	Hawaii .918	Hawaii .992

Table 4–4   The Environment of Inequality

	Median Family Income	Urban- ization	Industri- alization	Adult Educa- tion	Nonwhite Population Percentage
General income inequality (Gini)	−.77*	−.50*	−.36*	−.69*	−.72*
White-nonwhite differences					
Income	−.61*	−.53*	−.23	−.57*	−.41*
Unemployment	−.09	−.14	−.26	−.12	−.56*
Education	−.26	−.26	−.08	−.25	−.63*
Occupation	−.06	−.08	−.10	−.14	−.06
Discrimination in income					
Professional jobs	−.41	−.31	−.01	−.58*	−.29
Craftsmen jobs	−.69*	−.47*	−.31	−.74*	−.30*

NOTE: Figures are simple correlation coefficients for the fifty states; an asterisk indicates significant relationship.

lowing linkage: low *levels* of economic development bring about inequalities in the distribution of economic resources, which in turn result in *reduced* political participation and party competition.

Now let us examine the impact of inequality on civil rights policy in the states. Duane Lockard compiled a comprehensive list of state laws dealing with fair employment, fair housing, and open public accommodations.[9] According to Lockard, state laws prohibiting discrimination in employment, housing, and public accommodations are of little consequence if their enforcement must await lawsuits by victims of discrimination; Lockard attributes greater effectiveness to those states that established separate commissions to enforce antidiscrimination laws.

For the purposes of comparative analysis, a "civil rights score" was computed for each state based upon the comprehensiveness of

[9] Duane Lockard, *Toward Equal Opportunity* (New York: Macmillan Company, 1968).

Table 4–5   Inequality, Voter Participation,
            and Party Competition in the States

	Voter Turnout for Governor 1954–66	Party Competition for Governor 1954–66
Environmental variables		
Median family income	.52	.66
Urbanization	.17	.29
Industrialization	.05	.18
Education	.49	.61
Nonwhite percentage	.62	.62
Inequality measures		
General income (Gini)	−.71	−.72
Nonwhite-white income differential	−.68	−.70
Nonwhite-white education differential	−.70	−.67
Nonwhite-white occupation differential	−.19	−.16
Nonwhite-white unemployment differential	−.28	−.25
Discrimination, professional jobs	−.61	−.53
Discrimination, craftsmen jobs	−.60	−.68

NOTE: Figures are simple correlation coefficients for the fifty states.

their civil rights legislation.[10] The civil score for each state could range
as high as six, indicating that the state had passed fair employment, fair
housing, and open public accommodations laws, and had established
a commission or commissions to enforce all three types of antidiscrimi-

[10] A state was awarded one point for enacting a fair employment practices statute
and one for establishing a new commission with enforcement powers. It could
also receive one point for passing an open public accommodations law and an
additional point if the law was to be enforced by an independent commission.
Finally, one point was allotted for the enactment of a fair housing statute and
an additional point for the establishment of a commission to enforce the statute.

nation statutes; or as low as zero, indicating that a state had not passed any fair employment, fair housing, or open public accommodations laws nor established any commissions to enforce such laws. According to Lockard's data, as of 1966 thirteen states (Alaska, Colorado, Connecticut, Indiana, Massachusetts, Michigan, Minnesota, New Jersey, New York, Ohio, Oregon, Pennsylvania, and Rhode Island) possessed civil rights score of six. Thirteen states (Alabama, Arkansas, Florida, Georgia, Louisiana, Mississippi, South Carolina, North Carolina, Oklahoma, Tennessee, Texas, West Virginia, and Virginia) had civil rights scores of zero, indicating that they had no civil rights legislation whatsoever as of 1966. Other states fell between these extremes: for example, Arizona had a fair employment and open public accommodations law, a commission to enforce both statutes, but no fair housing law or commission, and therefore received a score of four. Iowa had a fair employment law and a public accommodations law, but no commissions to enforce them, and no fair housing law, and therefore received a score of two.

Civil rights legislation in the states is closely linked to economic development (see Table 4–6). Generally the states with the most comprehensive civil rights legislation are the wealthy, urban, industrial states with well-educated adult populations. Interestingly, income rather than education has the closest association with progress in state civil rights legislation. Civil rights legislation is also positively associated with voter turnout and party competition. Competitive two-party states with high voter turnout have more comprehensive civil rights laws than one-party states with low voter turnout.

As we expected, inequality is inversely related to the comprehensiveness of civil rights legislation in the states. But inequality is not as closely related to civil rights policy as the level of family income. Median family income is more closely correlated with civil rights scores than any of our measures of inequality. This suggests that civil rights policy is more a product of the general *level* of income than a product of equality or inequality in the *distribution* of income.

Some Thoughts about Inequality

The politics of equality no longer center about legal discrimination or even equality of opportunity. Today the issue of equality centers about

Table 4–6   Inequality and Civil Rights Policy in the States

Civil Rights Score Correlations		
With Environmental Variables	With Inequality Measures	
Median family income .71	General income inequality	−.63
Urbanization .52	Nonwhite-white income differential	−.50
Industrialization .45	Nonwhite-white education differential	−.38
Education .46	Discrimination, professional jobs	−.52
Nonwhite percentage −.42	Discrimination, craftsmen jobs	−.56

NOTE: Figures are simple correlation coefficients for the fifty states.

actual differences between blacks and whites in the allocation of valued resources—income, jobs, education, housing, and other valued commodities. Blacks are calling for a redistribution of these resources that will achieve actual equality between blacks and whites.

Research on the correlates of inequality suggests that economic development tends to reduce inequalities among men. Disparities between blacks and whites are greater in poor, rural, agricultural environments than in wealthy, urban, industrial ones. Moreover, civil rights legislation is also more likely to emerge from the political systems of economically developed societies with well-educated urban populations.

Occasionally one is tempted to view the problem of inequality somewhat optimistically, in the light of our knowledge about its relationship to economic development. For example, one might hope that continued economic affluence in this nation, with accompanying high levels of employment, income, and education, might gradually reduce black-white inequalities. This could be accomplished within the existing political and economic institutions. However, inequalities have been reduced only very slowly over time through the impact of economic development. While blacks have made important economic gains in recent years, disparities between blacks and whites have not been significantly reduced.[11] There is little reason to believe that the gap between black and white life chances will disappear in the foreseeable future.

Massive new public programs would be required to bring about a rapid redistribution of income and an early end to inequality in the life chances of blacks and whites. It is not clear whether existing political and economic institutions are capable of bringing about such changes. Current civil rights legislation has only dealt with equality of opportunity, not with actual equality. Comparative research suggests that civil rights legislation is a product of the general level of income and education, and it is not directly linked to reducing inequality.

Hence, the politics of equality in future years will center around programs designed to redistribute social and economic resources. The political goals of blacks will not be expressed in terms of the elimination of segregation and discrimination but rather in terms of achieving actual equality between blacks and whites in income, housing, jobs, education, and other life chances. This shift in goals will also mean a shift in the strategies, tactics, and styles of black politics.

[11] The components of "wealth" are very difficult to measure, and economists have not always agreed whether inequality in America has been diminishing or not. See Gabriel Kolko, *Wealth and Power in America* (New York: Praeger, 1962); W. H. Locke Anderson, "Trickling Down: The Relationship Between Economic Growth and the Extent of Poverty Among American Families," *Quarterly Journal of Economics* 78 (November 1964): 511–24; and Alan B. Batchelder, "Decline in the Relative Income of Negro Men," *Quarterly Journal of Economics* 78 (November 1964): 525–48.

chapter 5

Strategies
in Protest Politics

Goals and strategies in the struggle for equality are inextricably bound together. Ends shape means and means shape ends, and it is not really possible to view either independently. The politics of equality in America have involved a wide range of strategies, tactics, organizations, and leadership styles. In this chapter we shall attempt to describe the many varieties of protest politics—court litigation, mass protest, nonviolent direct action, congressional lobbying, black power, and black separatism.

The Strategy of Litigation

Brown v. *Board of Education of Topeka* marked the beginning of a new era in American politics. The *Brown* decision lent official legitimacy to the aspirations of black people. It encouraged them to believe that they could achieve full citizenship within the constitutional framework of American politics. It raised levels of expectation among black people and inspired them to insist upon their full constitutional rights. This important turning point in race relations in America was the product of a patient, reasoned, legalistic approach to racial problems.

While new styles, tactics, and approaches have been introduced into protest politics since the *Brown* case, the strategy of litigation continues to play a vital role in the politics of equality.

Let us examine the strategy of litigation with particular reference to the *Brown* v. *Topeka* decision.[1] It was no accident that in the fall of 1952 five separate cases posing the basic issue of racial segregation in public schools were on the Supreme Court's docket. The Legal Defense and Education Fund of the NAACP had coordinated a complex strategy of litigation that involved prosecuting various cases initiated by different plaintiffs from four states and the District of Columbia.

Since its founding in 1909, the NAACP had concentrated on the courtroom as its chosen battlefield in the struggle for Negro rights. From 1938 to 1961 Thurgood Marshall served as its principle legal counsel. Early in its history the NAACP had decided not to provide legal aid to individual blacks receiving unfair treatment at the hands of the law, but instead to concentrate on challenging segregation and discrimination in selected cases where a victory would bring about progress for the entire race.[2]

The Supreme Court heard three days of oral arguments on the desegregation cases in December 1952. Oral argument always involves an element of drama, and the Court's chambers are invariably filled to capacity when momentous cases are argued. Many talented attorneys appeared before the Court in the school desegregation cases, but the most interesting confrontation was that between Thurgood Marshall, the most famous and experienced black lawyer in the nation, representing the NAACP, and John W. Davis, the Presidential nominee of the Democratic party in 1924, representing South Carolina. In his oral argument Marshall concentrated on the theme that segregation in and of itself was unconstitutional and that segregation per se was psychologically more detrimental to black children than mere discrepancies in the physical plant or teaching standards of a school. In reply, Davis challenged the claim that segregation actually inflicted psychological

---

[1] For a complete description of the litigation process in this case, from the original suit to the final decision, see Daniel M. Berman, *It Is So Ordered* (New York: W. W. Norton, 1966).

[2] Class actions are authorized by Rule 23 of the Federal Rules of Civil Procedure for the United States District Courts.

damage. And he struck hard at the contention that Congress had intended to ban school segregation when it approved the Fourteenth
Amendment. If it did, he asked, why did that same Reconstruction Congress allow segregated schools to be maintained in the District of
Columbia? Davis also maintained that public education should not be
dealt with by the federal judiciary but instead by state and local governments exclusively. Following the first oral arguments in December
1952, the Court decided that it needed more time for research and
discussion before making its decision. New briefs and new oral arguments were presented to the Court in December 1953. Though many
of the briefs attempted to ascertain the original intent of Congress in
writing the Fourteenth Amendment, Marshall in his oral argument
asserted that the Court should apply the provisions of the Fourteenth
Amendment in the light of *contemporary* conditions regardless of historical precedent. Marshall clearly asserted the position of judicial
activism, urging the Court to interpret the Constitution itself and not
to be bound by past conditions.

On 17 May 1954 the Court handed down its brief and unanimous
decision of *Brown* v. *Board of Education of Topeka*.[3] The text of the
decision, including footnotes, was only a few pages long. The long and
patient work of the NAACP was clearly evident in the Court's decision.
The Court relied heavily on the sociological and psychological evidence
that had been presented to it, that separation inherently implied inequality. It accepted Thurgood Marshall's view that the historical arguments
regarding the original meaning of the Fourteenth Amendment were
irrelevant in the modern context. Thus did the strategy of litigation produce the Negro's most important legal victory since the Emancipation
Proclamation.

The Strategy of Mass Protest

Mass protest occurs when individuals in groups wishing to obtain concessions from established power holders but possessing little or no bargaining power seek to attain a bargaining position for themselves that
can induce the desired concessions. Often the protest is a means of

[3] *Brown* v. *Board of Education of Topeka,* 347 U.S. 483 (1954).

acquiring bargaining leverage for those who would otherwise be completely powerless. The protest may challenge established groups by threatening their reputations (in cases where they might be harmed by unfavorable publicity), their economic position (in cases where they might be hurt by a boycott), their peace and quiet (in cases where noise or disruption might upset their daily activities), or their security (in cases where violence or the threat of violence is involved). The protest strategy is one which appeals to powerless minorities who have little else to bargain vis-à-vis established majorities except their promise not to protest. Once mass protest has begun—or even before it has begun if the threat of protest is made credible—the minorities can then promise *not* to protest in exchange for the desired concessions. As James Q. Wilson correctly notes:

> Certain individuals and groups may wish to bargain, but they may lack the resources to do so—i.e., they may lack any stock of inducements (positive or negative) which they can use to influence other parties to act in accordance with at least *some* of their intentions. Others feel no need to bargain with these people. The question then becomes, how such a group (which I shall call the "excluded" group) can acquire a supply of compensations such that others will want to bargain. . . .
>
> The problem of many excluded groups is to create or assemble the resources for bargaining. Many often select a strategy of protest. *Protest* is distinguished from bargaining by the exclusive use of negative inducements (threats) that rely, for their effect, on sanctions which require *mass* action or response. . . . Bargaining might involve the use of negative inducements as compensation—i.e., a promise by one party *not* to act in a certain manner can be, relatively, a reward to the other party. This bargaining situation is based on protest only when these threats rely, for their effect, on the possibility of a mass response.[4]

In addition to threatening established groups, protest activity may also aim at motivating "third parties" possessing political resources that the protestors lack to enter the political arena on behalf of the

---

[4] James Q. Wilson, "The Strategy of Protest: Problems of Negro Civil Action," *Journal of Conflict Resolution* 5 (September 1961): 292.

protesters.[5] The protest calls the attention of formerly disinterested groups (for example, white middle class voters) to the existence of objectionable conditions. Even though the goals of the third party rarely coincide perfectly with those of the protesters, the third party may often be induced to join in concerted action on behalf of all or some of the protesters' goals.

Obviously in appealing to third parties for assistance, protesters desperately need the help of communications media. If protests are ignored by newspapers and television, they can hardly be expected to activate the support of an unknowing public. However, the news media seldom ignore protests with high audience appeal; protest leaders and newsmen share an interest in communicating "news" to the public.

The success of a mass protest depends, first of all, upon the designation of a clear goal or objective. Long-range, intangible, or complex goals do not lend themselves to mass protest tactics. For example, the passage of specific civil rights legislation, such as the Civil Rights Act of 1964 or the Voting Rights Act of 1965, presented a clear target for mass protest. But solutions to the many complex problems facing Negroes in urban slums—poverty, inadequate education, poor housing, unemployment, and crime—do not lend themselves easily to the mass protest approach. It is doubtful that one could conceive of any specific piece of national legislation that could cope with all of the many problems of the ghettos. For example, in 1968 after the death of Martin Luther King, Jr., a "poor people's march" on Washington failed to achieve any substantive results. This massive protest campaign on behalf of the nation's impoverished was supervised by experienced leaders, most notably the Reverend Ralph Abernathy, King's successor as head of the Southern Christian Leadership Conference. But the poor people's march failed at least in part because it had no clear legislative goal. The issues were confused and complex, and the campaign's leaders never made clear exactly what they wanted Congress to do. "Resurrection City, USA," the plywood and canvas shantytown hastily erected

[5] The following observations rely on an excellent essay on protest politics by Michael Lipsky, "Protest as a Political Resource," *American Political Science Review* 62 (December 1968): 1144–58.

on the park lands near the Lincoln Memorial, was eventually abandoned by the demonstrators without their having achieved any notable gains.

Not only must the goal of successful protest activity be specific, but a group capable of granting the desired goal must be readily identifiable. It is difficult to secure concessions if no one is really in a position to grant them. This dilemma is often posed when the goals of a protest action are too broad or too general for action by a specific governmental or private agency.

Obviously, successful protest depends upon the ability of protest leaders to organize the masses for protest activity. While the goal of a protest may be specific and tangible, protest leaders may attempt to generate mass participation by constantly referring to broad principles, ethics, or values. Such intangible allusions usually provide the incentive to mobilize the masses. However, in organizing a mass protest movement and in appealing to principle or morality, the protest leader correspondingly reduces his ability to bargain and to compromise. In other words, in stirring up the masses for protest activity, the protest leader must often resort to emotional appeals, inflammatory language, and attacks on "the enemy" or "the power structure" that later may make it difficult for him to deal with established elites without appearing to be a hypocrite to his followers. Moreover, protest leaders usually exhibit different skills than bargainers: protest leaders must inspire, inflame, and motivate the masses whereas bargainers must compromise, accommodate, and negotiate with elites.

The separate tasks of organizing the masses for protest activity and then bargaining with elites to gain concessions imply a division of labor between protest leaders and bargainers. Often this division of labor extends to organizations—some organizations specialize in bargaining, while others specialize in protest.[6]

Protest activity is more likely to be successful in gaining symbolic rewards than in winning significant, long-run changes in material conditions. Decision makers can respond to protest activity easily with

[6] See, for example, how protest leaders and established bargainers worked in tandem to desegregate public facilities in Atlanta in 1960 in Jack L. Walker, "Protest and Negotiation: A Case Study of Negro Leadership in Atlanta," *Midwest Journal of Political Science* 7 (May 1963): 99–124.

soothing verbal statements promising policy change. These statements may satisfy third party publics as well as many of the mass followers of protest leaders. Once the "crisis" is abated, the bargaining leverage of protest leaders diminishes considerably. Protesters find it difficult to maintain *sustained* pressures for long-term concrete gains.

Finally, we might note in this discussion the strategies available to decision makers who are faced with protest activity. They may dispense *symbolic* satisfactions giving the appearance of agreement with the goals of protesters without actually granting any tangible pay-offs to them. Or decision makers may dispense *token* satisfactions by responding, with much publicity, to one or more "crisis" cases, while doing little of a broad-based nature to alleviate conditions. Or decision makers may *appear to be constrained* in their ability to grant protest goals by claiming that they lack the financial resources or the legal authority to do so—the "I-would-help-you-if-I-could-but-I-can't" pose. Another common tactic is to *postpone action* by calling for further "study" while offering assurances of sympathy and interest; this tactic helps to remove the immediate pressures for action. Finally, the decision makers may attempt to *discredit* the protestors by stating or implying that the latter are violence-prone, "left-wing," or unrepresentative of the real aspirations of the people they seek to lead.

Nonviolent Direct Action

In 1963 a group of Alabama clergymen petitioned Martin Luther King, Jr., to call off mass demonstrations in Birmingham:

> . . . we are now confronted by a series of demonstrations by some of our Negro citizens. . . . We recognize the natural impatience of people who feel that their hopes are slow in being realized. But we are convinced that these demonstrations are unwise and untimely. . . .

> Just as we formerly pointed out that "hatred and violence have no sanction in our religious and political traditions," we also point out that such actions as incite to hatred and violence, however technically peaceful those actions may be, have not contributed to the resolution of our local problems. We do not believe that these days of new hope are days when extreme measures are justified in Birmingham. . . .

We further strongly urge our Negro community to withdraw support
from these demonstrations, and to unite locally in working peacefully
for a better Birmingham. When rights are consistently denied, a cause
should be pressed in the courts and in negotiations among local
leaders, and not in the streets.[7]

King, who had been arrested in the demonstrations, replied in his
famous "Letter from Birmingham Jail":

You may well ask, "Why direct action? Why sit-ins, marches, etc.?
Isn't negotiation a better path? You are exactly right in your call for
negotiation. Indeed, this is the purpose of direct action. Nonviolent
direct action seeks to create such a crisis and establish such creative
tension that a community that has constantly refused to negotiate is
forced to confront the issue. It seeks to so dramatize the issue that it
can no longer be ignored. . .

You express a great deal of anxiety over our willingness to break laws.
. . . One may well ask, "How can you advocate breaking some laws
and obeying others?" The answer is found in the fact that there are
unjust laws. I would be the first to advocate obeying just laws. One
has not only a legal but a moral responsibility to obey just laws.
Conversely, one has a moral responsibility to disobey unjust laws. . . .

In no sense do I advocate evading or defying the law as the rabid
segregationist would do. This would lead to anarchy. One who breaks
an unjust law must do it *openly, lovingly* (not hatefully as the white
mothers did in New Orleans when they were seen on television
screaming "nigger, nigger, nigger") and with a willingness to accept
the penalty. I submit that an individual who breaks a law that
conscience tells him is unjust, and willingly accepts the penalty by
staying in jail to arouse the conscience of the community over its
injustice, is in reality expressing the very highest respect for law.[8]

Nonviolent direct action is a technique requiring direct mass action against laws regarded as unjust, rather than court litigation, polit-

[7] A public statement by eight Alabama clergymen directed to Martin Luther
King, Jr., Birmingham, Alabama, 13 April 1963; the full text is reprinted in
Thomas R. Dye and Brett W. Hawkins, eds., *Politics in the Metropolis* (Colum-
bus, Ohio: Charles E. Merrill, 1967), pp. 68–69.

[8] A public letter by Martin Luther King, Jr., Birmingham, Alabama, 16 April,
1963; the full text is reprinted in Dye and Hawkins, *ibid.*, pp. 100–109.

ical campaigning, voting, or other conventional forms of democratic political activity. Mass demonstrations, sit-ins, and other nonviolent direct action tactics usually result in violations of state and local laws. For example, persons remaining at a segregated lunch counter after the owner ordered them to leave were usually violating trespass laws. Marching in the street frequently entailed the obstruction of traffic and resulted in charges of "disorderly conduct" or "parading without a permit." Mass demonstrations often involved "disturbing the peace" or refusing to obey the lawful orders of a police officer. Even though these tactics were nonviolent, they did entail disobedience to civil law.

Civil disobedience is not new to American politics. Its practitioners have played an important role in American history, from the patriots who participated in the Boston Tea Party, to the abolitionists who hid runaway slaves, to the suffragettes who paraded and demonstrated for women's rights, to the labor organizers who picketed to form the nation's major industrial unions, to the civil rights marchers of recent years. Civil disobedience is a political tactic of minorities: since majorities can more easily change laws through conventional political activity, they seldom have to disobey them. It is also a tactic attractive to groups wishing to change the social status quo significantly and quickly.

The political purpose of nonviolent direct action and civil disobedience is to call attention or "to bear witness" to the existence of injustices. Only laws regarded as unjust are broken, and these laws are broken openly without hatred or violence. Punishment is actively sought rather than avoided since punishment will further emphasize the injustices of the law. The object of nonviolent civil disobedience is to stir the conscience of an apathetic majority and to win support for measures that will eliminate the injustices. By accepting punishment for the violation of an unjust law, the person practicing civil disobedience demonstrates his sincerity. He hopes to shame the majority and to make it ask itself how far it will go to protect the status quo.

Clearly the participation of the mass news media, particularly television, has contributed immeasurably to the success of nonviolent direct action. Breaking the law made news; dissemination of the news called the attention of the public to the existence of unjust laws or practices; the public's sympathy was won when injustices were spotlighted; the willingness of the demonstrators to accept punishment provided evidence of their sincerity; and the whole drama laid the groundwork for changing unjust laws and practices. Cruelty or violence directed against the demonstrators by policemen or other defenders of the status quo played into the hands of the demonstrators by further emphasizing the injustices they were experiencing.

The first major application of the nonviolent direct action technique by blacks in modern times was prompted by events that began on 1 December 1955 when a black seamstress, Mrs. Rosa Parks, boarded a Montgomery, Alabama, public bus. Mrs. Parks took a seat in the Negro section of the bus, but shortly thereafter she was ordered to give up her seat so that a white man could sit down. She refused and was arrested. Word of the arrest spread through the black community, and a relatively unknown black minister, Martin Luther King, Jr., soon organized a black boycott of Montgomery buses. The bus boycott lasted for more than a year, finally ending when the Supreme Court outlawed racial segregation on public buses. The successful bus boycott led to the creation of the Southern Christian Leadership Conference (SCLC), headed by King, and provided the inspiration for Southern blacks to begin a long campaign of nonviolent direct action to end segregation.

In February 1960 four black students from North Carolina Agricultural and Technical College sought service in the segregated Woolworth's lunch counter in Greensboro, North Carolina. When they were denied service, they remained seated; they kept their seats even after being ordered out by the manager and subjected to abuse by whites. They did not respond when kicked, shoved, or attacked by whites, and they did not resist when arrested by police. Their actions attracted nationwide attention, and soon the "sit-in" movement spread throughout the Southern states. Students were organized for sit-ins by a new civil rights organization, the Student Nonviolent Coordinating Committee (SNCC). Thousands of black and white college students were jailed for violating segregation laws. The efforts of the sit-in demonstrators forced many of the larger chain stores to abandon the segregation of their eating facilities. The sit-in technique soon expanded to other areas: wade-ins were held at public swimming pools and kneel-ins at segregated churches.

In 1961 the Congress of Racial Equality (CORE) organized a series of "freedom rides" throughout the South in an attempt to desegregate interstate travel facilities. Earlier the Interstate Commerce Commission and the Supreme Court had ruled that racial segregation of passengers in buses, waiting rooms, and other interstate travel facilities violated the constitutional rights of passengers. Even so, most bus lines and bus terminals throughout the South had remained segregated. When integrated black and white riders reached Anniston, Alabama, on a trip from Washington, D.C., to New Orleans, their bus was burned by local whites and the riders were beaten. They received the same treatment in Montgomery, Alabama, and President Kennedy was obliged to send a force of federal marshals to that city to keep order. Both the freedom riders and the sit-in demonstrators succeeded in dramatizing segregationist practices and exposing the full extent of white hostility toward integration in the South. News of freedom rides, sit-ins, and white violence directed against demonstrators, combined with the nonviolent conduct of the young people involved in these incidents helped to win the sympathy of whites throughout the nation.

Perhaps the most dramatic application of nonviolent direct action occurred in Birmingham, Alabama, in the spring of 1963. Under the direction of Martin Luther King, Jr., the SCLC chose Birmingham as a major site for desegregation demonstrations during the centennial year of the Emancipation Proclamation. Birmingham was by its own description the "Heart of Dixie"; it was the most rigidly segregated large city in the United States. King believed that if segregation could be successively challenged in Birmingham, it might begin to crumble throughout the South. Thousands of Negroes, including school children, staged protest marches in Birmingham from 2 to 7 May. In response, policemen and firemen under the direction of Police Chief "Bull" Connor attacked the demonstrators with fire hoses, cattle prods, and police dogs—all in clear view of national television cameras. Pictures of police brutality were flashed throughout the nation and the world, doubtless touching the consciences of many white Americans. The demonstrators conducted themselves in a nonviolent fashion. Thousands were dragged off to jail, including Martin Luther King, Jr. (It was at this point that King wrote his famous "Letter from Birmingham City Jail," explaining and defending nonviolent direct action.)

The most massive application of nonviolent direct action was the great "March on Washington" in August 1963, during which more than two hundred thousand black and white marchers converged on the nation's capital. The march ended in a formal program on 28 August at the Lincoln Memorial in which Martin Luther King, Jr., delivered his most eloquent appeal, entitled "I Have a Dream." Shortly after this march President John F. Kennedy introduced a comprehensive civil rights bill; this bill was enacted the following year, after his death, as the Civil Rights Act of 1964.

Another very significant application of nonviolent direct action occurred in Alabama in the spring of 1965 during the SCLC-organized march from Selma to Montgomery to protest voting inequities. Thousands of blacks and whites converged on Selma for the march. On 7 March the first attempt to begin was broken up by Alabama state troopers using tear gas and night sticks. White segregationists subsequently murdered two demonstrators, both white, and committed other acts of violence against the demonstrators. On 21 March President Johnson ordered the Alabama National Guard into federal service to protect the marchers during their four-day trek. The Selma march served as a stimulus for the Voting Rights Act of 1965.

White racial violence in the early 1960s contributed measurably to the success of the nonviolent direct action movement in winning the nation's sympathy and support. In addition to the violent acts already mentioned, several other murders and bombings shocked and disgusted whites in both the North and in the South. On 12 June 1963 Medgar Evers, NAACP state chairman from Mississippi, was shot to death by a sniper as he entered his Jackson home. Evers had been leading a series of sit-ins and other demonstrations in Jackson prior to the shooting. Jackson police jailed a white man, and charged him with murder; but Mississippi juries were unable to agree on a verdict, and two trials ended in mistrials. On 15 September 1963 a bomb killed four black girls attending Sunday school in Birmingham, Alabama. This tragic incident marked the twenty-first time in eight years that blacks had been the victims of bombings in Birmingham, and (as in the previous cases) the crime went unsolved. In the summer of 1964 three young men (Michael Schwerner and Andrew Goodman, both white, and James Chaney, a black) were murdered in Philadelphia, Mississippi, while working on a civil rights project in education and voter registration. The FBI arrested twenty-one Mississippians in connection with these murders, including a county sheriff, a deputy, a city policeman, and a Baptist minister. No charges were brought by the Mississippi law enforcement officials, but eighteen of the men arrested were charged by a federal grand jury with conspiring to violate the constitutional rights of the victims, a violation of an 1870 civil rights law. In 1967 a federal jury in Meridian, Mississippi, convicted seven of the men, including a deputy sheriff and a Ku Klux Klan imperial wizard, acquitted eight others, and failed to reach a decision on three defendants.

In 1965 a black educator from Washington, D.C., Lemuel Penn, was murdered as he drove through Athens, Georgia, while returning from military duty as a reserve officer. Four Klansmen were arrested and charged with murder; when tried by a local jury, they were acquitted. Later the same Klansmen were convicted by a federal jury for violating the civil rights of Penn, a charge that then carried a maximum sentence of 5 years.

On 4 April 1968 Martin Luther King, Jr., was shot and killed by a white man in Memphis, Tennessee. James Earl Ray was apprehended in England and later convicted and sentenced to life imprisonment for this crime. The murder of the nation's leading advocate of nonviolence was a tragedy affecting all Americans.

In summary, nonviolent direct action has played a vital part in the civil rights movement in America. It has helped to dramatize the injustices of segregation and to touch thereby the conscience of America's white majority. Nonviolent direct action was instrumental in the passage of both the Civil Rights Act of 1964 and the Voting Rights Act of 1965. These major legislative breakthroughs on behalf of civil rights would not likely have come about in the absence of massive nonviolent protests by tens of thousands of black and white Americans in the early 1960s. President Johnson, in his message to Congress requesting enactment of the Voting Rights Act of 1965, publicly acknowledged the contribution that nonviolent direct action had made to progress in civil rights legislation:

> The real hero of this struggle is the American Negro. His actions and protests, his courage to risk safety and even to risk his life, have awakened the conscience of this nation. His demonstrations have been designed to call attention to injustice, designed to provoke

change, designed to stir reform. He has called upon us to make good the promise of America. And who among us can say that we would have made the same progress were it not for his persistent bravery and his faith in American democracy?[9]

Despite its successes, nonviolent direct action does pose several serious problems. This tactic is capable of arousing extreme passions on either side of an issue and exciting and provoking masses to act without thinking, perhaps ultimately making disrespect for the law a commonplace attitude. If undertaken too frequently or directed against laws or practices that are not really serious injustices, the tactic may have the effect of alienating the majority, whose sympathies are so essential to the success of the movement. Success can be achieved by actions that arouse the conscience of a majority against injustice or that discomfort a majority to the point where it is willing to grant the demands of the minority rather than to experience further discomfort. But actions that provoke hostility or a demagogic reaction from the majority merely reduce the opportunities for progress.

Even in a *nonviolent* movement the risk of violence is always very great. Though violence on the part of policemen or counter-demonstrators can assist in achieving the movement's objectives, violence by demonstrators usually has the opposite effect. Unfortunately, mass followers do not always fully understand or appreciate the distinction between nonviolent demonstrations directed against injustice, and rioting, looting, and violence directed against society itself.

Finally, while nonviolent direct action may be effective against direct discrimination, or an obvious injustice, this strategy is less successful against very subtle discrimination or de facto segregation. Few Americans approve of direct discrimination or cruelty against a nonviolent minority, and direct action tactics that spotlight such injustice can arouse the conscience of the white majority. But the white majority is less likely to become conscience-stricken over subtle forms of discrimination or de facto segregation or inequalities not immediately the product of direct discrimination.

[9] President Lyndon B. Johnson, 15 March 1965, message to the Eighty-ninth Congress assembled in joint session; reprinted in Henry Steele Commager, *The Struggle for Racial Equality: A Documentary History* (New York: Harper & Row, 1967), p. 213.

Civil Rights in Congress

Next we will examine Congressional politics in the field of civil rights, with particular reference to the passage of the Civil Rights Act of 1964. In Chapter 2 we described the *policies* contained in this act; let us now examine the *process* by which these policies were enacted.[10]

The immediate impulse for the Civil Rights Act of 1964 was a series of nonviolent direct action protests and demonstrations that spread throughout the country in 1963. By the end of the year, demonstrations had taken place in over eight hundred cities and towns, climaxed by the gigantic "March on Washington" on Sunday, 28 August. In February 1963 President Kennedy had asked Congress for a very modest civil rights bill, the first civil rights measure that the young President had sent to Congress. Its purposes were to broaden existing laws protecting Negro voting rights and to extend the life of the U.S. Commission on Civil Rights. But with millions of black and white Americans turning to protest activities in 1963, Kennedy was moved in June to submit a bill including the above requests, plus legislation to guarantee Negroes access to public accommodations, to allow the Justice Department to file suits in school desegregation cases, to allow federal programs to be cut off in any area where discrimination was practiced, and to strengthen fair employment practices by government contractors. In a nationwide address on June 11 the President said: "We are confronted primarily with a moral issue. . . . The fires of frustration and discord are burning in every city, North and South. Where legal remedies are not at hand, redress is sought in the streets in demonstrations, parades and protests, which create tensions and threaten violence—and threaten lives."[11] Of course, the public accommodations section immediately became the "heart" of the President's bill and the focal point for the 1963 civil rights demonstrations.

---

[10] Excellent summaries of the Congressional activity leading up to the Civil Rights Act of 1964, the Voting Rights Act of 1965, and the Civil Rights Act of 1968 (fair housing), are available in Congressional Quarterly Service, *Revolution in Civil Rights*, 4th ed. (Washington, D.C.: Congressional Quarterly, Inc., 1968).

[11] Quoted in Commager, *The Struggle for Racial Equality*, p. 165.

The Kennedy Administration realized that Republican support was essential if the civil rights bill was to overcome the expected opposition from Southern Congressmen. The Administration stood ready to compromise on the bill and even to label it "bipartisan" in order to win Republican support. The Senate, with its filibuster rule and entrenched conservative leadership, was considered to be a more difficult obstacle than the House. Hence the Administration chose to push for House passage first in order to confront the Senate with the maximum possible pressure for passage. Negotiations between Attorney General Robert F. Kennedy and the ranking House Judiciary Committee Republican, William M. McCulloch of Ohio, and Republican House Leader Charles A. Halleck of Indiana had already resulted in a redrafting of the bill and a favorable recommendation from the House Judiciary Committee before President Kennedy's assassination on 22 November. Actually the House bill was stronger than the original Kennedy proposal for it included provisions for an Equal Employment Opportunity Commission and barred discrimination not only by government contractors but also by private employers, and unions. Thus, House Republicans could rightfully claim that they had strengthened the bill and that it was not solely the product of a Democratic Administration. In his first address to Congress following President Kennedy's assassination, President Johnson named civil rights as the priority item for Congressional action: "No memorial eulogy or oration could more eloquently honor President Kennedy's memory than the earliest possible passage of the Civil Rights Bill for which he fought so long."[12]

To mobilize support for civil rights legislation the major civil rights organizations had earlier formed a Leadership Conference on Civil Rights. Roy Wilkins of the NAACP acted as chairman of the group, which also included representatives from the Urban League, Congress on Racial Equality, Southern Christian Leadership Conference, AFL-CIO, National Council of Churches, Americans for Democratic Action, American Civil Liberties Union, and even the Student Nonviolent Coordinating Committee. During the House battle on civil rights, the Conference set up a special office adjacent to

---

[12] Congressional Quarterly, *Revolution in Civil Rights* (Washington, D.C.: Congressional Quarterly, Inc., June 1968), p. 4.

the House Office Building and participated in an extensive lobbying campaign. The Conference coordinated the efforts of civil rights groups, labor unions, and church groups into a very effective coalition. Key participants in this coalition during the civil rights debate in 1963–64 were Clarence Mitchell (director of the NAACP's Washington office), A. Philip Randolph (president of the Brotherhood of Sleeping Car Porters), Andrew Biemiller (legislative director of the AFL-CIO), James Hamilton (National Council of Churches of Christ in America), Joseph Rauh (Americans for Democratic Action), and Jack Conway (associated with Walter Reuther's United Auto Workers). These organizations kept close tabs on members of Congress, ensuring that they would be present for key votes.

A "Coordinating Committee for Fundamental American Freedoms" was formed in 1963 for the purpose of defeating the civil rights bill; this was the only organization to lobby extensively against the measure. Its chairman was William Loeb, publisher of the *Manchester* (N.H.) *Union Leader,* and its active participants included John C. Satterfield, former president of the American Bar Association, and John J. Synon, director of Americans for Constitutional Action. A major portion of the group's funds were furnished by the Mississippi Sovereignty Commission, a state agency partially tax-supported that had been created by the Mississippi legislature. The organization distributed great quantities of materials, but in no way could it match the intensity of effectiveness of the lobbying activities of the Leadership Conference on Civil Rights. Significantly, such conservative organizations as the National Association of Manufacturers and the United States Chamber of Commerce chose not to involve themselves in the civil rights controversy, despite the fact that the bill placed important restrictions on the activities of private businessmen.

In the House of Representatives, leadership for the bill was provided by Judiciary Committee Chairman Emanuel Celler (D., N.Y.) and the ranking minority member of the Committee, Congressman McCulloch, as well as by the liberal-oriented Democratic Study Group (DSG), composed of more than one hundred House Democrats. The DSG's civil rights effort was headed by Congressman Richard S. Bolling (D. Mo.,); Democratic Whip Hale Boggs of Louisiana did not function during the debate on the bill. Bolling spearheaded the effort to force the bill out of the Rules Committee by initiating a discharge petition (the Rules Committee was chaired by Howard W. Smith, a Virginia Democrat and opponent of the measure).

On 30 January 1964 the House Rules Committee granted the bill a rule allowing ten hours of debate after which the bill would be open to floor amendments. The major effort of the bill's proponents was to beat back numerous amendments offered on the floor by Southerners. Congressmen Celler and McCulloch, respectively, managed to keep most Democrats and Republicans from supporting any major changes in the bill. The civil rights lobbyists made certain that the bill's supporters were all present on the floor to vote down a barrage of amendments. On 10 February the House passed the historic bill by a vote of 290–130. Of the 256 House Democrats, 152 (59 percent) voted in favor of the bill and 96 against. (Seven Democrats were absent, and the Speaker of the House normally does not vote.) Northern Democrats supported the bill 141–4. Southern Democrats opposed it by a 92–11 margin, with all of the Southern supporters representing Border states. Of the 177 Republicans, 138 (78 percent) voted for the bill and 34 against (5 not voting).

When the House-passed bill came to the Senate, the central problem for its proponents was to muster the two-thirds majority needed to impose cloture, thereby cutting short the expected Southern filibuster. Over the years the Southern bloc in the Senate had always depended upon the support of a number of Northern, Western, and Border state Democrats and Republicans who, cherishing the tradition of unlimited debate in the Senate, opposed cloture as a matter of principle. Never in its history had the Senate closed off debate on a civil rights measure despite eleven cloture attempts dating from 1938.

In 1964 the venerable Republican leader of the Senate, Everett McKinley Dirksen of Illinois, appeared to be the pivotal man who could make the difference between the success or failure of the cloture motion. Majority Whip Hubert H. Humphrey (D., Minn.) was chosen by President Johnson to guide the bill through the Senate. Humphrey's strategy was to avoid bitter or contentious debate, to accommodate most of Dirksen's suggestions on the bill, and to share credit for the bill with the Republican leadership. In February Humphrey managed to bypass the Senate Judiciary Committee headed by civil rights opponent James O. Eastland (D., Miss.), and on a 54-37 vote placed the House-passed bill directly on the Senate calendar for action. In late March Senate Majority Leader Mike Mansfield (D., Mont.) brought the bill to the floor for Senate consideration, and the Southern filibuster began. Southern opposition was led by Senator Richard B. Russell (D., Ga.). Russell declined to negotiate an end to the filibuster in exchange for a softer bill, as had been his strategy in the earlier civil rights acts of 1957 and 1960. Instead, he chose to hold out against any bill and to try to prevent cloture.

Behind-the-scenes negotiations took place between Dirksen, Humphrey, Mansfield, and Johnson Administration officials during April and May while the Southern filibuster continued. Eventually a substitute bill was developed that was more acceptable to the Republican leader. The major differences between the House-passed bill and Dirksen's substitute was that more emphasis was placed on conciliatory efforts by the Equal Employment Opportunity Commission in achieving desegregation in private businesses. On 19 May Dirksen, who had remained notably silent on the issue, made his first public statement: "Civil rights—here is an idea whose time has come. . . . Let editors rave at will and states fulminate at will, but the time has come, and it can't be stopped."[13]

With Dirksen's support, cloture was voted on 10 June by a 71–29 margin. Thirty-four Democrats and twenty-seven Republicans joined in voting to end the Southern filibuster. The cloture motion was opposed by twenty-three Democrats (twenty-one from the South, plus Bible of Nevada and Hayden of Arizona, who both opposed cloture on principle) and six Republicans (Bennett of Utah, Goldwater of Arizona, Mechem of New Mexico, Simpson of Wyoming, Tower of Texas, and Young of North Dakota). The battle was over after the important cloture vote. On June 19 the Senate passed the Civil Rights Bill by a 73–27 roll-call vote. Public attention focused on the vote of Republican Senator Barry Goldwater, who was then the leading contender for the Republican Presidential nomination. Goldwater said he had voted against the bill because he believed that Titles II (public accommodations) and VII (equal employment opportunity) were unconstitutional expansions of federal control over privately owned businesses. His vote was widely interpreted as part of a strategy to win him the support of the Southern states in the upcoming Presidential election. Following

---

13 *Ibid.*, p. 60.

its passage, the Senate version of the bill was sent back to the House, where it was adopted by a 289–126 roll-call vote. Voting to approve the Senate-amended bill were 153 Democrats and 136 Republicans; voting against it were 35 Republicans and 91 Democrats, 88 of them Southerners. In a momentous nationwide television broadcast from the White House, President Johnson signed the civil rights bill into law on 2 July, a few hours after receiving it from the House.

Black Power

The civil rights legislation of the 1960s had relatively little impact on the black masses in urban ghettos. The breakthroughs that the civil rights movement made in open public accommodations, fair employment, fair housing, and voting rights may have opened new opportunities to the educated black middle class, but the undereducated black poor living in the ghetto environment could not really take advantage of these new opportunities. Moreover, the established black leadership of the civil rights movement did not carry great influence with the black masses in urban ghettos. Even Martin Luther King, Jr., was unable to attract a great following in the Northern ghettos. The philosophy of nonviolent direct action was little understood in the ghettos. Moreover, the established organizational style of big-city politics left many urban blacks with a feeling of powerlessness. It was inevitable that sooner or later the deplorable conditions of the black masses in urban ghettos would spawn new political styles.

Black power began not as a program of political action but simply as a slogan. In June 1966 James Meredith, who in 1962 had been the first black to enroll in the University of Mississippi, was shot on a lone freedom march through Mississippi. Leaders of several civil rights organizations, including Martin Luther King, Jr., of SCLC and Stokely Carmichael, chairman of SNCC, continued Meredith's march. During this march Carmichael and his associates employed the slogan "black power," although King and others disapproved of its use.

The meaning of this slogan has been widely debated, and there is really no concise definition of what black power means as a political program. However, it is possible to identify several recurrent themes in militant black politics. In a book entitled *Black Power: The Politics of Liberation in America,* Carmichael and Charles V. Hamilton write:

> Black Power . . . is a call for black people in this country to unite, to recognize their heritage, to build a sense of community. It is a call for black people to begin to define their own goals, to lead their own organizations and to support those organizations. It is a call to reject the racist institutions and values of this society. . . .
>
> . . . black people must lead and run their own organizations. Only black people can convey the revolutionary idea—and it is a revolutionary idea—that black people are able to do things themselves. . . .
>
> It does not mean *merely* putting black faces into office.[14]

Thus we see that one prominent theme in militant black politics is the necessity of *fostering black pride and dignity.* One of the worst effects of segregation and discrimination is that members of the minority group begin to doubt their own worth as human beings. Kenneth Clark writes:

> Human beings who are forced to live under ghetto conditions and whose daily experience tells them that almost nowhere in society are they respected and granted the ordinary dignity and courtesy accorded to others will, as a matter of course, begin to doubt their own worth. Since every human being depends upon his cumulative experiences with others for clues as to how he should view and value himself, children who are consistently rejected understandably begin to question and doubt whether they, their family, and their group really deserve no more respect from the larger society than they receive.[15]

To overcome these effects, black leaders endeavor to develop a positive image toward blackness. Carmichael and Hamilton write:

> Throughout this country, vast segments of the black communities are beginning to recognize the need to assert their own definitions, to reclaim their history, their culture; to create their own sense of com-

[14] Stokely Carmichael and Charles V. Hamilton, *Black Power: The Politics of Liberation in America* (New York: Random House, 1967), pp. 44 and 46.
[15] Kenneth B. Clark, *Dark Ghetto: Dilemmas of Social Power* (New York: Harper & Row, 1965), pp. 63–64.

munity and togetherness. There is a growing resentment of the word "Negro," for example, because this term is the invention of our oppressor; it is *his* image of us that he describes. Many blacks are now calling themselves African-Americans, Afro-Americans or black people because that is *our* image of ourselves.[16]

The effort to assert pride in blackness is often accompanied by African dress, African hair styles, "soul food," "soul music," and the like.

An important political theme of black militancy is a general *condemnation of white society as "racist."* This condemnation of racism in society extends far beyond individual acts of bigotry (for example, the bombing of a Negro church) to encompass nearly all of the values and institutions of white society. Charles E. Silberman in *Crisis in Black and White* writes:

> What we are discovering, in short, is that the United States—all of it, North as well as South, West as well as East—is a racist society in a sense and to a degree that we have refused so far to admit, much less face. . . . The tragedy of race relations in the United States is that there is no American dilemma. White Americans are not torn and tortured by the conflict between their devotion to the American creed and their actual behavior. They are upset by the current state of race relations, to be sure. But what troubles them is not that justice is being denied but that their peace is being shattered and their business interrupted.[17]

Black militants argue that the institutions of American society are inherently racist because blacks are kept segregated in slums, because black unemployment is twice as great as white unemployment, because black incomes are only half those of whites, because the infant mortality rate among blacks is twice that among whites, because the educational level of blacks is below that of whites, and so on. In other words, the condition of blacks in American society is itself considered sufficient proof of the racism of established institutions. Moreover, these conditions also inspire black militants to condemn the value structure of American society, which either has supported these conditions or at least has failed to eradicate them.

[16] Carmichael and Hamilton, *Black Power*, p. 37.

[17] Charles E. Silberman, *Crisis in Black and White* (New York: Random House, 1964), pp. 9–10.

The black militant's condemnation of existing societal values and institutions as racist leads him to reject traditional democratic and organizational politics. This disparagement of democratic politics is usually accompanied by a *rejection of the ideal of coalition with white liberals*. Carmichael and Hamilton specifically reject coalition politics and identify three "major fallacies" of the "coalitionists":

> *First,* that in the context of present-day America, the interests of black people are identical with the interests of certain liberal, labor and other reform groups. Those groups accept the legitimacy of the basic values and institutions of the society, and fundamentally are not interested in a major reorientation of society. . . . *The second myth* is the fallacious assumption that a viable coalition can be effected between the politically and economically secure and the politically and economically insecure. *The third myth* assumes that political coalitions are or can be sustained on a moral, friendly, sentimental basis; by appeals to conscience.[18]

In other words, white liberals want to reform the system, while black radicals want to do away with it. While "limited, short-term coalitions on relatively minor issues" are possible, "such approaches seldom come to terms with the roots of institutional racism." In addition to black militants' concern that most white liberals are insufficiently radical in their politics, there is also the fear that black people will be "absorbed or swallowed up" in white-controlled liberal organizations. There is the fear that white liberals will use black people to further white liberal objectives, claiming all the while that these objectives coincide with the aspirations of black people.

This line of reasoning inevitably leads to the conclusion that *black organizations must be led by black people* rather than by white people. The participation of whites in black organizations should be limited to "supportive roles" involving "specific skills and techniques," as for example that typified by lawyers. The black militants do not welcome the participation of the

> many young, middle-class, white Americans [who], like some sort of Pepsi generation, have wanted to "come alive" through the black community and black groups. They have wanted to be where the action is

[18] Carmichael and Hamilton, *Black Power*, p. 60.

—and the action has been in those places. They have sought refuge among blacks from the sterile, meaningless, irrelevant life in middle-class America. They have been unable to deal with the stifling, racist, parochial, split-level mentality of their parents, teachers, preachers and friends. . . . The black organizations do not need this kind of idealism, which borders on paternalism.[19]

The emphasis on black pride and solidarity, and the hostility toward existing social values and institutions frequently lead to a *rejection of integration*. To the militants, integration means co-optation into the white middle class society that they so vigorously condemn. It means the loss of black identity and the submergence of black culture into the prevailing culture of white society. According to the militants:

The goals of integrationists are middle-class goals, articulated primarily by a small group of Negroes with middle-class aspirations or status. Their kind of integration has meant that a few blacks "make it," leaving the black community, sapping it of leadership potential and know-how. . . . This is why SNCC—and the concept of Black Power—affirms that helping *individual* black people to solve their problems on an *individual* basis does little to alleviate the mass of black people. Secondly, while color blindness *may* be a sound goal ultimately, . . . [there] is no black man in this country who can live "simply as a man." His blackness is an ever-present fact in this racist society, whether he recognizes it or not. . . .

"Integration" as a goal today speaks to the problem of blackness not only in an unrealistic way but also in a despicable way. It is based on complete acceptance of the fact that in order to have a decent house or education, black people must move into a white neighborhood or send their children to a white school. This reinforces, among both black and white, the idea that "white" is automatically superior and "black" is by definition inferior. For this reason, "integration" is a subterfuge for the maintenance of white supremacy.[20]

Another important theme of black militants is their *political identification with African independence movements*. In *Black Man's Burden*, John Oliver Killens writes:

The one thing we black Americans have in common with the other colored peoples of the world is that we have all felt the cruel and

[19] Carmichael and Hamilton, *Black Power*, p. 83.
[20] *Ibid.*, pp. 53–54.

ruthless heel of white supremacy. We have all been "niggerized" on one level or another. And all of us are determined to "deniggerize" the earth. To rid the world of "niggers" is the Black Man's Burden; human reconstruction is the grand objective.[21]

Yet the black power movement is by no means synonymous with black separatism. Once the prevailing values and institutions of white society are radically altered or abolished, genuine racial integration would then presumably be possible. The black power movement generally does not envision a separate black nation but merely asserts that black pride and black solidarity are preconditions for bringing about the kinds of social conditions requisite for genuine integration. The kind of integration envisioned by black power advocates is one in which the black masses will become an integral part of a radically different society, rather than one in which individual Negroes will be absorbed into the existing culture.

Although the black power movement does not advocate violence, it does not celebrate "nonviolence" either. The black militants concept of self-defense involves not an open, loving acceptance of punishment but rather an aggressive response to perceived white-inspired violence. Yet, black militants generally regard black power as an approach quite different from protracted black-white guerilla warfare. In fact, the black power position is sometimes defended as an alternative to urban guerilla warfare.

Black militancy has won widespread acceptance among black college students. At many major colleges and universities black students have organized all-black clubs whose activities have frequently reflected black power philosophy. These students have been critical of established values and institutions of American society; they have demanded greater emphasis on black history and culture, including the establishment of separate black studies curricula, which frequently they insist must be taught only by black instructors; they have demanded that more black students be accepted for admission, often irrespective of previous academic record; they have demanded that universities hire more black faculty; and they have generally rejected integration into the white social life on campus. The black student unions have stressed black consciousness and black pride among their members and have

[21] John Oliver Killens, *Black Man's Burden* (New York: Trident Press, 1965), pp. 175–76.

frequently expressed interest in supporting revolutionary movements in Asia, Africa, and Latin America.

The political influence of black power philosophy is often reflected in demands for "community control" in ghetto areas. Within big-city ghettos the idea of community control of public institutions and services clearly implies black control. Local autonomy has long been a conservative tenet of government, but increasingly it is attractive to militant blacks who see in it an opportunity to gain control of governmental institutions, particularly schools and police, operating in the ghetto. Of course, decentralization of government is also appealing to reformers interested in making bureaucracy more responsive to popular needs. But black militants have equated community control with the "liberation" of black people from the "colonialism" of white governmental administrators, white welfare workers, white policemen, white school teachers, and white businessmen—people who, through influencing the lives of ghetto residents in important ways, need not respond to their needs and desires.

Malcolm X and the Nation of Islam

Like other nationalist movements, black nationalism asserts a common identity, heritage, language, culture, and religion among American Negroes. Black nationalists believe they ought to rule themselves and to shape their own destinies, meaning that they aspire to establish and to control their own social, economic, and political institutions. The only notable difference between black nationalism and other nationalist movements is that the former has not yet produced a political program for the establishment of a separate geographically defined national home.

The Nation of Islam is the most important black nationalist movement in the United States. The Nation of Islam was founded in America by the prophet Wallace Fard Muhammad in Detroit in the 1930s. When Prophet Fard disappeared in 1933, Elijah Muhammad became the leader of the movement. Under his leadership the movement has flourished, establishing temples throughout the United States, with the largest located in Detroit, Chicago, and Washington, D.C. Until the 1960s the movement was small and highly secretive, but today

Elijah Muhammad bids openly for the allegiance of the Negro masses. Members of the Nation of Islam are known as "Muslims"—chosen people selected by Allah as his special instrument for the redemption of the entire black nation.

Black nationalism, as represented in the Nation of Islam, rejects white political, social, and religious culture. Belief in Allah and the acceptance of Islam, as taught by Elijah Muhammad, are minimal requirements for membership. Muslims reject the Christianity of the Caucasian race so that they may "return" to their own religion and their own fulfillment of the covenant that Allah made in the Old Testament: only the Nation of Islam provides the true road to redemption; ultimately Allah will destroy the Caucasian race and its civilization, overturning the white man's domination of black people.

Black nationalism is truly separatist. The Nation of Islam is "a nation within a nation." Muslims believe that they can only enjoy freedom, fraternity, justice, and equality within their own nation. They affirm that their lives have been morally and materially bettered since they have accepted Islam as a way of life. Only nonwhites can join the Nation of Islam. Muslims are not supposed to vote in local or national elections, and they are urged to resist induction into the United States armed forces. Muslims have endeavored to establish their own businesses, their own farms, and even their own private schools. Insofar as possible, these Muslim institutions are intended to remain free from white participation or control.

Muslims, in common with other black militants, assert pride in blackness. Indeed, for the Muslim, an awareness of one's black identity—his separate black self, nation, religion—is considered the true meaning of redemption, while ignorance of blackness is the meaning of hell. Muslims trace their heritage to Islamic African civilization, which they assert was infinitely superior in morality, justice, and equality to any other way of life. Muslims believe that the subordination and humiliation of the black man in America for two centuries has resulted in a Negro subculture that is "uncivilized." The Nation of Islam seeks to restore the shaken pride and confidence of the black man. Muslims see themselves as a "nation," and they seldom use the word "race" and never the word "Negro" unless it is qualified by "so-called" or used contemptuously. Muslims deplore the lack of solidarity and internal cohesion among the black masses. They endeavor to overcome the heritage of slavery, the centuries of abuse and indignities, and "Negro-ness" through total identification—religious, political, and economic—with the Nation of Islam.

Muslim self-pride carries with it the responsibility to lead a disciplined, righteous life as prescribed by the "laws of Islam." Elijah Muhammad has denounced the matriarchal character of Negro society, the lack of masculine parental authority and discipline within the family, and the lack of savings habits. These characteristics, together with personal indolence, are believed to lead to dependence on the white man. For this reason, habits of hard work and thrift are emphasized. Moreover, the laws of Islam forbid extramarital sexual relations, gambling, dancing, moviegoing, long vacations, unnecessary sleeping, discourtesy (especially toward women), lying, stealing, and the use of alcohol, tobacco, or narcotics. Cleanliness is a moral duty. The eating of pork, the straightening of hair, conspicuous cosmetics, or intemperance of any kind is strictly forbidden. Ordinarily, Muslims are advised to respect civil authority unless it conflicts with religious teachings.

Perhaps the most important spokesman for the Nation of Islam was Malcolm X, a former follower of Elijah Muhammad, who in 1963 formed his own movement.[22] Malcolm X was a fiery orator and a popular leader of the Muslims in Harlem. Following his break with Elijah Muhammad, he organized his own black nationalist organization, the Organization of Afro-American Unity. A struggle for leadership of the Muslim movement resulted in his assassination by other blacks in 1965.

Malcolm X was one of the first articulate leaders of the black masses to teach pride in blackness, to advocate racial solidarity, to stress the Negro's African heritage, and to urge black people in America to link their struggle with that of their African brothers. In a document presented to a meeting of delegates of thirty-four African nations, Malcolm X requested the delegates to raise the issue of discrimination in America on the floor of the United Nations.

Malcolm X did not directly advocate violence against whites, but

---

[22] Accounts of the activities and public statements of Malcolm X are available in Malcolm X, *Autobiography of Malcolm X* (New York: Grove Press, 1965), and *Malcolm X Speaks* (New York: Grove Press, 1966).

he was a strong proponent of armed self-defense. He urged blacks to retaliate in kind against any attacks made upon them. The Muslim position on violence was "never be the aggressor. Never look for trouble; but if the man molests you, may Allah bless you!" Malcolm X expanded the idea of self-defense to include "the right of maximum retaliation." (We shall discuss violence as an ideology in greater detail in Chapter 7.)

Malcolm X has assumed greater eminence after his death than he ever enjoyed during his lifetime. He has been elevated to the status of folk hero among many militant black youth.

"Who Speaks for Black America?"

It is unrealistic to expect any single organization or individual to "speak for the Negro"; certainly no single organization or individual "speaks for the white man." The variety of strategies, philosophies, organizations, and leadership styles among black is not necessarily a weakness. The resulting competition, the multiple goals and strategies, and the ability of different individuals and groups to perform different roles in protest politics may all be sources of strength and resilience to the black man in America.

To date it seems clear that the overwhelming majority of blacks in America want integration and not separatism. Whether the question involves employment, housing, or schools, the overwhelming majority of American blacks prefer integration to separatism (see Table 5–1). Among blacks negative attitudes toward separatist movements, black nationalists, and Muslims are widespread. William Brink and Louis Harris reported these comments as typical:

> "I do not like the theory of black supremacy—it's just as wrong as white supremacy. I don't like their spirit of violence and disrespect of law and government. Hate will never solve anything and they appear to be a hate organization."
>
> "I go along with Mr. King, you have to be friendly. Bloodshed is just no good."
>
> "I am impressed with the way they give Negroes a sense of race pride and the desire to achieve despite the hardships. I believe, in time, when they are more sophisticated, they will soften their notion

Table 5-1   Black Preference for Integration

	1969	1966	1963
Preference at work			
Mostly other Negroes	13%	10%	11%
Mixed group	78	80	76
Not sure	9	10	13
Preference in neighborhood			
Negroes	16	17	20
Whites and Negroes	74	68	64
Not sure	10	15	16
Preference for children in schools			
Go with whites	78	70	70
Not go with whites	9	11	10
Not sure	13	19	20

SOURCE: Derived from data in William Brink and Louis Harris, *Black and White: A Study of U.S. Racial Attitudes Today* (New York: Simon & Schuster, 1967), and updated to 1969 in *Newsweek*, 30 June 1969. Copyright 1966, 1967 by Newsweek, Inc. Reprinted by permission of Simon & Schuster, Inc.

on race to the point where they will agree with me that not all white people are devils. Just most of them."

"We all came here together and we should stay here together, because we go to war for our country together."

"You can't advocate racial superiority without advocating racial inferiority."

"I just don't like them with all that fuzz around their faces."[23]

This, despite the constant barrage of separatist rhetoric, the goals of most of the nation's black people remain unchanged: an equal—but integrated—place in American life.

Of course, conflicts and strains persist within the civil rights movement. Until recently black leaders were consistently reluctant to attack other black leaders on the grounds that only hostile whites could profit from the ensuing scuffle. But the rise of black militancy fractured what-

[23] William Brink and Louis Harris, *Black and White: A Study of U.S. Racial Attitudes Today* (New York: Simon & Schuster, 1967), pp. 50-51.

ever unity existed among blacks. The militants frequently referred to the established leaders of the NAACP, the Urban League, and the Southern Christian Leadership Conference as "Uncle Toms" and "handkerchief-head niggers." Not until 1968 did the NAACP speak out "loud and clear" against what it called "extremists who are shrilly and insistently espousing apartheid; racism, including anti-Semitism; intimidation and violence." In an obvious reference to black power advocates, it condemned "a reversal of the trend toward integration." The statement went on to assert:

> Let it be known that the preachers of hate, the defeatists afraid to compete in the open market, the name callers who substitute epithets and slogans for reason, the exhorters who summon Negro youth to death in futile shoot-outs with the police and the military—let it be known that these media-created "leaders" are not our spokesman.

> Dissent, protest and militancy, yes. Intimidation, disruption, suppression of free speech, extremism and violence, no![24]

[24] *The Crisis* 75 (November 1968): 312.

chapter 6

From Protest
to Politics

In an article significantly entitled "From Protest to Politics: The Future of the Civil Rights Movement," Bayard Rustin argues that the problems of blacks today—the fundamental social and economic disabilities afflicting the black masses—cannot be resolved by the same type of protest activities that eliminated Jim Crow. According to Rustin, progress in overcoming the problems facing blacks today requires broad-based political power.

> The future of the Negro struggle depends on whether the contradictions of this society can be resolved by a coalition of progressive forces which becomes the *effective* political majority in the United States. I speak of the coalition which staged the March on Washington, passed the Civil Rights Act, and laid the basis for the Johnson landslide—Negroes, trade unionists, liberals, and religious groups.[1]

Whether black leaders can organize a radical majority coalition of church, labor, and liberal groups—radical enough to support massive public programs in education, housing, and income redistribution

---

[1] Bayard Rustin, "From Protest to Politics: The Future of the Civil Rights Movement," *Commentary* 42 (February 1965): 28.

—is a serious political question. Attempts to build a black–poor white coalition have floundered before, as have efforts to build a black-labor alliance. However, blacks play a much more important role in national politics today than ever before. Undoubtedly, blacks today exert a considerable liberalizing influence on American politics—hence the importance of examining the role of blacks in democratic politics.

Black Political Participation

Traditionally blacks have exhibited lower levels of political participation than whites. If political participation is defined as casting votes in federal, state, and local elections, running for public office, and belonging to voluntary organizations and associations, then blacks have engaged in less political activity than whites. For example, Table 6–1 indicates that black nonvoting percentages in Presidential elections have been more than twice as great as white nonvoting figures. However, voting surveys divulge that in recent years black voter turnout has increased considerably, both in Presidential elections and in state and local elections, reflecting gains attributable not only to increased voting rights in the South (see Chapter 2) but also to increased political awareness among blacks throughout the nation.

One explanation of lower black participation notes that people of low socioeconomic standing in American society—regardless of color—participate less actively in elections and voluntary associations than those of middle and high socioeconomic status. Another explanation recalls that blacks have been prevented from participating in elections, parties, and voluntary organizations by racial discrimination and asserts that the effects of past discrimination linger on in poor participation rates. In other words, since blacks were traditionally conditioned against participating politically, they have subsequently failed to develop regularized habits of voting or joining organizations. Associated with this explanation is the idea that blacks are "alienated" from the political system, their nonparticipation representing disillusionment with democratic politics.

In order to sort out the effects of lower socioeconomic status on nonparticipation from the effects of race itself, we must compare the political activity of blacks and whites *at equivalent socioeconomic*

Table 6–1   Black and White Voting Preferences
             in Presidential Elections

| | Percentage of Voters | | | Percentage |
	Democratic	Republican	Other*	Not Voting
1952				
White	40	59	1	22
Negro	79	19	2	67
1956				
White	39	60	1	24
Negro	63	35	2	65
1960				
White	47	52	1	19
Negro	66	27	7	47
1964				
White	63	35	2	21
Negro	98	0	2	35
1968				
White	36	49	15	22
Negro	96	3	1	32

Source: Surveys of the American electorate immediately following each of last five
Presidential elections by the Survey Research Center, University of Michigan.

* Includes persons preferring minor party candidates as well as those whose preference
could not be ascertained. In 1968, American Independent Party candidate George C.
Wallace received 13.6 percent of the votes cast, almost all of which are presumed to
be white votes.

levels. In other words, only if we control for the effects of socioeconomic status can we determine whether or not black nonparticipation
is a product of socioeconomic disabilities which also affect whites at
the same socioeconomic level or rather a response to present or past
racial discrimination.

On the whole, blacks do not belong to as many voluntary organizations as whites. But if blacks and whites with the same educational
level are compared, a different pattern emerges. Poorly educated blacks
are slightly *more* likely to belong to organizations than poorly educated whites (see Table 6–2). Comparing higher education groups,

Table 6–2   Membership in Organizations by Race and Education

	Percentage Belonging to One or More Organizations	
	White	Negro
Education		
Grade school	30	45
Some high school	36	36
High school graduate	51	43

SOURCE: Anthony M. Orum, "Social and Political Participation of Negroes," *American Journal of Sociology* 72 (July 1966): 37; compiled from data supplied by the National Opinion Research Center, University of Chicago, and based on a national sample of adults. Reprinted by permission of The University of Chicago Press.

we find that better educated whites are somewhat more likely to belong to organizations than their black counterparts. Thus, differences between black and white participation in voluntary organizations are greatly reduced when a socioeconomic variable such as education is controlled.

Studies of voter turnout also suggest that blacks and whites at the same socioeconomic level behave similarly. The presence of strong political party organizations in Northern urban areas has encouraged Negro voter registration and turnout. For many years there has been a consistently high turnout among urban Negroes in the North.[2] One study of black voters in Northern cities reports

"that non-voting is *not* significantly disproportionate between Negroes and comparable whites in the North, and that if there is any difference it is that Negroes vote more. It is true that lower class people vote less than higher class ones, so that there is some validity to the argument that the Negro voting potential is reduced by the larger proportion of Negroes in the lower income group. But the effect of this on Negro turnout is not very great since class by class there is no difference in Negro and white turnout.[3]

[2] See Oscar Glantz, "The Negro Voter in Northern Industrial Cities," *Western Political Quarterly* 13 (December 1960): 1107.

[3] Ithiel de Sola Pool et al. *Candidates, Issues and Strategies: A Computer Simulation of the 1960 Presidential Election* (Cambridge, Mass.: MIT Press, 1964), pp. 94–95.

Table 6–3   Voting in a Presidential Election
             by Region, Race, and Education

	Percentage of Registered Voters who Voted in the 1960 Presidential Election	
	White	Negro
Non-South		
Part high school or less	76	70
High school graduate	85	83
South		
Part high school or less	56	55
High school graduate	77	82

SOURCE: Anthony M. Orum, "Social and Political Participation of Negroes," *American Journal of Sociology* 72 (July 1966): 44; compiled from data supplied by the National Opinion Research Center, University of Chicago, and based on a national sample of adults. Reprinted by permission of The University of Chicago Press.

There is less voter turnout among both whites and blacks in the South than in other regions of the nation (see Table 6–3). Overall, Negro registration in the South is less than that of whites, although the gap has been closing rapidly in recent years. If we consider only Negroes in the South who are registered and eligible to vote, simultaneously controlling for socioeconomic status, we find that Negroes vote just as often as whites in similar circumstances.[4] Table 6–3 shows that in the 1960 Presidential election the turnout of Negro registered voters in the North was only slightly less than that of white registered voters, and in the South the turnout of Negro registered voters was slightly more overall than the turnout of white registered voters.

In summary, while blacks as a whole vote less often than whites and belong to fewer voluntary associations, most of the differences between blacks and whites in political participation can be explained by differences in the socioeconomic levels of blacks and whites in this nation. In both the North and the South, blacks and whites in similar socioeconomic categories exhibit approximately the same degree of

[4] Anthony M. Orum, "Social and Political Participation of Negroes," *American Journal of Sociology* 72 (July 1966): 44.

political participation. This suggests that blacks are no more "alienated" from the political system than whites at the same socioeconomic
level. Even in the South, with its history of legal barriers to black voting, the differences between black and white participation are diminishing. Among blacks in both the North and the South, the higher the
educational level, occupational status, or income of a person, the more
likely he is to participate actively in politics. Of course, the same relationship holds true for whites: the higher the socioeconomic status,
the higher the level of political participation.

Though black and white political participation levels differ little
once socioeconomic variables have been controlled, the attitudes of
blacks and whites toward the political system diverge significantly.
Even blacks and whites sharing comparable socioeconomic backgrounds differ in their perceptions of government. For example, when
asked whether government officials were likely to give them "equal
treatment" in matters like housing regulations or taxes, only 49 percent of a national black sample, as compared to 90 percent of a comparable white sample, replied affirmatively (see Table 6–4). In addition, substantially fewer blacks believed that public officials would
listen to or take their views "seriously." In summary, blacks are much
more cautious and distrustful of representatives of the government than
are whites with a similar background.

While blacks place approximately the same importance on the
impact of local government on their daily lives as whites (approximately one-third of the Negro and white matched subsamples feeling
that government actions had "great impact"), only 50 percent of the
blacks, as compared to 72 percent of the whites, felt that government
had generally been helpful in their lives. Blacks were also more likely
to feel ineffectual politically than whites. A larger proportion of Negroes than whites believed that it was almost impossible to change a
bad law, or attempted to influence a local policy decision.

Unfortunately most scholars studying political participation have
concentrated their attention on traditional democratic forms of participation such as voting and organizational membership. Participation
in nonviolent direct action demonstrations and in riots has been largely
overlooked by political scientists until very recently. Yet obviously
this form of political participation has been very effective. A national
survey conducted by Louis Harris at the height of the nonviolent direct

Table 6–4   Expectations about Government by Race

	National White	Matched Subsamples	
	Cross-section	Negro	White
Government officials would give equal treatment	87%	49%	90%
Police would give equal treatment	88	60	85
Officials would listen and take views seriously	50	30	45
Police would listen and take views seriously	58	36	48
Local government has "great impact" on daily lives	35	31	37
Local government actions are usually helpful	71	50	72
It is almost impossible to change a bad local regulation by own efforts	24	38	31
Very unlikely to try to change bad local regulation	26	43	38
Never have tried to influence local policy decision	70	86	73

SOURCE: Dwaine Marvick, "The Political Socialization of the American Negro," *Annals of the American Academy of Political and Social Science* 361 (September 1965): 112–27. Reprinted by permission of the publisher.

action campaign in 1963 reported the following figures on participation in direct action:[5]

Negro participation in direct action:

Marched in a demonstration	12%
Picketed in a store	9
Taken part in a sit-in	8
Gone to jail	4

[5] See William Brink and Louis Harris, *The Negro Revolution in America* (New York: Simon & Schuster, 1964), p. 216.

Negro willingness to:

March in a demonstration	51%
Take part in a sit-in	49
Go to jail	47
Picket a store	46

The urban riots of the 1960s are also a form of political participation, albeit a criminal one. We shall examine "The Politics of Rioting" in greater detail in Chapter 7. It is sufficient to note here that the rioters were not "a tiny minority," nor were they just "agitators," "criminals," or "riff-raff." Postriot survey information indicates that roughly 20 percent of the blacks in Watts in 1965 and Detroit in 1967 actually participated to some degree in the riots in those cities. More importantly, a majority of the black residents in those areas supported or were sympathetic to the activities of the rioters. The vast majority of blacks in ghettos viewed the riots as a form of protest rather than as a meaningless disregard for law and order.

The Black Vote and the Democratic Party

Black voters are heavily committed to the Democratic party. The black vote for Democratic candidates in Presidential elections in recent years has never been less than 63 percent (except in 1956) and has ranged as high as 98 percent (in 1964). National surveys reveal that among blacks registered to vote, 79 percent regard themselves as Democrats, 10 percent as Republicans, 5 percent as independents, with 6 percent failing to express a preference.[6]

The pro-Democratic sentiment of blacks can be traced back to the 1930s and the Presidential administration of Franklin D. Roosevelt. Detroit Negro leader Albert B. Cleage, Jr., polled in a Louis Harris interview, explained: "Roosevelt changed the tempo for the Negro struggle, gave the Negro a sense of being a participating part of American life. He recognized the political power of Negroes. He

[6] William Brink and Louis Harris, *Black and White: A Study of U.S. Racial Attitudes Today* (New York: Simon & Schuster, 1967), p. 92.

put together the Democratic Party which was made of basic elements in American life—the Negro was one of them. Negroes have built upon this."[7] Harry Truman maintained the pro-Democratic bias of Negroes, and many older Negro leaders recognize his contributions in desegregating the armed forces and in advocating fair employment laws. Kennedy had a strong personal following among blacks, and even though Johnson enjoyed little personal appeal among blacks, nonetheless his efforts on behalf of the Civil Rights Act of 1964 (in contrast to Barry Goldwater's opposition) won him the greatest margin of black electoral support ever received by a Presidential candidate. Thus, the record of Democratic Presidents in recent decades in promoting civil rights progress goes a long way toward explaining the loyalty of black voters to the Democratic party.

Blacks also tend to look upon themselves as poor people and to regard the Democratic party as the friend of the underprivileged. Blacks view the Democratic party as the "champion of the underdog" and view themselves as "the underdog." Louis Harris reported that a number of black interviewees cited economic reasons for their Democratic voting: "The Democratic party raises wages and makes it possible for everyone to live on a higher level. The Republican party lowers wages." "The Democrats work for the masses, the Republicans for the major industrial people, the bosses." "Republicans won't do anything. Republicans are rich."

Blacks in the South face some cross-pressures in supporting the Democratic party because local and state Democratic party organizations in many Southern states have traditionally been committed to white supremacy and many still are. The Democratic party of the South led the confederacy during the Civil War and was a bulwark of segregation for nearly a century thereafter. Southern Democratic party leaders include strong segregationists such as Governor Lester Maddox of Georgia, Senator James O. Eastland of Mississippi, and others. Yet Professors Donald R. Matthews and James W. Prothro reported that Negroes in the South are strongly committed to the Democratic party,[8]

[7] *Ibid.*, p. 93.

[8] Donald R. Matthews and James W. Prothro, "Southern Images of Political Parties," *Journal of Politics* 26 (February 1964): 82–111, and *Negroes and the New Southern Politics* (New York: Harcourt, Brace, 1966).

identifying themselves as Democrats in roughly the same proportion
as whites. This agreement on party identification exists despite the
sharp division over policy. Regarding Negro and white support for the
Democratic party in the South, Matthews and Prothro remark: "Perhaps nowhere is the cliche about bedfellows in politics more true than
in the South today."[9]

The explanation for this seeming paradox lies in the differing
images that Negroes and whites in the South have of the Democratic
party. White Southerners associate the party with their state and
region, while blacks look to its national image. The most popular
aspect of the Democratic party's image among white Southerners is
that it is good to the common people and the working man (see Figure
6–1). The Democratic party is also viewed as the party of "good living, good jobs, and good times." However, many white Democrats
complained of the "liberalism" of the party, citing most frequently the
view that the party is "too good to Negroes."

Among blacks, the image of the Democratic party has elements
similar to those described by whites but also some significant differences. Blacks agreed that "conditions are good" under the Democrats
and that the Democratic party is "good to workers." Blacks favorably
viewed the party as "good to Negroes" whereas whites deplored rather
than applauded that perception. Moreover, the blacks' image of the
Democratic party was far less ambivalent than the whites' image.
Blacks liked almost everything about the party as they conceived it
whereas white Southerners harbored many negative images.

Estimating the impact of black voting on Southern politics is
difficult. For many years winning the "Battle of the Ballots" was
thought essential to the Negro's struggle for citizenship and social and
economic equality. It was believed that once blacks in the South voted
in substantial numbers, white politicians would become responsive to
the desires of the black community.[10]

[9] Matthews and Prothro, "Southern Images of Political Parties," p. 96.

[10] Believers in the utility of the black vote often cite the 1964 Presidential election, in which President Johnson's plurality in five Southern states (Florida,
Tennessee, Virginia, Arkansas, and North Carolina) was smaller than the black
registration—the implication being that black votes were decisive in pushing
these states into the Democratic column.

Figure 6–1

SOUTHERN IMAGES OF THE DEMOCRATIC PARTY
(in percentage of all respondents expressing attitudes toward parties)

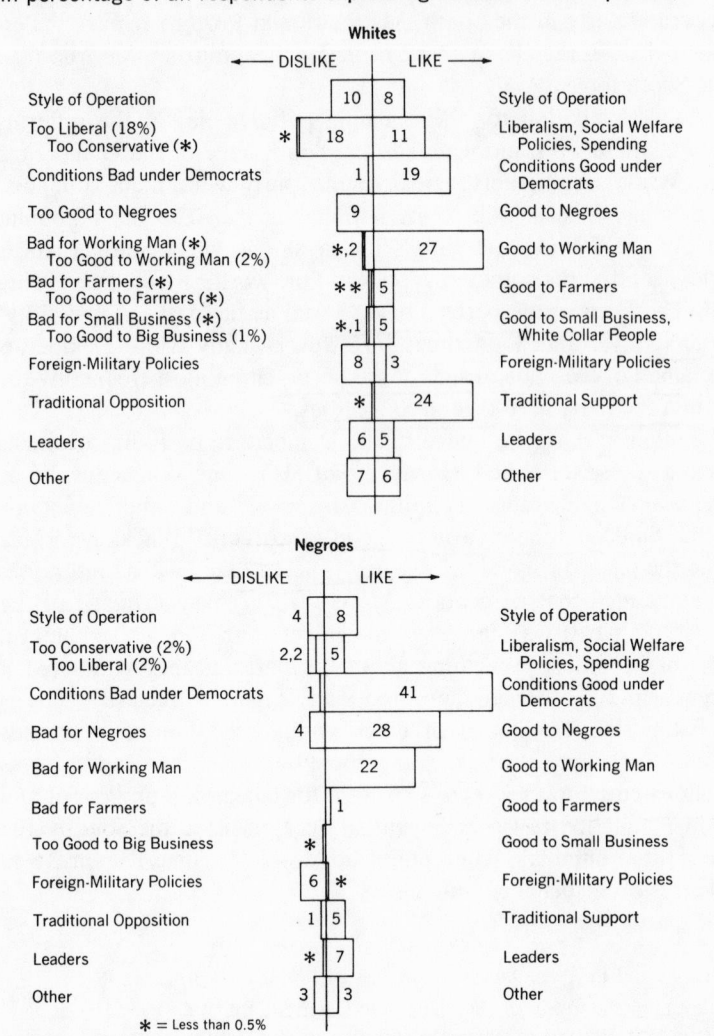

SOURCE: Donald R. Matthews and James W. Prothro, "Southern Images of Political Parties," *Journal of Politics* 26 (February 1964): 93. Reprinted by permission of the publisher.

Certainly at the *local* level the increase in black voting will result in the election of blacks to public office in many areas where they constitute an electoral majority for the first time since Reconstruction. For example, a black man was elected sheriff of Macon County, Alabama, in 1966; and Charles Evers, brother of the murdered Mississippi NAACP director Medgar Evers, was elected mayor of Fayette, Mississippi, in 1969. There were twelve Negro state legislators in Georgia in 1968, more than in any other state except Illinois. Georgia state representative Julian Bond became a nationally known figure in 1967 when the Georgia legislature barred him from taking his seat. Bond later led a challenging delegation to the Democratic National Convention of 1968 and succeeded in splitting Georgia's convention votes between his own delegation and that of segregationist governor Lester Maddox. Black voters have also been responsible for the election of some white Southern moderates.[11] For many years Mayor Ivan Allen, Jr., of Atlanta, the only Southern mayor to testify before Congress in favor of the Civil Rights Act of 1964, was kept in office by a coalition of Negroes and moderate middle class whites. In 1969 an even more liberal coalition of blacks and whites in Atlanta elected a Jewish mayor and a Negro vice-mayor.

However, a careful analysis of the black voting potential in the South suggests that few dramatic changes will occur in Southern *statewide* politics, or in the general posture of the Southern states in *national* politics. The major problem confronting effective black voting in the South is the fact that blacks constitute a minority in every Southern state. Moreover, the black proportion of the population in every Southern state is declining. Blacks cannot "win"—that is, elect either black candidates or white candidates sympathetic to black problems—in statewide elections without substantial assistance from white voters. And to date most white voters in the South have been unwilling to commit themselves to a coalition with black voters. If any statewide candidate becomes clearly associated with black aspirations, or if black bloc voting on behalf of a candidate becomes obvious, the white majority will unite at the ballot box to frustrate black hopes, at least

[11] See, for example, Kent Jennings and Harmon Zeigler, "A Moderate's Victory in a Southern Congressional District," *Public Opinion Quarterly* 28 (Winter 1954): 595–603.

for the foreseeable future. In most Southern states there are still more votes to be won by playing on the racial fears of whites than by openly campaigning for black votes.

"Uncle Tom" Politics

Styles of black politics have been changing rapidly in recent years. In part these changes reflect the massive migration of blacks from the rural South into Northern metropolitan slums, but they reflect equally the differing perspectives of successive generations of blacks.

The political style that we have labeled " 'Uncle Tom' politics" has been well described by Dwaine Marvick:

> Traditionally, Negro civic leaders occupying symbolic positions of respect were "tapped" by leaders in the white community as contact points. The influence of such "annointed" figures often depended more on their near monopoly over liaison channels to the all important white communities' decision-makers than on any spontaneous following within the Negro community which they might have generated. Undertakers, insurance men, bankers, teachers, a few professional men—above all, ministers of Negro churches; these were the men who traditionally were treated as spokesmen for their local Negro communities. Accommodationist, conservative, dignified, personally successful men: they have been for more than half a century the prime models for Negro children asking to be shown local "men of influence."[12]

This style of black political leadership was quite common in Southern communities until very recently. Sociologist Floyd Hunter has described the traditional black leadership of Atlanta, Georgia, in detail. The white leadership of that city normally communicated with only a small number of black professionals—educators, ministers, and social workers.[13] The black "subcommunity" of Atlanta could express

[12] Dwaine Marvick, "The Political Socialization of the American Negro," *Annals of the American Academy of Political and Social Science* 361 (September 1965): 123.

[13] Floyd Hunter, *Community Power Structure* (Chapel Hill, N.C.: University of North Carolina Press, 1953), chap. 5.

its desires (not demands) to the white governing power structure through middle class black representatives. A brief quote from one of these representatives reveals the style of accommodationist leadership: "All of the leaders [in the black subcommunity] have one or two white men they can go to and discuss various matters that concern us. Whenever there is a threat of trouble or when the police get too brutal, we can get help from some of the men we know personally."[14] Thus, the power of these black leaders was based upon their exclusive control of the channels of communication to the white power structure. These middle class black political leaders did not participate in policy decisions themselves except when their advice on black matters was solicited by whites. They were generally powerless to influence basic community decisions.

It is important to note that this traditional black leadership was almost exclusively middle class in character. Since most blacks found themselves in lower class circumstances, this middle class leadership could hardly be genuinely representative of the black community. Often these middle class leaders were completely out of touch with the black masses since their acceptability to the white community, not their popularity among the black masses, was the crucial criterion for selection.

The traditional black leadership did not make "demands," but simply "requests," of the white community. Black leaders were dependent upon white leaders: only by appealing to the latter's interests and beliefs could Negroes gain their objectives. The ability of Negroes to make "demands" was severely limited. Black leaders had to manipulate and to persuade whites. They had to "behave themselves." Compliance with white-imposed behavioral norms was necessary to make any headway, even when fellow blacks called it "Tomming."

Traditionally black political participation centered about *local* issues and offices. National politics was "white man's business." Blacks were concerned with facilities in their own segregated schools, the conditions of the streets in black neighborhoods, and the leniency of local law enforcement. The sheriff's office was often the center of black concern.

14 *Ibid.*, p. 127.

Everett C. Ladd, Jr., writes:

> This was the period of the "Uncle Tom," the "handkerchief head,"
> the "white man's nigger." Whites wanted passive Negroes who would
> be faithful servants and efficient workers. They rewarded "good" Ne-
> groes who said the right things and who showed proper respect for
> the system of race relations. The rewards . . . took the form of con-
> sulting with these "good" Negroes, listening to their appeals for help,
> and then channeling certain tangible benefits through to the Negro
> community.
>
> In this way Negro leaders were "made." Negro communities accepted
> these white-designated leaders because they had no choice. They
> needed people who could talk to influential whites and secure from
> them certain goods and services, and who could obtain small favors
> and personal protection in a white-dominated society.[15]

Organizational Politics

The massive infusion of blacks from the rural South to the urban centers of seven key Northern industrial states—New York, Pennsylvania,
New Jersey, Ohio, Michigan, Illinois, and California—provided American Negroes with an important measure of political leverage, especially in Presidential elections. This leverage derives from the pivotal
nature of these states in Presidential politics: they are characterized
by strong two-party competition and they possess a large bloc of electoral votes. Black votes in the North provided crucial support for black
protests in the South and for the passage of federal legislation protecting the rights of Southern blacks.

   The increase in black voting populations in Northern cities in the
1920s and 30s and the increase in black voter registration in the South
in the 1940s and 50s brought about a gradual modification of the
"Uncle Tom" style of Negro politics. The mobilization of black electoral strength in both the North and the South gradually improved the
bargaining position of black leaders. They were no longer required to
depend exclusively upon white good will; an expanded black elec-

[15] Everett C. Ladd, Jr., *Negro Political Leadership in the South* (Ithaca, N.Y.:
Cornell University Press, 1966), p. 43.

torate provided a new political instrument and gave rise to an "organizational style" of black politics.

Disadvantaged black masses provide a pool of support for a machine style of politics that relies upon personal and material rewards to control behavior. Among black masses in large cities, the ward leaders' offers of jobs, favors, and patronage have a great deal of appeal. Organizational politics avoids ideologies and issues, instead concentrating on personal friendships, favors, jobs, and material rewards. Black political machines have emerged in large cities where the prevailing style of white politics was the machine model. In these cities the black machine was tied closely to the existence of the white machine. The political machine was essentially a business organization, devoid of ideologies and issues, whose business was to get votes and to control elections by trading off social services, patronage, and petty favors to the urban masses. To get the money to pay for the social services and favors, it traded off city contracts, protection, and privileges to business interests that paid off in cash. The organizational style of politics does not stress "racial" issue, but instead concentrates its attention on material rewards. For example, the organization is not likely to oppose the location of a new public hospital in a black residential area merely because the hospital would contribute to segregation; the machine would rather have the jobs and material rewards of the hospital, even if it were segregated, than the ideological victory of building an integrated hospital in a white neighborhood.

For many years the most powerful black organizational leader in the nation has been Congressman William L. Dawson of Chicago. Dawson exercises predominant influence over five all-black wards in that city and therefore controls a large contingent of local officials and state representatives as well as his own safe seat in Congress. The Dawson organization is a part of the larger political organization controlled by Mayor Richard J. Daley. Dawson depends upon Daley for support and vice versa. Dawson delivers a heavy black vote to the Daley machine, and in return Daley provides the jobs, favors, protection, and material rewards that enable Dawson to hold his organization together. Edward C. Banfield and James Q. Wilson write of the Dawson style:

> Dawson maintains his machine in the usual way, by exchanging jobs, favors, and protection for votes. Almost every weekend he flies to

Chicago to sit in a shabby ward office in the midst of the slums and to listen to all who come to him. Where the direct, material interests of his constituents are at stake, he and his organization are ready to help; they will get a sick man into the county hospital, find out why an old lady's welfare check has not arrived, defend a beleaguered homeowner against the urban renewal authority, and go to the police commissioner, and if necessary the mayor, to see to it that a case of alleged police brutality is properly investigated. Matters involving Negro rights in the abstract do not interest them, however. These concern the militants, but they are not the base upon which the machine builds.[16]

Black organizational politics is most likely to be found in cities where the prevailing style of white politics is organizational. In other words, the style of black politics depends largely upon the style of white politics. Organizational politics is strengthened by the concentration of blacks in one or a few all-black geographical areas in the city, and it is further strengthened when the political system is based on a large number of relatively small wards or other geographic subdivisions. Of course organizational politics is closely tied to the existence of strong party organizations. In summary, organizational politics is strengthened by residential segregation, ward organization, and strong partisan politics. In contrast, it is weakened by residential integration, at-large elections, and nonpartisan politics.

Organizational styles of black politics are usually associated with Northern cities, where the blacks have long enjoyed the right to vote and where their numbers rose sufficiently after World War I to make that vote large enough to support machine politics. But the expansion of voting rights and the increased black registration in the South have contributed to the emergence of a political style resembling organizational politics among blacks in Southern cities. In Southern communities where voter registration has progressed to a point sufficient to create a substantial bloc of black voters, organizational Negro leaders have begun to emerge. In the 1950s political scientists reported the emergence of black community leaders who were able to barter black votes with white politicians in exchange for material rewards. H. D. Price reports that "street lights, side walks, and paved streets are more

---

16 Edward C. Banfield and James Q. Wilson, *City Politics* (Cambridge, Mass.: Harvard University Press and MIT Press, 1963), pp. 304–305.

common in communities where blacks vote in substantial numbers. Such things as Negro civic centers, bandshells, playgrounds, libraries, hospital annexes, and even swimming pools are found in increasing numbers."[17] John H. Fenton and Kenneth N. Vines describe an alliance of "shady white and underdog Negro" elements in Louisiana communities. White sheriffs charged with corruption by middle class white residents occasionally offset their electoral threat by catering to Negroes for support. "The reward . . . is respect from the politicians and attendance at Negro political meetings, cessation of police brutality, and promises made and often kept regarding such matters as street improvements and better school facilities."[18] Effective black-white vote bargaining in Southern communities often requires special political tactics. Black leaders have to identify to their black constituents the white candidates designated for support; yet they simultaneously have to avoid hurting those same candidates' standing with anti-Negro white constituents. In other words, blacks have to cast a bloc vote for a white candidate without letting too many white voters know what they are doing. In this style of Southern politics, blacks do not attempt to elect black representatives to office. Instead, they trade votes for commitments from white politicians.

Regarding the importance of expanded black voting in Southern communities, political scientist William R. Keech writes:

> To what extent has the evidence supported the contention that votes protect the rights of minorities in a democracy? The conclusion is not encouraging. . . . The vote is a far more potent instrument for achieving legal justice than social justice. The gains I have found [in Tuskegee, Alabama, and Durham, North Carolina] most susceptible to Negro voting have consistently been those which most clearly involve fair and just administration of existing laws. Social justice, however, demands more than this. It often demands changes in existing laws. . . . With few exceptions, the vote has failed Durham and Tuskegee Negroes when they sought to change the law in order to eliminate existing discrimination.[19]

[17] Hugh D. Price, "The Negro and Florida Politics," *Journal of Politics* 17 (May 1955): 219.

[18] John H. Fenton and Kenneth N. Vines, "Negro Registration in Louisiana," *American Political Science Review* 51 (September 1957): 712.

[19] William R. Keech, *The Impact of Negro Voting* (Chicago: Rand McNally, 1968), pp. 106–107.

Thus, in the South the organizational style of black political participation has been successful in achieving legal justice within the existing system, but it has failed to bring about significant changes in the socioeconomic conditions of blacks. In the North, black political organizations in big cities have been successful in winning material rewards—jobs, favors, public works—and these organizations have provided a strong incentive for the Democratic party to support civil rights legislation at the national level. But these organizations have not been able to bring about significant changes in the lives of the masses of ghetto dwellers.

"Good Government" and Black Politics

It seems fair to say that blacks are frequently a victim of governmental reform. "Good government" or "reform" movements in American municipal politics, in their zeal for efficiency, democratic government, and elimination of corruption, have led to political systems that frequently operate to the detriment of minorities. The good government movement is concerned largely with efficiency, economy, and the saving of the tax dollars of the middle class; it offers very little to low income, low status elements of the large metropolis. The good government movement prefers nonpartisan elections to party competition, at-large elections to ward representation, and professional city management to mayor-council control. The good government movement promotes the belief that government should be honest, impartial, efficient, and operated by professional administrators directly responsible to the citizens, and that the institutions of government should be structured to bring "good" people into control. It deplores boss rule, machines, and partisan politics. The good government movement is more likely to be supported by white middle class voters than by blacks or the poor.[20]

Blacks and other minorities are disadvantaged by the formal institutional arrangements of middle class reform government—nonpartisanship, at-large elections, and professional city management.

[20] See Thomas R. Dye, *Politics in States and Communities* (Englewood Cliffs, N.J.: Prentice-Hall, 1968), chap. 10.

Commenting on reformed cities, Banfield and Wilson observe: "In a city with a nonpartisan, at-large system the nature of Negro politics is radically affected by the fact that the candidate must face the whole (predominantly white) electorate and must do so without benefit of a party label."[21] Where candidates are elected at large without party labels, the support of newspapers and civic associations becomes crucial to their election. In cities where blacks constitute a numerical minority, the result is that the black community will either be unable to elect a black representative to the city council or school board or other decision-making body, or at best white leaders will allow blacks to have token representation. Moreover, those blacks elected in at-large nonpartisan cities will probably be either moderate or conservative on racial issues, since they must be acceptable to middle class whites. According to Banfield and Wilson: "Not only are few Negroes elected to office, but those who *are* elected generally find it necessary to be politicians first and Negroes second. If they are to stay in office, they must often soft-pedal the racial issues that are of the most concern to Negroes as Negroes."[22]

Banfield and Wilson go on to note the dilemma faced by Negro councilmen facing reelection in a nonpartisan at-large system:

> Without a strong Negro vote he cannot hope to be re-elected, and to get a strong Negro vote he must . . . be aggressive on at least some racial issues. But he must also have the support of the press and the civic associations in order to be re-elected, and he will not have this unless he is "reasonable" from the standpoint of conservative, middle-class whites.[23]

On the basis of this analysis, it appears that minority groups, especially blacks, are generally better represented in a partisan ward system of elections. Given the prevalence of residential segregation, this system seems to assure genuine black representation.

The good government movement provides a relatively "legitimate" method by which whites can protect themselves against black influence in city government. The good government movement enables

---

[21] Banfield and Wilson, *City Politics*, p. 307.

[22] *Ibid.*, p. 293.

[23] *Ibid.*, p. 308.

whites to reduce black influence in city government, yet at the same time to avoid pangs of conscience by easy resort to an ideological defense of reform government. Table 6–5 indicates that ward elections in the nation's largest cities have guaranteed blacks representation on city councils in approximate proportion to their percentage of the population. But black representation in cities with at-large and combination at-large and ward elections is very uneven. Sociologist Lee Sloan writes that "if black Americans today were to seek governmental reform in local politics, they could perhaps do worse than ask for a repeal of certain institutional arrangements established and defended in the name of good government."[24]

Racial Politics

Traditionally it was the middle class Anglo-Saxon Protestant old residents of the city who led the fight against the machine. But in recent years black militants have also attacked organizational politics. An uncomplimentary description of Congressman William L. Dawson re-

Table 6–5   1969 Black Representation on City Councils
for U.S. Cities with Estimated Population
of 500,000 or more (by Type of Council Election)

City	Total Council Seats[1] (Ward Seats)	Seats Held by Blacks[1]	Percentage of Seats Held by Blacks	Percentage of Blacks in 1965 Population[2]
At-large elections				
Washington, D.C.	9 (–)[3]	5	56	66
Atlanta	16 (0)	1	6	44
Detroit	9 (0)	2	22	34
Houston	8 (0)	0	0	23
Dallas	11 (0)	1	9	21

[24] Lee F. Sloan, "Good Government and the Politics of Race," *Social Problems* (in press).

Table 6–5 *(continued)*

City	Total Council Seats[1] (Ward Seats)	Seats Held by Blacks[1]	Percentage of Seats Held by Blacks	Percentage of Blacks in 1965 Population[2]
Pittsburgh	9 (0)	1	11	20
Columbus	7 (0)	0	0	18
Boston	9 (0)	1	11	13
San Francisco	11 (0)	1	9	12
San Antonio	9 (0)	1	11	8
San Diego	8 (0)[4]	1	13	7
Seattle	9 (0)	1	11	7
Phoenix	6 (0)	1	17	9
Combination				
(At-large and ward elections combined)				
New Orleans	7 (5)	0	0	41
Memphis	13 (7)	3	23	40
Philadelphia	17 (10)	3	18	31
Indianapolis	9 (6)	—[5]	—[5]	23
Kansas City, Mo.	13 (6)	2	15	22
New York	37 (27)	2	5	18
Buffalo	15 (9)	3	20	17
Ward Elections				
Baltimore	19 (18)[6]	4	21	38
St. Louis	28 (28)	8	29	36
Cleveland	33 (33)	11	33	34
Chicago	50 (50)	8	16	28
Los Angeles	15 (15)	3	20	17
Milwaukee	19 (19)	2	11	11
Denver	9 (9)	1	11	9

[1] Written communication with city government officials. Data are for January 1969.
[2] National Advisory Commission on Civil Disorders, *Report* (Washington, D.C.: Government Printing Office, 1968), p. 248.
[3] Councilmen in Washington are appointed by the President of the United States.
[4] Councilmen are nominated by district but elected at-large.
[5] Data unavailable.
[6] Mayor or President of the Council only is elected at-large.

SOURCE: Data compiled by Lee F. Sloan, Department of Sociology, Florida State University.

flects the attitudes of many militants toward successful black organization politicians:

> Chicago provides an excellent example of how Negroes can be co-opted into inactivity. . . . Dawson surrendered far more than he has obtained for the Negro community. What Dawson obtained were the traditional benefits of the big-city political machine: low-paying jobs for a lot of followers; political intervention with the police and with bail bondsmen, social workers, housing officials, and other bureaucrats whose decisions can affect a poor constituent's life; and a slice of the "melon" in the form of public housing projects, welfare payments, and the like.
>
> What Dawson surrendered was the pride and dignity of his community; he threw away the opportunity to force Chicago's political and civic leaders to identify and deal with the fundamental problems of segregation and oppression.[25]

In contrast to organizational styles of black politics, the "racial style" emphasizes ideological values rather than material rewards. Appeals are made to principle, to lofty moral and racial goals, to the wishes and fears of black masses, but not to their material welfare. The political style depends upon the existence of an "enemy"—discrimination, "racism," injustice against Negroes. Black status and black power are the goals of the racial leader; the improvement of the material welfare of the black is of secondary importance. The racial leader derives his support from his appeal to principle, and therefore it is difficult for him to engage in bargaining with white leaders.

James Q. Wilson describes Congressman Adam Clayton Powell, Jr., of Harlem as the prime example of a racial politician.[26] Powell's base of support is the Abyssinian Baptist Church, a church of ten thousand members who had been his father's congregation before him. Powell's appeal is almost entirely personal and ideological. He has a personal organization of his own, but he does not rely upon the estab-

---

[25] Charles E. Silberman, *Crisis in Black and White* (New York: Random House, 1964), pp. 204 and 206; quoted with approval by Stokely Carmichael and Charles V. Hamilton, *Black Power: The Politics of Liberation in America* (New York: Random House, 1967), pp. 11–12.

[26] James Q. Wilson, "Two Negro Politicians: An Interpretation," *Midwest Journal of Political Science* 4 (November 1960): 346–69; see also idem., *Negro Politics* (New York: Free Press, 1960).

lished party organization in New York. Powell is handsome, eloquent, and flamboyant; in his public appearances he is passionately and uncompromisingly dedicated to the cause of his race. Powell frequently makes charges of racial discrimination and injustice. He mingles his political, religious, and civic roles; there are elements of both charisma and ideology in Powell's appeal to his followers. Powell has not succeeded to any great extent in obtaining material benefits for his constituents. But material rewards are not the basis of his appeal to his followers. His politics are not pragmatic but ideological. Powell's appeal is based on his ability to express the fears, demands, and resentments of the black masses. His unpredictable personal behavior and flamboyant style of life actually endear him to his constituents. Powell lives well: he drives sports cars, owns several homes and boats, entertains extravagantly, and frequently takes prolonged vacations in the Bahamas. But his followers do not resent the sight of Powell in expensive restaurants and night clubs; instead, they appear to be gratified that he is living as they would like to live. When Congress deprived Powell of his Congressional seat for allegedly mishandling funds from his Congressional committee, the effect was to solidify further Powell's popularity with his followers. They believed that his actions were no more improper than those of other Congressmen, but that he was singled out for discipline because he was black.

James Q. Wilson draws an interesting contrast between the organizational style of politics of William L. Dawson and the more flamboyant racial politics of Adam Clayton Powell:

> The one is an orator, the other an organizer; one is flamboyant, the other is conservative; one is militant on the race question, the other is moderate. One seeks publicity and speaks almost always "on the record"; the other shuns publicity and speaks to interviewers only off the record. One is considered by most of his House colleagues to be demagogic and unreliable; the other has the confidence and respect of many influential Congressmen. . . . One raises the race issue on every occasion; the other goes out of his way to avoid discussing race or race questions. One is light-skinned, handsome, boyish, gregarious, fun-loving; the other is brown-skinned, aged, reserved, quiet. One spends his free time (of which he has a great deal) in world travel, entertaining, and night life; the other rarely travels, devotes himself completely to politics, and leads a home life carefully

screened by privacy and silence. The two most prominent Negro politicians are radically dissimilar, avoid each other's company, speak disparagingly of one another, and elicit the violent attitudes of love and hate from their friends and enemies.[27]

It is possible to make a further distinction between militant and organizational styles of racial politics. The militant is likely to cast racial issues into simplistic terms such as a fight between good and evil and to see white racism as the sole difficulty facing blacks. The moderate is more likely to see racial issues in the broader context of complex social problems and to recognize that the black faces other problems besides white racism. The militant is more likely to assume the posture of protest and agitation, regardless of whether any tangible results might accrue from such activity. The moderate is proud of past accomplishments. The militant wants massive legislative action to resolve race problems. The moderate is more likely to accept informal agreements or bargains with white leaders. The militant is willing to agitate for sweeping reform, while the moderate concentrates on more specific or limited goals. The militant wants immediate change, while the moderate is more willing to wait a longer period of time for progress. The militant emphasizes how bad the conditions are at the present time, while the moderate is more likely to look backward and to compare present conditions with the even worse conditions of the past.

Blacks in Public Office

Blacks do not occupy public office in America in proportion to their percentage of the nation's population. However, in recent years black candidates have been more successful at the polls than at any time since Reconstruction. No blacks served in the national Congress from the Fifty-seventh Congress (1901–1903) to the Seventy-first Congress (1929–31). But the black population migration to Northern cities, the concentration of black people in ghettos, the increase in black registration, and finally the legislative reapportionment of the 1960s prompted by *Baker* v. *Carr,* have all combined to promote black office holding. Since 1929 one or more blacks from Northern cities have served in Congress. The number of blacks in Congress has gradually

[27] Wilson, "Two Negro Politicians," p. 347.

increased to the point where the Ninety-first Congress (1969–71) included nine black Representatives and one Senator. In 1967 two blacks were elected mayors of large cities for the first time: Carl B. Stokes in Cleveland and Richard Hatcher in Gary, Indiana. Blacks have also been winning state and local offices with increasing frequency; in 1967–69 an estimated 4 percent of the state legislative seats in the nation were held by blacks. In 1967 President Lyndon B. Johnson appointed Thurgood Marshall to the United States Supreme Court, the first Negro ever to serve on that high tribunal.

Observing the political styles of the national black officeholders is an instructive exercise. Most successful black candidates to date have avoided racial militancy, pledging instead to represent "all of the people." Most have avoided positions that would be threatening to whites. They have been generally willing to form electoral and political alliances with white groups. Let us compare the political careers and styles of three prominent Negro officeholders—Edward Brooke, Carl Stokes, and Thurgood Marshall—and the political settings in which they gained office.[28]

Edward W. Brooke was the first black to serve in the United States Senate since Reconstruction. He was elected as a Republican in 1966 by a solid 62 percent of the voters of Massachusetts, a state that has only a 5 percent black population. Throughout his career Brooke has pledged "to serve all of the people of Massachusetts," and he has never espoused militancy for the black cause. Brooke once referred to the term "black power" as "a response to white irresponsibility. . . . The answer to extremism is clear. Government at all levels must respond to legitimate requests of responsible civil rights leadership. . . . The very public officials who most deplore the rise of militant civil rights leadership are often its unwitting partners." On another occasion he insisted that "we will not tolerate killing, looting, burning, sniping, or other acts of violence. Those on the lunatic fringe who make statements to incite riots do a disservice to their nation and to the cause they profess to serve." Brooke has generally voted with the most liberal members of his party.

[28] Background material on Edward W. Brooke is available in *Congressional Quarterly Weekly Report*, 7 June 1968, p. 1316; material on Carl B. Stokes can be found in Louis Masotti, Jeffrey K. Hadden, Victor Thiessen, "The Making of Negro Mayors, 1967," *Transaction* (January 1968): 21–30.

Brooke's background includes education at Howard University and a law degree from Boston University; he served with the "partisans" in Italy as a captain in the U.S. Army Infantry, and he is married to a white Italian whom he met while serving abroad. In 1952 he was narrowly defeated in a race for state representative, and he declined a job offered as secretary to the governor's council, a job traditionally held by a black. Brooke said that he refused the offer because "I don't believe in Negro jobs. I want to be elected on my own ability. Only then do you have progress." In 1960 he narrowly lost in the race for Secretary of State, but in 1962 he won election as Attorney General of Massachusetts. Brooke was an active attorney general; he even indicted a former Democratic governor and a number of high state officials. In Brooke's 1966 campaign for the U.S. Senate, he was pitted against former governor Endicott Peabody, a liberal with a strong civil rights record. Peabody did not exploit the racial issue during the campaign, despite the widespread feeling that the Northern racial riots would provoke a sizable white "backlash." Brooke said only that "I do not believe any voter in Massachusetts holds me responsible for the riots in Chicago or Atlanta or San Francisco. They have always known that I have stood for law and order." There was no backlash discernible in Brooke's overwhelming election.

Race was much more of an issue in the election of Carl B. Stokes as mayor of Cleveland in 1967. Negroes comprised an estimated 36 percent of Cleveland's population in that year. Thus, even though race was an issue in the election, Stokes clearly had substantial white support.

The political circumstances surrounding Stokes' victory suggest that black candidates can win high office if they can secure the near-unanimous support of the black community while at the same time appealing to a substantial number (though not necessarily a majority) of white voters. Stokes defeated the incumbent mayor Ralph S. Locher in the Democratic primary, despite Locher's endorsement by party leaders. At the time, Locher's administration as mayor was generally considered to have been uninspiring; the Cleveland *Plain Dealer*, the largest daily newspaper in Ohio, endorsed Stokes over Locher. Stokes mounted a massive voter registration drive in Negro wards, but at the same time he campaigned in white wards, speaking in churches, clubs, and homes.

Stokes won the Democratic primary with 52.5 percent of the vote. An analysis of returns leaves little doubt that race was the principal determinant in the voting. Recognized black wards gave Stokes 96.2 percent of their vote while recognized white wards gave him only 15.2 percent; predictably, mixed black and white wards divided their votes, giving Stokes a combined total of 54.4 percent. Stokes' victory was the product of three factors: (1) an unprecedented number (73.4 percent) of registered blacks turned out at the polls to vote for him; (2) many whites were unenthusiastic about Locher, and only 58.4 percent turned out to vote; and (3) Stokes was able to win about 20 percent of the white vote.

In the general election when Stokes as a Democratic candidate faced his Republican opponent Seth Taft, race again became the principal issue—despite the fact that Taft did not exploit the issue. Normally, Taft as a Republican would have had little chance in a Democratic city. The *Plain Dealer* again endorsed Stokes, as did organized labor. Taft attempted to project the image of the new breed of liberal Republican *à la* John Lindsay and Charles Percy, pointing proudly to his own record on civil rights (he was one of the authors of the Ohio Fair Housing Law). His attacks on Stokes were all legitimate: he accused him of absenteeism in the state legislature and charged that Stokes himself was a slum lord who owned dilapidated rental properties in the ghetto.

Again, Stokes' problem in the campaign was to hold on to his high turnout of Negro voters while at the same time winning over some whites. Stokes opened his campaign with an overt racial appeal: "The personal analysis of Seth Taft . . . is that Seth Taft may win the November 7 election, but for only one reason. Taft's reason is that his skin happens to be white." When whites reacted negatively to this approach, Stokes quickly changed his strategy and played down the racial issue. But even though both Taft and Stokes said little about race during the campaign, it turned out to be the most important issue in the election.

Stokes won the general election by holding on to his near-unanimous high-turnout Negro vote while at the same time winning about 20 percent of the white vote. With large numbers of white Democrats voting for a Republican mayor for the first time in their lives, Stokes barely squeaked by with only 50.5 percent of the total vote. He received 95 percent of the vote in black wards while Taft received 80 percent of the vote in white wards; again the mixed wards were divided, with Stokes receiving 54 percent of the vote in these wards.

Thus Stokes' victory in Cleveland was not a great victory for racial tolerance. Four out of five whites voted against the black candidate, and blacks were nearly unanimous in their opposition to the white candidate. In his term of office Stokes will be faced with policy problems similar to those he faced in the election. He must demonstrate to blacks that his presence in city hall does make a difference, but his programs must not seem so preferential toward blacks as to run the risk of unifying white opposition.

Thurgood Marshall built his brilliant legal career upon a record of unparalleled success in civil rights litigation. Marshall was the son of a pullman car steward. He was educated at Lincoln University and Howard University Law School. Shortly after graduation from law school in 1933, he became counsel for the Baltimore chapter of the NAACP. From 1940 to 1961 Marshall served as director and chief counsel of the NAACP's semiautonomous Legal Defense and Educational Fund. During that period Marshall argued thirty-two cases before the Supreme Court, winning twenty-nine of them. His most notable victory—indeed, perhaps the black man's most notable judicial victory—came in *Brown* v. *Board of Education of Topeka* in 1954 (see Chapter 2).

President Kennedy chose Marshall as a judge for the U.S. Circuit Court of Appeals in 1961, and President Johnson appointed him Solicitor General of the United States in 1965. As Solicitor General, Marshall argued nineteen more cases before the U.S. Supreme Court. When President Johnson announced Marshall's appointment to the Supreme Court in 1967, he accurately noted that "probably only one or two other living men have argued as many cases before the court—and perhaps less than half a dozen in all the history of the nation."

Probably no other Justice ever came to the Supreme Court with so much experience in constitutional law as Thurgood Marshall. In approving the appointment of Marshall, the Senate Judiciary Committee described his style in championing the civil rights cause in glowing terms: "Marshall has demonstrated those qualities which we admire in members of our highest judicial tribunal: thoughtfulness, care, moderation, reasonableness, a judicial temperament, and balanced approach to controversial and complicated national problems." Only eleven Senators voted against the Marshall nomination, all of them from the South.

Edward Brooke, Carl Stokes, and Thurgood Marshall are different types of black leaders whose careers have followed substantially different paths. But each has acquired position and influence *within* the present political, social, and economic system, and each has employed his influence to advance the interests of Negroes. Of course, none has succeeded in radically transforming the conditions of the black masses. All have accepted "the system" substantially as it is and have endeavored to achieve legal, political, economic, educational, and welfare goals that are within the capacity of the existing system to grant.

What Can Blacks Get Out of Politics?

It is easy to overestimate the value of voting and political activity in our society. Traditionally, textbooks in American government have asserted the value of the vote, but in so doing they are reflecting the American creed more than describing the actual impact of voting. Serious scholarship suggests that elections are primarily symbolic exercises that help to tie the masses to the political system and to give them a feeling of participation. According to Murray Edelman, elections are primarily a form of "symbolic reassurance" that serves "to quiet resentment and doubts about particular political acts."[29] The impact of voting on public policy is still relatively unclear.[30] Thus, a serious evaluation of the impact of black political activity must proceed with caution.

A generation ago Gunnar Myrdal wrote an essay entitled "What the Negro Gets Out of Politics" for his book *An American Dilemma*. He observed that "unquestionably the most important thing that Negroes get out of politics where they vote is legal justice—justice in the courts; police protection and protection against the persecution of the police."[31] John Stuart Mill, the political philosopher, once wrote: "Men, as well as women, do not need political rights in order that they

[29] Murray Edelman, *The Symbolic Uses of Politics* (Urbana, Ill.: University of Illinois Press, 1964), p. 17.

[30] See Gerald Pomper, *Elections in America* (New York: Dodd, Mead, 1968).

[31] Gunnar Myrdal, *An American Dilemma: The Negro Problem and Modern Democracy*, 2 vols. (New York: Harper, 1944), I:497.

might govern, but in order that they not be misgoverned." Contemporary research suggests that blacks can indeed help to ensure justice before the law through the exercise of their franchise. And Professor William R. Keech correctly asserts that the vote is a symbol of full citizenship and equal rights contributing to black self-respect.[32] Though legal justice is extremely important, we must nevertheless ask whether this is *all* that blacks can expect to gain from politics?

In addition to minimum of standards of justice, we have suggested that blacks can achieve *specific, although only marginal, material rewards* from political activity. These material rewards include jobs, patronage, favors, and public works projects. In 1961 the U.S. Commission on Civil Rights reported that segregated black schools in Southern counties *where blacks voted* were noticeably better in quality than those in counties where *blacks did not vote*.[33] But the kinds of tangible rewards that political activity can secure are largely "token" in character. There is no evidence that black voting can bring about significant changes in income, housing, employment, or other basic conditions of life.

There is some evidence that black political activity has assisted in bringing about the legal and the symbolic victories of the civil rights movement. The elimination of Jim Crow—direct, lawful discrimination—was primarily a political accomplishment. American Presidents and the Democratic party have been cognizant of the strategic location of large numbers of voting blacks in the big cities of Northern industrial states. Presidential candidates and nominating conventions have been more "pro civil rights" on the whole than Congress, suggesting their appreciation of the blacks' pivotal power in the large urban states with big blocs of electoral votes. And the Democratic party, which includes most big-city black voters, has been particularly interested in civil rights issues. Finally, there is some evidence that Northern Congressmen from districts with large numbers of blacks are, in general, more "liberal" than Northern Congressmen from districts with fewer blacks.[34]

---

[32] Keech, *The Impact of Negro Voting*, p. 3.

[33] U.S. Commission on Civil Rights, *1961 Report* (Washington, D.C.: Government Printing Office, 1961), p. 187.

[34] See Lewis A. Froman, *Congressmen and Their Constituencies* (Chicago: Rand McNally, 1963), p. 93.

However, even the symbolic victories of the civil rights movement cannot be attributed solely to black political activity. In the past, support for civil rights legislation came from a broad spectrum of the white community—from liberals, laborers, intellectuals, clergymen, and urban middle class voters. For example, the Northern states with the earliest and strongest record of civil rights legislation are not necessarily the states with the most black voters. In Chapter 4 we noted that state civil rights legislation was *inversely* related to black population percentages: the larger the bloc of black voters in a state, the less comprehensive its civil rights legislation. Thus, a large, politically active black population can arouse white fears to the point where paranoia more than cancels out the impact of black voting. The larger the black population, the greater the perceived threat to whites and the greater the unity and intensity of white opposition to black political demands. This relationship must also be considered in any honest evaluation of what blacks can gain from political activity.

Despite these reservations, it is clear that blacks can exercise a liberalizing influence on public policy through political activity. They can join in coalitions with whites—urban, labor, liberal, intellectual, and church groups—on behalf of public programs aimed at urban problems, low income housing, welfare assistance, health care for the poor, manpower training and job placement, economic opportunity, legal services for the poor, and problems of hunger. But political coalitions can achieve only marginal benefits for blacks. There are no large white voter groups interested in radically changing the character of our society or in embarking upon the massive public programs required to abolish ghettos and to eliminate differences in black-white life chances in the immediate future.

Professor James Q. Wilson provides a realistic summary of what blacks can expect to gain from political activity:

Viewed as a whole, Negro political activity must be judged as a strategy of limited objectives. Where Negroes can and do vote, they have it in their power to end the indifference or hostility of their elected representatives, but these representatives do not have it in their power to alter fundamentally the lot of the Negro. The vote is a legally important, morally essential weapon for the protection and advancement of individual and group interests, but it cannot protect or advance all the relevant interests. It can force the passage of laws, the ending of obvious forms of state-sanctioned discrimination, and the removal from office of race-baiters and avowed segregationists. It can only marginally affect the income, housing, occupation, or life chances of Negro electorates.[35]

[35] James Q. Wilson, "The Negro in American Politics: The Present," in *The American Negro Reference Book* (Englewood Cliffs, N.J.: Prentice-Hall, 1966), p. 456.

chapter 7
Violence
in the Ghettos

The Ghetto Riots

Civil disorder and violence are not new to the American scene. On the night of 16 December 1773 a group of "agitators" in Boston, Massachusetts, illegally destroyed 342 chests of tea—and violence as a form of political protest has continued intermittently in America to the present day. The nation itself was founded in armed revolution. Shortly thereafter, in 1786, indebted farmers led by Daniel Shay forcibly stopped the trials of debtors in many Massachusetts cities and laid siege to the court house in Springfield, Massachusetts. The state militia was required to put down Shay's Rebellion. Nat Turner's slave insurrection in 1831 resulted in the deaths of fifty-seven white persons and the later execution of Turner and his followers. On 13 July 1863 New York City was the scene of the nation's first major draft riot. Negroes were the object of much of the rioters' wrath, since many whites attributed conscription to Lincoln's attempt to free the slaves. Federal troops finally restored order. Violence was also the constant companion of the early labor movement in America. In a bitter railroad strike in Pittsburgh, Pennsylvania, in 1887 an estimated sixteen soldiers and fifty strikers were killed, and more than 125 locomotives,

2,000 freight cars, and other property were destroyed. The famous Homestead strike of 1892 turned Homestead, Pennsylvania, into an open battlefield. The Pullman strike of 1893 in Chicago resulted in twelve deaths and the destruction of a great deal of railroad property. On 20 April 1914 Ludlow, Colorado, was the scene of the famous Ludlow massacre in which company guards burned a miners' tent city and killed nearly one hundred persons, including women and children. During World War II serious racial violence erupted in Detroit. Black and white mobs battled in that city on 20 and 21 June 1943, the conflict resulting in thirty-five deaths, hundreds of injuries, over a thousand arrests, and finally the dispatch of federal troops to the scene.

Even though domestic violence has played a prominent role in America's history, the ghetto riots of the 1960s shocked the nation beyond measure. Violence flared in cities as dissimilar as Los Angeles, Des Moines, Cleveland, Buffalo, Milwaukee, New York, Atlanta, Chicago, Tampa, Cincinnati, Erie, Detroit, and New Haven. More than 150 major riots were reported in American cities from 1965 to 1968, all these riots involving black attacks on established authority —on policemen, firemen, National Guardsmen, whites in general, and property owned by whites. Three of these riots—Watts in 1965 and Newark and Detroit in 1967—amounted to major civil disorders.

The Watts riot from 11 to 17 August 1965 was set off when a white motorcycle officer arrested a black youth for drunken driving in a black district of Los Angeles known as Watts. In the words of the McCone Commission's report on the Watts violence:

> In the ugliest interval . . . perhaps as many as 10,000 Negroes took to the streets in neurotic bands. They looted stores, set fires, beat up white passers-by whom they had hauled from stopped cars, many of which were turned upside-down and burned, exchanged shots with law enforcement officers, and stoned and shot at firemen. The rioters seemed to have been caught up in an insensate rage of destruction. By Friday, disorder spread to adjoining areas, and ultimately, an area covering 46.5 square miles had to be controlled with the aid of military authority before public order was restored. . . .
>
> When the spasm passed, 34 persons were dead, and the wounded and hurt numbered 1,032 more. Property damage was about 40 million dollars. Arrested for one crime or another were 3,952 persons, women as well as men including over 500 youths under 18. Lawless-

ness in this one segment of the metropolitan area had terrified the entire county and its 6 million citizens. . . .

Of the 34 killed, one was a fireman, one was a deputy sheriff, and one a Long Beach policeman. . . . [the remainder were Negroes.]

More than 600 buildings were damaged by burning and looting. Out of this number, more than 200 were completely destroyed by fire. The rioters concentrated primarily on food markets, liquor stores, furniture stores, clothing stores, department stores, and pawn shops. . . . We note with interest that no residences were deliberately burned, that damage to schools, libraries, churches and public buildings was minimal, and that certain types of business establishments, notably service stations and automobile dealers, were for the most part unharmed.[1]

The Newark riot was set off when police arrested a black cab driver for reckless driving, driving without a license, and resisting arrest. Fellow black cab drivers led a crowd to the police station in the overwhelmingly black central ward of Newark. Soon rocks and bottles were clattering against the station house walls. Tension mounted throughout the ghetto, some fires were set, some windows were broken, looting began, and when police and firemen arrived at the scenes of disturbances they were met with hostility and violence. Frequently police, untrained in riot control, responded in a heavy-handed and undisciplined fashion. Within twenty-four hours Newark was in the throes of a major civil disorder. For four consecutive days and nights, snipers fired at police and firemen, looters made off with the inventories of scores of stores, and arsonists set fire to large portions of commercial property in the black section of Newark. New Jersey's governor proclaimed Newark a city "in open rebellion," declared a state of emergency, and called out the National Guard. More than four thousand city policemen, state troopers, and National Guardsmen were required to restore order. Before the riot was over, twenty-three persons had been killed, and property damage was widespread. Of the

[1] Governor's Commission on the Los Angeles Riots, *Violence in the City—An End or a Beginning?* (Sacramento, Calif.: Office of the Governor, State of California, 1965), pp. 3–5. The Commission was headed by John A. McCone, former Director of Central Intelligence.

dead, only two were white—a policeman and a fireman. Of the Negro dead, two were children and six were women.

In the violent summer of 1967 Detroit became the scene of the bloodiest racial violence of the twentieth century. A week of rioting in Detroit, from 23 to 28 July, left forty-three dead and more than one thousand injured. Whole sections of the city were reduced to charred ruins and smoke. Over thirteen hundred buildings were totally demolished and twenty-seven hundred businesses sacked. Detroit's upheaval began when police raided an after-hours club and arrested the bartender and several customers for selling and consuming alcoholic beverages after authorized closing hours. A force of fifteen thousand city and state police, National Guardsmen, and finally federal troops fought to quell the violence. Most of the looted retail businesses were liquor, grocery, and furniture stores. Many black merchants scrawled "Soul Brother" on their windows in an attempt to escape the wrath of the black mobs. Eventually homes and shops covering a total area of fourteen square miles were gutted by fire. Firemen who tried to fight fires were stoned and occasionally shot by ghetto residents.

In all, more than seventy-two hundred persons were arrested in the Detroit riots. Out of the forty-three persons killed during the riot, thirty-three were black and ten were white. Among the dead were one National Guardsman, one fireman, one policeman, and one black private guard. Both the violence and the pathos of the ghetto riots were reflected in the following report from Detroit:

> . . . a spirit of carefree nihilism was taking hold. To riot and destroy appeared more and more to become ends in themselves. Late Sunday afternoon it appeared to one observer that the young people were "dancing amidst the flames."

> A Negro plainclothes officer was standing at an intersection when a man threw a Molotov cocktail into a business establishment at the corner. In the heat of the afternoon, fanned by the 20 to 25 m.p.h. winds of both Sunday and Monday, the fire reached the home next door within minutes. As its residents uselessly sprayed the flames with garden hoses, the fire jumped from roof to roof of adjacent two- and three-story buildings. Within the hour the entire block was in flames. The ninth house in the burning row belonged to the arsonist who had thrown the Molotov cocktail. . . .

. . . Employed as a private guard, 55-year-old Julius L. Dorsey, a Negro, was standing in front of a market when accosted by two Negro men and a woman. They demanded he permit them to loot the market. He ignored their demands. They began to berate him. He asked a neighbor to call the police. As the argument grew more heated, Dorsey fired three shots from his pistol in the air.

The police radio reported: "Looters, they have rifles." A patrol car driven by a police officer and carrying three National Guardsmen arrived. As the looters fled, the law enforcement personnel opened fire. When the firing ceased, one person lay dead.

He was Julius L. Dorsey . . .[2]

The National Advisory Commission on Civil Disorders concluded:

1. No civil disorder was "typical" in all respects. . . .

2. While the civil disorders of 1967 were racial in character, they were not *inter*racial. The 1967 disorders, as well as earlier disorders of the recent period, involved action within Negro neighborhoods against symbols of white American society—authority and property—rather than against white persons.

3. Despite extremist rhetoric, there was no attempt to subvert the social order of the United States. Instead, most of those who attacked white authority and property seemed to be demanding fuller participation in the social order and the material benefits enjoyed by the vast majority of American citizens.

4. Disorder did not typically erupt without preexisting causes, as a result of a single "triggering" or "precipitating" incident. Instead, it developed out of an increasingly disturbed social atmosphere, in which typically a series of tension-heightening incidents over a period of weeks or months became linked in the minds of many in the Negro community with a shared network of underlying grievances.

5. There was, typically, a complex relationship between the series of incidents and the underlying grievances. For example, grievances about allegedly abusive police practices . . . were often aggravated in the minds of many Negroes by incidents involving

[2] National Advisory Commission on Civil Disorders, *Report* (Washington, D.C.: Government Printing Office, 1968), p. 4.

the police, or the inaction of municipal authorities on Negro complaints about police action. . . .

6. Many grievances in the Negro community result from the discrimination, prejudice, and powerlessness which Negroes often experience. . . .

7. Characteristically, the typical rioter was not a hoodlum, habitual criminal, or riff-raff. . . . Instead, he was a teen-ager or young adult, a lifelong resident of the city in which he rioted, a high-school drop-out—but somewhat better than his Negro neighbor —and almost invariably underemployed or employed in a menial job. He was proud of his race, extremely hostile to both whites and middle-class Negroes and, though informed about politics, highly distrustful of the political system and of political leaders.

8. Numerous Negro counter-rioters walked the street urging rioters to "cool it." . . .

9. Negotiations between Negroes and white officials occurred during virtually all the disorders surveyed. . . .

10. . . . Some rioters . . . may have shared neither the conditions nor the grievances of their Negro neighbors; some may have coolly and deliberately exploited the chaos created by others; some may have been drawn into the melee merely because they identified with, or wished to emulate, others. . . .

11. The background of disorder in the riot cities was typically characterized by severely disadvantaged conditions for Negroes, especially as compared with those for whites. . . .

12. In the immediate aftermath of disorder, the status quo of daily life before the disorder generally was quickly restored. Yet, despite some notable public and private efforts, little basic change took place in the conditions underlying the disorder. In some cases, the result was increased distrust between blacks and whites, diminished interracial communication, and the growth of Negro and white extremist groups.[3]

The areas of the city where rioting occurred were the ghettos—areas of high concentrations of impoverished blacks. Table 7–1 compares the socioeconomic character of seventeen disturbance areas with the corresponding cities and metropolitan areas as a whole.

---

[3] *Ibid.,* pp. 110–12.

Table 7–1   Characteristics of Disturbance Areas

	Disturbance Areas	Cities		SMSA's	
	Nonwhites	Nonwhite	White	Nonwhite	White
Median school years completed	8.7	8.8	10.6	8.9	11.2
Median unemployment rate, male (%)	11.1	9.7	4.7	10.1	3.8
Median family income ($)	4218	4336	6243	4338	6697
Families with annual income less than $3,000 (%)	32.0	29.0	14.0	32.8	11.6
Children under 18 living with both parents (%)	66	67	89	68	92

CITIES: Atlanta, Cincinnati, Dayton, Detroit, Elizabeth, Englewood, Grand Rapids, Jersey City, Milwaukee, Newark, New Brunswick, Patterson, Phoenix, Plainfield, Rockford, Tampa, and Tucson.

SOURCE: National Advisory Commission on Civil Disorders, *Report* (Washington, D.C.: Government Printing Office, 1968).

The Politics of Rioting

Any interpretation of the urban violence of the 1960s requires a complex and difficult unravelment of both the actions and motivations of the participants. Interpretation of the riots is a political activity itself, since the ideological views of the interpreter and the considerations of practical politics often influence the conclusions. For example, elected public officials concerned with the preservation of the established order are likely to label the riots as "criminal" and "lawless," deliberately deemphasizing their political and racial aspects. Some tactical advantage in stemming disorder may be gained by downgrading the seriousness of the riots and by branding the participants as "hoodlums," "riffraff," and "a tiny minority." Law enforcement officials are likely to see the events simply as problems of law enforcement and the maintenance of peace and quiet, requiring merely the restoration of law and order.

In contrast, black militants accentuate the racial character of the riots as well as their seriousness. They are likely to hail the riots as "a black revolt," a "rebellion," or an "insurrection." Often radical rightists in the white community join in supporting this interpretation in order to justify extreme repressive measures.

Our own interpretation is that the riots were a form of political protest. The riots expressed the hostility many blacks feel toward white people in general and toward established authority. They reflected the frustration most blacks harbor at their entrapment in the cellar of American society. To be sure, this form of political protest is a criminal one. And it may be irrational and self-defeating. The great majority of casualities of the riots—the dead, the injured, and the arrested—were rioters themselves. Much of the property destroyed belonged to the ghetto residents. Many businesses and other conveniences will never again venture into the ghetto. Moreover, the riots may have changed the attitudes of some whites toward the civil rights movement from sympathy to opposition. Certainly violence itself cannot solve the complicated social problems facing ghetto residents. But nonetheless the riots were not "senseless" or without purpose.

Our interpretation of the riots as purposeful protest is supported by evidence indicating that a large percentage of the black population in the ghettos supported the riots. As noted in the last chapter, a post-riot survey determined that roughly one-fifth of the blacks in the Watts area actually participated in the riot and that more than one-half of the residents supported the activities of the rioters.[4] Interviewers found that 58 percent of the Watts residents felt that the long-run effect of the riots would be favorable; 84 percent said that whites were now more aware of black problems; 62 percent regarded the riot as a black protest. In the eyes of a large proportion of blacks, the riots were a legitimate protest against white society, and this protest is expected to produce an improvement in the conditions of blacks. Of those blacks who claimed that the riots had a political purpose, each cited one or more of the following "purposes": (1) to call attention

---

[4] President's Commission on Law Enforcement and Administration of Justice, *Crime and Its Impact—An Assessment* (Washington, D.C.: Government Printing Office, 1967), p. 116, reporting findings of the Los Angeles Riot Study, Institute of Government and Public Affairs, University of California at Los Angeles.

to black problems; (2) to express black hostility to whites; or (3) to serve as an instrument for improving conditions, ending discrimination, of communicating with the "power structure."[5]

There is also evidence that the active rioters were not necessarily the poorest among the ghetto residents. It would be difficult to maintain that the riots were merely an economic revolt by poor people and thus were devoid of racial implications. In fact, the evidence suggests that rioters were slightly better off economically than most of their fellow blacks living in the ghettos.[6]

The political nature of the riots is further implied by survey information indicating that rioters were more politically active and racially conscious than nonrioters (see Table 7-2). According to the National Commission on Civil Disorders, the rioter

> feels strongly that he deserves a better job and that he is barred from achieving it, not because of lack of training, ability, or ambition, but because of discrimination by employers.
>
> He rejects the white bigot's stereotype of the Negro as ignorant and shiftless. He takes great pride in his race and believes that in some respects Negroes are superior to whites. He is extremely hostile to whites, but his hostility is more apt to be a product of social and economic class than of race; he is almost equally hostile toward middle-class Negroes.
>
> He is substantially better informed about politics than Negroes who were not involved in the riots. He is more likely to be actively engaged in civil rights efforts, but is extremely distrustful of the political system and of political leaders.[7]

The rioting was not simply another form of lawless activity in-

---

[5] See William McCord and John Howard, "Negro Opinions in Three Riot Cities," in *Riots and Rebellion,* eds. Louis H. Masotti and Don R. Bowen (New York: Sage Publications, 1968).

[6] The National Advisory Commission on Civil Disorders reported that in Newark rioters were more likely to be skilled (as opposed to unskilled) workers than nonrioters. In Detroit 61.4% of the persons identified as rioters had annual incomes exceeding $5,000, while in Newark the comparable figure was 67.4%. Approximately 70% of the rioters in both cities held jobs. Persons with some high school education were more likely to participate in riots than those with only grade school educations. National Advisory Commission on Civil Disorders, *Report,* pp. 129–33.

[7] *Ibid.,* pp. 133–34.

Table 7–2 The Political Views of Rioters and Nonrioters

	Newark	
	Rioters	Noninvolved
Do you feel your job is appropriate considering the education you have?		
Yes	29.3%	44.4%
No	70.7	55.6
Perceived opportunity		
Possible to obtain desired job	32.4	43.9
Not possible to obtain desired job	67.6	56.1
Perceived obstacles to employment		
Lack training	18.3	41.2
Lack experience	12.7	8.8
Discrimination	69.0	50.0
Sometimes I hate white people		
Agree	72.4	50.0
Disagree	27.6	50.0
Political information score		
High	68.9	51.2
Low	31.1	48.8
	Detroit	
	Rioters	Noninvolved
How much did anger with politicians have to do with causing riot?		
Great deal	43.2	19.6
Something	31.8	39.1
Nothing	18.2	24.5
Don't Know	6.8	16.8

Table 7–2 *(continued)*

	Detroit		Newark	
	Rioters	Noninvolved	Rioters	Noninvolved
Who do you think are more dependable?				
Negroes	48.6	22.4	45.0	27.8
Whites	21.7	27.6	35.2	49.1
Same	29.7	50.0	19.8	23.1
Who do you think are nicer?				
Negroes	61.0	36.3	78.1	57.3
Whites	4.9	5.0	21.9	37.3
Same	34.1	58.7	0.0	5.4
Civil rights groups with white and Negro leaders would do better without whites				
True	36.1	21.1	51.4	33.1
False	63.9	78.9	48.6	66.9
Is the country worth fighting for in major world war?				
Yes	55.3	75.0	33.0	50.8
No	39.4	15.5	52.8	27.8
Don't Know	5.3	9.5	14.2	21.4

SOURCE: National Advisory Commission on Civil Disorders, *Report* (Washington, D.C.: Government Printing Office, 1968).

distinguishable from murder, robbery, or other criminal acts. Though the rioters engaged in criminal activities during the riots, they did not destroy indiscriminately but instead directed their efforts specifically against white political and economic institutions. The targets of the violence were representative of the political and economic order. Generally the looting and sniping were directed toward white merchants and white policemen, and the rioters were almost uniformly black.

When black residences or businesses burned, it was usually the acci-
dental product of arson directed against white businesses, schools, or
precinct stations. Moreover, the riots were not simply a "psychological
release"—that is, "rioting for kicks"—although the motivations of
many individual participants may have taken this form. One is tempted
to view some aspects of the rioting as divorced from political purposes
—a social sickness causing individuals temporarily to lose their
inhibitions against violence and theft and to become caught up in
crowd hysteria. It is true that there is some evidence of rioters experiencing a sense of "freedom" or "joy" in a riot as a result of release
from inhibitions against destruction and aggression. Some observers
characterize the crowd-gathering and looting stages of a riot as a "Roman holiday" or "carnival." Doubtless these psychological factors
were present in some of the riots. But again this explanation fails to
account for the political and racial aspects of the riots.

Assessing the Causes of Riots

One explanation of the urban violence is that it is a product of the
"relative deprivation" of ghetto residents.[8] "Relative deprivation" is
the discrepancy between people's expectations about the goods and
conditions of life to which they feel themselves justifiably entitled, and
what they perceive to be their chances of getting and keeping what
they feel they deserve. Relative deprivation is not merely a complicated way of saying that people are deprived and therefore angry
because they have less than they want; it is more complex than that.
Relative deprivation focuses on (1) what people think they *deserve,*
not just what they want in an ideal sense, and (2) what they think they
have a *chance* of getting, not just what they have.

Relative deprivation differs considerably from the "absolute deprivation" hypothesis. The absolute deprivation idea suggests that individuals who are the most deprived are those most likely to rebel.

[8] For a full discussion of the "relative deprivation" explanation as well as alternative explanations, see Don R. Bowen and Louis H. Masotti, "Civil Violence:
A Theoretical Overview," in *Riots and Rebellion,* eds. Masotti and Bowen; see
also James C. Davies, "Toward a Theory of Revolution," *American Sociological
Review* 27 (February 1962): 6.

Of course it is true that ghetto conditions provide the necessary environment for violence. Racial imbalance, de facto segregation, slum housing, discrimination, unemployment, poor schools, and poverty— all of these are excellent kindling for the flames of violence. But these underlying conditions have existed for decades in America, and yet the nation never experienced simultaneous violent uprisings in its major cities until the 1960s. This observation suggests that deprivation itself is not a sufficient condition for violence: some new ingredients must have been added to the incendiary conditions in American cities to touch off the violence of the 1960s.

Relative deprivation focuses on the distance between current status and levels of expectation. According to this hypothesis, neither the wholly downtrodden (who have no aspirations) nor the very well-off (who can satisfy their aspirations) represent a threat to civil order, but rather those whose expectations about what they deserve out-distance the capacity of the political system to satisfy them. Often, rapid increases in expectations are the product of symbolic or token improvements in conditions. This situation leads to the apparent paradox of violence and disorder occurring precisely at the time that improvements in the conditions of blacks are being made. Hope, not despair, generates civil violence and disorder. As Louis H. Masotti and Don R. Bowen assert, "The reason why black Americans riot is because there has been just enough improvement in their condition to generate hopes, expectations, or aspirations beyond the capacities of the system to meet them."[9]

The civil rights movement made many blacks acutely aware of discrimination in American society and reduced their tolerance for injustice. The civil rights movement increased the levels of aspiration among the black masses and heightened their impatience with, and hostility toward, the "white establishment." The civil rights movement had to awaken blacks to their plight in American society before progress could be made in eliminating discrimination; but the price of this awakening was a major increase in levels of aspiration and the concomitant risk of frustration and bitterness once aspirations went unfulfilled. The breakthroughs that the established civil rights movement made in public accommodations, employment, voting, and office-

[9] Bowen and Masotti, "Civil Violence," pp. 24–25.

holding in the 1960s may have opened new opportunities for the educated middle class. But the undereducated black poor living in the ghetto environment could not really take advantage of many of these opportunities. The movement increased their expectations but it failed utterly to alter their conditions in life. Thus, it was not by coincidence that the most serious urban disorders followed on the heels of some of the most significant legislative gains in the civil rights struggle.

Several additional propositions can be derived from the relative deprivation model.[10] In a psychological analysis of civil strife, Ted Gurr developed a series of interrelated propositions.

> The first proposition is that the greater the extent of discrepancy that men see between what they seek and what seems to be attainable, the greater their anger and consequent disposition to aggression.

This proposition may explain why dissatisfied people often revolt just when things seem to get better. A little improvement accompanied by promises that a great deal of improvement will soon follow raises expectations, and if insufficient proof of improvement follows, consternation and militancy increase rapidly among the "cheated."

> A second proposition relates to "opportunities": men who feel that they have many ways to attain their goals are less likely to become angry when one is blocked than those who have few alternatives. . . . but this [may be dangerous] since those who invest their energies in what appear to be opportunities but fail to make progress toward their goals tend to become more bitterly angry than those who do nothing.

This proposition suggests that if government programs in job training (e.g., the Job Corps and Manpower Development, among others) promise opportunities to disadvantaged blacks but then fail to deliver on those promises after blacks have invested their energies and hopes, the effects can be explosive.

> A third general proposition is that the greater the intensity of men's expectations, the greater their anger when they meet unexpected or increased resistance.

10 The following analysis is based upon Ted Gurr, "Urban Disorder: Perspectives from the Comparative Study of Civil Strife," in *Riots and Rebellion*, eds. Masotti and Bowen. See also Ted Gurr, "A Casual Model of Civil Strife," *American Political Science Review* 62 (December 1968): 1104–24.

Expectations are most intensely held among the young, among Northern blacks, and among black leaders; these are the groups most dissatisfied with the pace of improvement in Negro life.

> If men think that deprivation is legitimate, i.e., justified by circum-
> stances or by the need to attain some greater end, the intensity and
> perhaps the level of expectations decline and consequently depriva-
> tion tends to be accepted with less anger.

This observation may explain why most blacks, like most whites, accept tax increases and the risk of military service without opting for
open rebellion. On the other hand, if deprivation is labeled by black
leaders as illegitimate, the result may be an increase in frustration
and aggression.

Gurr himself tested several of his propositions in a cross-national
study of correlates of civil strife. From news reports and dispatches,
Gurr constructed an index of civil strife in 114 nations. The United
States ranked forty-second among the 114 nations in total magnitude
of strife. He then proceeded to measure such factors as short-term
deprivation (economic fluctuations), persistent deprivation (low levels
of income and education), the size and loyalty of police and military
forces, the availability of political institutions to channel strife, and
the levels of past civil strife.

The conclusions from Gurr's cross-national research are as
follows:

> Among nations generally—the qualification that applies to all these—
> only three variables are direct and important causes of turmoil: long-
> term deprivation, a history of strife, and the legitimacy of the political
> system. These three variables control or mediate the effects of all
> others. . . . If coercive forces are large and loyal, if few facilitative
> conditions are present, and most important if there is no tradition of
> civil violence, short-term deprivation is unlikely to lead to violence. If
> the intervening conditions are substantially different, however, even
> mild deprivation is likely to result in turmoil. . . . We have considerable
> evidence, comparative and specific, that police or military repression
> has effects similar to deprivation; it infuriates its victims, the more
> so to the extent that they believe that their acts are legitimate, and
> their fury is likely to be contained only by the strongest of internal
> or external controls. . . . Legitimacy seems to be causally related to
> strife in 114 polities, independent of either deprivation or the other

intervening variables. . . . One implication for urban racial violence in the United States can be drawn from this. Although most Americans regard their political system as a legitimate one, a growing minority of Negroes say they do not because of what they regard as its deliberately dilatory progress toward racial equality. Whatever the merit of their judgment, it seems likely to persist; and insofar as the general principle applies to the United States, higher levels of turmoil can be expected as a consequence.[11]

Once racial violence breaks out anywhere in the nation, the mass media immediately begin disseminating images of violence as well as the symbols and rationalizations of the rioters. Television offers rioters the assurance of a mass audience. In the past rioters have been known to leave the riot scene temporarily to rush to watch themselves on TV. Moreover, TV images may reinforce a viewer's predisposition to participate in riots and may even legitimize in his own mind such participation. Television coverage forces the blacks in one ghetto to see what blacks in another ghetto are doing, thus helping to explain simultaneous rioting in ghettos across the nation.

The National Advisory Commission on Civil Disorders

In July 1967, in the midst of widespread urban disorder, President Lyndon B. Johnson appointed a National Advisory Commission on Civil Disorders to study the riots and to make necessary recommendations. Democrat Otto Kerner, Governor of Illinois, was named Chairman of the Commission, and Republican John Lindsay, Mayor of New York, was named Vice-chairman.[12] There were no real radicals or militants on the Commission. In many ways, the fact that the Com-

---

11 Gurr, "Urban Disorder," pp. 61–65.

12 Other Commission members were Senator Fred R. Harris, Democrat of Oklahoma; Congressman James C. Corman, Democrat of California; Congressman William M. McCulloch, Republican of Ohio; Miss Katherine Graham Peden, former Commissioner of Commerce of Kentucky; I. W. Abel, President of United Steel Workers of America; Herbert Jenkins, Chief of Police in Atlanta; Charles B. Thornton, Chairman of the Board of Litton Industries; Senator Edward W. Brooke, Republican of Massachusetts; and Roy Wilkins, Executive Director of NAACP.

mission's membership was so moderate in character made its conclusions so shocking to the nation.

In its official report, the Commission, attempting perhaps to jolt the nation's white majority into action on urban problems, asserted that "white racism" was responsible for urban rioting. In Chapter 4 of its report, entitled "The Basic Causes," the Commission enumerated "three of the most bitter fruits of white racial attitudes":

> *Pervasive discrimination and segregation.* The first is surely the continuing exclusion of great numbers of Negroes from the benefits of economic progress through discrimination in employment and education, and their enforced confinement in segregated housing and schools. The corrosive and degrading effects of this condition and the attitudes that underlie it are the source of the deepest bitterness and at the center of the problem of racial disorder.

> *Black migration and white exodus.* The second is the massive and growing concentration of impoverished Negroes in our major cities resulting from Negro migration from the rural South, rapid population growth and the continuing movement of the white middle-class to the suburbs. The consequence is a greatly increased burden on the already depleted resources of cities, creating a growing crisis of deteriorating facilities and services and unmet human needs.

> *Black ghettos.* Third, in the teeming racial ghettos, segregation and poverty have intersected to destroy opportunity and hope and to enforce failure. The ghettos too often mean men and women without jobs, families without men, and schools where children are processed instead of educated, until they return to the street—to crime, to narcotics, to dependency on welfare, and to bitterness and resentment against society in general and white society in particular.[13]

However, the Commission admitted that "these facts alone—fundamental as they are—cannot be said to have caused the disorders." The Commission identified three "powerful ingredients" that had "begun to catalyze the mixture":

> *Frustrated hopes.* The expectations aroused by the great judicial and legislative victories of the civil rights movement have led to frustration, hostility and cynicism in the face of the persistent gap between

[13] National Advisory Commission on Civil Disorders, *Report*, pp. 203–204.

promise and fulfillment. The dramatic struggle for equal rights in the South has sensitized Northern Negroes to the economic inequalities reflected in the deprivations of ghetto life.

Legitimation of violence. A climate that tends toward the approval and encouragement of violence as a form of protest has been created by white terrorism directed against nonviolent protest, including instances of abuse and even murder of some civil rights workers in the South; by the open defiance of law and federal authority by state and local officials resisting desegregation; and by some protest groups engaging in civil disobedience who turn their backs on nonviolence, go beyond the Constitutionally protected rights of petition and free assembly, and resort to violence to attempt to compel alteration of laws and policies with which they disagree. This condition has been reinforced by a general erosion of respect for authority in American society and reduced effectiveness of social standards and community restraints on violence and crime. This in turn has largely resulted from rapid urbanization and the dramatic reduction in the average age of the total population.

Powerlessness. Finally, many Negroes have come to believe that they are being exploited politically and economically by the white "power structure." Negroes, like people in poverty everywhere, in fact lack the channels of communication, influence and appeal that traditionally have been available to ethnic minorities within the city and which enabled them—unburdened by color—to scale the walls of the white ghettos in an earlier era. The frustrations of powerlessness have led some to the conviction that there is no effective alternative to violence as a means of expression and redress, as a way of "moving the system." More generally, the result is alienation and hostility toward the institutions of law and government and the white society which controls them. This is reflected in the reach toward racial consciousness and solidarity reflected in the slogan "Black Power."[14]

The Commission warned that "our nation is moving toward two societies, one black, one white—separate and unequal." The principal "blame" for the riots was placed upon whites rather than blacks: "What white Americans have never fully understood—but what the Negro can never forget—is that white society is deeply implicated in

[14] *Ibid.*, pp. 204–205.

the ghetto. White institutions created it, white institutions maintain it, and white society condones it."[15] The Commission recommended massive federal aid programs in employment, education, welfare, and housing, but it suggested no new departures from traditional programs in these areas. The Commission called for the creation of two million new jobs in the ghettos, the elimination of de facto segregation, the construction of six million new units of public housing, and more liberal welfare benefits. In the Commission's words: "These programs will require unprecedented levels of funding and performance, but they neither probe deeper nor demand more than the problems which called them forth. There can be no higher priority for national action and no higher claim on the nation's conscience."[16]

The Commission's account of events during the riots seemed to focus more on police brutality than on the actions of rioters. The Commission also concluded that "the urban disorders of the summer of 1967 were not caused by, nor were they the consequence of, any organized plan or 'conspiracy.'"[17] While recognizing that militant organizations and individual agitators repeatedly forecast and called for violence, the Commission concluded that ghetto conditions were the basic cause of the riots.

Violence as an Ideology

It is not easy to determine what role the ideology of violence plays in urban rioting. Doubtless some ghetto blacks believe that violence is justified, indeed even necessary, in the interests of black freedom. But violence as an ideology appears to be limited to a very small minority. Only if conditions are otherwise ripe for violence will violence-prone leaders likely have any real impact on the black masses.

As early as 1963 Malcolm X was speaking in urban ghettos against Martin Luther King's philosophy of nonviolence:

> The white man . . . wants to put knots on your head and take advantage of you and not have to be afraid of your fighting back. To keep

---

[15] *Ibid.*, p. 2.
[16] *Ibid.*, p. 2.
[17] *Ibid.*, p. 202.

you from fighting back, he gets these old religious Uncle Toms to teach you and me, just like novocaine, to suffer peacefully. Don't stop suffering—just suffer peacefully. . . . This is a shame. . . .

There is nothing in our book, the Koran, that teaches us to suffer peacefully. . . . Be peaceful, be courteous, obey the law, respect everyone; but if someone puts his hand on you, send him to the cemetery. . . . That's a good religion.[18]

As late as 1964 Malcolm X reiterated the theme that violence might be necessary for self-defense:

The only thing that I've ever said is that in areas where the government has proven itself either unwilling or unable to defend the lives and the property of Negroes, it's time for Negroes to defend themselves. Article number two of the constitutional amendments provides you and me the right to own a rifle or a shotgun. This doesn't mean you're going to get a rifle and form battalions and go out looking for white folks, although you'd be within your rights—I mean, you'd be justified; but that would be illegal and we don't do anything illegal.[19]

After traveling in Asia and Africa, Malcolm X acquired greater sympathy for violent revolutions, contending that "black brothers" throughout the world had to resort to violence to gain their independence. In his public speeches he began to talk of giving the white man "alternatives"—either freedom or violence. Typically, he would spend a great deal of time talking about white atrocities, such as Ku Klux Klan murders; then he would exclaim:

He's talking the language of violence while you and I are running around with this little chicken-picking type of language—and think that he's going to understand.

Let's learn his language. If his language is with a shotgun, get a shotgun. Yes, I said if he only understands the language of a rifle, get a rifle. If he only understands the language of a rope, get a rope. But don't waste time talking the wrong language to a man if you want to really communicate with him. Speak his language—there's nothing wrong with that. If something was wrong with that language, the federal government would have stopped the cracker from speaking it to you and me.[20]

[18] Malcolm X, *Malcolm X Speaks* (New York: Grove Press, 1965), p. 12.
[19] *Ibid.,* p. 43.
[20] *Ibid.,* p. 108.

Thus, some black leaders have sought to legitimize violence, leading many blacks to believe that violence is justified. In 1967 H. Rap Brown came to Cambridge, Maryland, during an extended period of racial tension and violence in that city. Brown was indicted for inciting to riot after delivering an inflammatory speech to an assembly of blacks who later the same evening rioted in the downtown business district of Cambridge. Excerpts from Brown's speech indicate the development of the ideology of violence:

> They run around and tell you: "Don't start no fight with the honky picker 'cause you can't win." And he outnumbers you. Hell! Don't you know they always outnumber us. David was outnumbered when he fought the lions. He was outnumbered. Daniel in the lion's den, when he fought the lion. All of us is outnumbered. That don't make no difference. . . .

> America is killing people down south by starving them to death in Alabama. Babies die. Five hundred people die a year for lack of food and nourishment. And yet we got enough money to go to the moon. Think about that. . . .

> You got no business letting your brother, your sons, your nephews go to that war [Vietnam]. That ain't your war. All right, you'd better get you some guns. You'd better get you some guns. The man's moving to kill you. The only thing the honky respects is force. . . .

> And don't let them come into your community. Ain't got no reason for white folks to be leisurely walking up and down your community. He's got no business coming over, talking and taking black women out of your community. You ain't a man if you let that animal come over here and take a black woman out of your community. . . .

> I mean, don't be trying to love that honky to death. Shoot him to death. Shoot him to death, brother, cause that's what he's out to do to you. Like I said in the beginning, if this town don't come around, this town should be burned down. It should be burned down, brother.[21]

If conditions are ripe for violence, a fiery speaker like Brown can doubtless trigger a riot. But Brown and other militants do not

[21] U.S. Congress, Senate, Committee on the Judiciary, *Hearings on H.R. 421, "Antiriot Bill,"* 90th Cong., 1st sess., 2 August 1967, pp. 31–32.

"cause" riots; rather Brown *and* riots are both "caused" by the same set of conditions and emotions in the ghettos.

Police in the Ghetto

Nearly all riots are accompanied by charges of "police brutality." Incidents involving police action have often been the trigger for riots. Police-black tensions are always high in ghetto areas since to many ghetto dwellers the police are a symbol of white oppression. "Police brutality" has become a theme with enormous emotional impact among blacks.

While the actual events at any particular riot can probably never be untangled to the full satisfaction of both sides, perceptually the policeman stands as a symbol of oppression for blacks and a symbol of law and order for whites. Police themselves are not immune to social prejudice. The policeman's attitude toward ghetto residents is often affected by the high crime rates in ghetto areas (see Table 7–3). The policeman is suspicious of ghetto residents because crime rates tell him that his suspicions are often justified. Sociologists interviewing policemen in the cities that experienced riots in 1967 reported that 79 per-

Table 7–3   Crime and Police Assignments
in Three Chicago Police Districts, 1965
(Rates per 100,000 Residents)

	High Income, White	Low-Middle-Income, White	Very Low Income, Black
Crimes against persons	80	440	1615
Crimes against property	1038	1750	2508
Patrolmen assigned	93	133	243

SOURCE: National Advisory Commission on Civil Disorders, *Report* (Washington, D.C.: Government Printing Office, 1968).

cent of the policemen did not think that Negroes were treated un-equally.[22] However, police accurately perceived the hostility directed at them in the ghettos. They believed that only a small minority of blacks, as compared to a substantial majority of whites, regard them as friends. Moreover, the police viewed themselves much as blacks view them—as unwelcome aliens in the ghetto: they reported feeling iso-lated in a hostile atmosphere, but could not understand why blacks resent them. Finally, antiblack attitudes among the policemen inter-viewed were fairly strong; for example, 49 percent did not approve of socializing between whites and blacks, and 56 percent were disturbed by the movement of blacks into white neighborhoods.

Ranking with police discrimination and police brutality as com-plaints of ghetto residents is the charge that police fail to protect resi-dents and to enforce the law among blacks. Blacks are more frequently the victims of crime than whites (see Table 7–4).

Policemen tend to view ghetto riots as acts of criminal irresponsi-bility rather than social or political protest.[23] A large majority of the policemen interviewed in 1967 believed that the riots "are caused by nationalists and militants" (77 percent) and that "criminal elements are involved in riots" (69 percent); fewer than one-third of the policemen (31 percent) believed that "unheard Negro complaints are involved in riots." Policemen are not particularly sensitive to the under-lying social and economic problems of the ghetto. They tend to regard a riot as primarily a problem in mob control and the suppression of criminal activity. Policemen frequently view judges as too lenient in law enforcement. They often look upon civil rights groups as contribu-tors to violence and upon social agencies as misguided social reform institutions that do not understand the legitimacy of force. Policemen are recruited from those social classes most likely to have anti-Negro prejudices, the lower-middle and working classes. Very few have had college training. It would be unrealistic to expect policemen to possess more tolerant social attitudes than the middle and lower class high-school educated white populations from which most of them are re-cruited. High crime rates in the ghettos and the element of danger in

---

[22] *Supplemental Studies for the National Advisory Commission on Civil Dis-orders* (Washington, D.C.: Government Printing Office, 1968), p. 44.
[23] *Ibid.*, p. 96.

Table 7–4   Victims of Crime by Race
                  (Rates per 100,000 Population)

	White	Nonwhite
Total	1,860	2,592
Forcible rape	22	82
Robbery	58	204
Aggravated assault	186	347
Burglary	822	1,306
Larceny	608	367
Motor vehicle theft	164	286

SOURCE: President's Commission on Law Enforcement and Administration of Justice, *Crime and Its Impact—An Assessment* (Washington, D.C.: Government Printing Office, 1967), p. 80.

the policeman's job makes him naturally suspicious of ghetto residents, particularly young people. Policemen are engaged in rule enforcement as members of a semimilitary organization. They are concerned with authority themselves, and they expect ghetto residents to respect authority. It is often difficult for even the most well-meaning police officer to develop respect or sympathy for ghetto residents.[24] One policeman described this problem as follows:

> The police have to associate with lower class people, slobs, drunks, criminals, riff-raff of the worst sort. Most of these . . . are Negroes. The police officers see these people through middle class or lower middle class eye-balls. But even if he saw them through highly sophisticated eye-balls he can't go in the street and take this night after night. When some Negro criminal says to you a few times, "you white mother-fucker, take that badge off and I'll shove it up your ass," well it's bound to affect you after a while. Pretty soon you decide they're all just niggers and they'll never be anything but niggers. It would take not just an average man to resist this feeling, it would take an extraordinary man to resist it, and there are very few ways by which the police department can attract extraordinary men to join them.[25]

[24] See J. H. Skolnick, *Justice Without Trial* (New York: John Wiley, 1967).

[25] James Q. Wilson, *Varieties of Police Behavior* (Cambridge, Mass.: Harvard University Press, 1968), p. 43.

One commentator described the dilemma of police-ghetto relations as follows:

> First, the police department recruits from a population (the working class) whose numbers are more likely than the average population to hold anti-Negro attitudes; second, the recruits are given a basic classroom training program that is unlikely to change the anti-Negro sentiments; third, the recruit goes out on the street as a patrolman and is more likely than not to have his anti-Negro attitudes reinforced and hardened by the older officer; fourth, in the best departments, the most able officers are soon transferred to specialized administrative duties in training, recruitment, juvenile work, etc., or are promoted after three to five years to supervisory positions; fifth, after five years the patrolman on street duty significantly increases in levels of cynicism, authoritarianism, and generalized hostility to the non-police world. Finally, it is highly likely that the worst of the patrolmen will wind up patrolling the ghetto, because that tends to be the least wanted assignment.
>
> If this is an accurate description of the urban police system (and my personal observations over the past five years tell me this is so), then the reason is clear why every poll of black citizens shows the same high level of distrust and hostility against policemen.[26]

The National Advisory Commission on Civil Disorders found that even the most routine and legitimate police action can lead to disorder in the ghetto. On sweltering summer nights the front steps and the streets become a refuge from the stifling, non-air-conditioned, unventilated rooms of tenement houses in the ghettos. A large number of people are on the streets on such nights, including a high proportion of young people. Attracting a crowd is easy in this setting. Though stopping a car for speeding might be a routine police action that would pass unnoticed anywhere else, in the ghetto that action can attract a crowd immediately. Ghetto residents watching a white policeman arrest a black man in their neighborhood are "quick to misunderstand, quick to characterize the police action as unfair, quick to

[26] Burton Levy, "Cops in the Ghetto," in *Riots and Rebellion,* eds. Masotti and Bowen, p. 353; see also Arthur Niederhoffer, *Behind the Shield: The Police in Urban Society* (New York: Doubleday, 1967).

abandon curiosity for anger."[27] The Commission made a series of recommendations regarding city police and law enforcement, including the following:

> The police department should have a clear and enforced policy that the standard of law enforcement in ghetto areas is the same as in other communities. . . .
>
> A specialized agency with adequate funds and staff should be created separate from other municipal agencies, to handle, investigate and to make recommendations on city complaints [against policemen].
>
> Police departments should intensify their efforts to recruit more Negroes. . . . [See Table 7–5.]
>
> Police officers should be so assigned as to insure that the police department is fully and visibly integrated. Some cities have adopted a policy of assigning one white and one Negro officer to patrol cars, especially in ghetto areas. . . .
>
> The basic rule, when applying force, is to use only the minimum force necessary to effectively control the situation. Unwarranted application of force will incite the mob to further violence, as well as kindle seeds of resentment for police that, in turn, could cause a riot to recur. Ill-advised or excessive application of force will not only result in charges of police brutality, but also may prolong the disturbance.[28]

The Commission recommended neither that the looters should be shot on sight nor that law enforcement personnel should stand idly by during looting or withdraw their forces from riot areas. The Commission took the view that civil disorders are not simply police matters but are ultimately the responsibility of elected governmental officials. It recommended that mayors should control and coordinate police activities and that, insofar as possible, they should "maintain close personal contact with the ghetto."

The Black Panthers

The ghetto riots were unplanned, property-oriented, mass disorders.

---

[27] National Advisory Commission on Civil Disorders, *Report,* p. 325.

[28] *Ibid.,* p. 17. The last paragraph is a quotation from the FBI riot control manual.

Table 7–5   Black Policemen in Large Cities, 1967

	Estimated Nonwhite Percentage of City Population	Nonwhite Policemen as Percentage of Total Force
Atlanta	38	10
Baltimore	41	7
Boston	11	2
Buffalo	18	3
Chicago	27	17
Cincinnati	28	6
Cleveland	34	7
Dayton	26	4
Detroit	39	5
Hartford	20	11
Kansas City	20	6
Louisville	21	6
Memphis	38	5
Michigan State Police	9	—
New Haven	19	7
New Orleans	41	4
New York	16	5
New Jersey State Police	9	—
Newark	40	10
Oakland	31	4
Oklahoma City	15	4
Philadelphia	29	20
Phoenix	8	1
Pittsburgh	19	7
St. Louis	37	11
San Francisco	14	6
Tampa	17	3
Washington, D.C.	63	21

SOURCE: National Advisory Commission on Civil Disorders, *Report* (Washington, D.C.: Government Printing Office, 1968), p. 321.

But a new form of ghetto violence is now haunting the nation's cities. It is planned, deliberate, person-oriented violence involving small numbers of well-armed blacks in conflict with the police. Loosely organized Black Panther groups have sprung up in the nation's largest cities, and tension between these militant armed blacks and the city police has resulted in several bloody "shoot-outs."

The Black Panther leaders speak the rhetoric of violence. Panther newspapers contain "recipes" for Molotov cocktails and "peoples hand grenades"—aerosal cans filled with explosives. They declare "All self-defense groups must strike blows against the slavemaster until we have secured our survival as a people, and if this takes shooting every pig and blowing up every pigsty, then let's get on with it."[29] And there has been enough association of Panthers (Eldridge Cleaver, Huey Newton, Bobby Seale, and others) with acts of violence (against both police and fellow blacks) to suggest that many Panthers are prepared to go beyond the mere rhetoric of violence. Large quantities of weapons have been seized at various Panther headquarters.

Since police are generally the objects of Panther wrath, they are understandably touchy in approaching Panther "turf." In several violent confrontations between police and Panthers, most notably in Chicago in December 1969, police have not hesitated to use heavy fire power against Panthers. The result has been the development of some sympathy for the Panthers among blacks. Louis Harris reported in 1970 that a majority of blacks agree that "Panthers give me a sense of pride."[30]

Shoot-Out in Cleveland

Violence erupted in Cleveland in 1968 that was similar in nature to several later violent confrontations between Black Panthers and policemen. On the night of 24 July 1968 a small well-equipped army of black nationalists led by Fred "Ahmed" Evans engaged in a two-hour gun battle with Cleveland policemen. Blacks with automatic weapons and bandoliers of ammunition strapped around their chests killed three policemen and wounded twelve others; a civilian who attempted to help a wounded policeman was also killed; at least three black nationalists were killed. Ahmed Evans was later convicted of conspiring with other black nationalists to purchase weapons and to plan their at-

[29] Reprinted in *Time*, 11 May 1970, p. 25.
[30] *Ibid.*, p. 30.

tack on the police. The anger and extremism of the small band of black nationalists in Cleveland was apparently unaffected by the fact that the city's mayor, Carl Stokes, was a black. Since earlier violence both in Cleveland and elsewhere had been spontaneous and unplanned, the deliberate and premeditated nature of the violence of the black nationalists in Cleveland signaled an ominous development in race relations.[31]

Race relations in Cleveland offer a particularly interesting case study. In 1963 a United Freedom Movement (UFM) was organized in the city from some fifty separate civil rights groups, including local chapters of NAACP and CORE, to protest de facto school segregation. In 1964 the UFM led a series of demonstrations, sit-ins, picketing campaigns, and school boycotts in support of demands to bus more black pupils to predominantly white schools. The UFM also demonstrated against the construction of any more schools in the ghetto area. During one demonstration at a school construction site the Reverend Bruce Klunder, a white minister, lay down behind a bulldozer and in the confusion was run over and killed. By 1965 "black power" had gained popularity among militant blacks and some of the pressure for integration shifted to an increasing emphasis on black control over ghetto schools. At the same time, outbreaks of violence were increasing, particularly between black and white teenage gangs.

In July 1966 Cleveland experienced a major upheaval in its Hough (pronounced "huff") area that resembled the ghetto riots then sweeping through other cities. Four persons (all blacks) were killed; looting, vandalism, burning, and sniping occurred over a four-day period. Whole blocks of buildings were leveled, and National Guardsmen patrolled the streets. But the summer of 1967 was surprisingly quiet in Cleveland. While other cities were experiencing their worst racial convulsions, Cleveland was calm. Perhaps the black community was channeling its hopes and grievances into the election campaign of Carl Stokes. Stokes' November victory was hailed initially as a great victory over bigotry and as the beginning of a new era of racial

---

[31] The following description of racial violence in Cleveland is based upon Louis H. Masotti and Jerome R. Corsi, *Shoot-Out in Cleveland: Report to the National Commission on the Causes and Prevention of Violence* (Washington, D.C.: Government Printing Office, 1968).

harmony in the cities. Only later did the voting data reveal that Stokes had won only one white vote in five. The mayor initiated a "Cleveland Now" program combining private contributions with some public money to finance youth employment and ghetto development projects. In the early summer of 1968 Ahmed Evans received $10,300 from "Cleveland Now" to develop African crafts in his Afro Culture Shop and Bookstore.

The actual sequence of events on the night of 24 July is difficult to determine. It is not clear whether the policemen or whether the nationalists fired the first shot, nor whether the policemen were lured into an ambush or were attacked while watching Ahmed's apartment. But there is little doubt that Ahmed and his followers were well armed and well prepared to do battle. The black nationalists had automatic weapons (submachine guns), while the police did not. During the shoot-out large crowds of blacks formed in the streets surrounding the battle area. Ahmed surrendered shortly after midnight. The police succeeded in suppressing most of the firing from the area held by Ahmed and his followers, but meanwhile widespread looting and burning and stoning of police and firemen had begun. Hundreds of policemen, and later National Guardsmen, were mobilized to deal with the disorder.

The following day Mayor Carl B. Stokes met with black leaders and decided to withdraw white policemen and National Guardsmen from the riot area. In their place Stokes sent in a hastily organized group of black citizens known as the Mayor's Committee. This "all-black" strategy was strongly resented by the police. No one was killed on the second night, but looting and burning continued. Merchants and property owners accused Stokes of selling them out to the looters. Stokes replied that saving lives was more important than saving property. However, on the third night Stokes sent regular police and National Guard forces into the riot area, and the disorder flickered out.

As a result of the shoot-out and its aftermath, racial attitudes in Cleveland became more polarized than ever before. The Fraternal Order of Police bitterly denounced the mayor while mourning their dead comrades. The National Guard commander accused the mayor of "surrender to the black revolutionaries." Rumors of more black nationalist activity spread fear into the white community. In March 1969 a jury found "Ahmed" Evans guilty of conspiring to kill a police officer and sentenced him to death. Many blacks were enraged by the decision, asserting that the police were just as violence-prone as Ahmed and his followers.

Public Reaction to Racial Violence

Negroes and whites disagree over both the causes and the cures of urban violence. This fact alone presents a serious obstacle to the development of a viable public policy to deal with the problem.

In a study commissioned by the National Advisory Commission on Civil Disorders (see Table 7–6), researchers found that whereas whites were likely to believe that the main instigators of civil disorders were "radicals," looters and other undesirables, and "communists," very few blacks took this view.[32] Blacks tended to cite discrimination and unfair treatment, unemployment, inferior jobs, and substandard housing as causes. Only about one-half as many whites as blacks cited these underlying, socioeconomic conditions as "the main cause" of the riots. A clear majority of the blacks interviewed believed that the civil disturbances were "mainly a protest against unfair conditions" with few blacks believing that the riots were "mainly a way of looting and things like that." Though many whites recognized the protest nature of the riots, they were far more likely than Negroes to believe that the disturbances were mainly a way of looting. Blacks and whites differed even more sharply on how to prevent future riots: whites more often called for repressive measures (more police control) than blacks, who instead called for improvements in socioeconomic conditions (better employment and an end to discrimination). Whites and blacks also differed greatly in their assessments of the impact of the riots: though a slim plurality of Negroes believed that the disturbances had helped rather than hurt the cause of Negro rights, the overwhelming majority of whites felt that the riots had hurt the black cause.

Despite many blacks' belief that the riots had helped their cause, it is important to point out that the great majority of urban blacks do not believe that violence is "the best way for Negroes to try to gain

[32] The following analysis is based upon figures reported in *Supplemental Studies for the Commission on Civil Disorders.*

Table 7–6   Black and White Perceptions
of Civil Disorders in Large Cities

| | Negro | | White | |
	Men	Women	Men	Women
Some people say these disturbances are mainly a protest by Negroes against unfair conditions. Others say they are mainly a way of looting and things like that. Which seems more correct to you?				
Mainly protest	56%	59%	38%	48%
Mainly looting	9	10	33	24
50/50 mixture	30	25	25	24
Don't know	5	6	4	4
On the whole, do you think the disturbances have helped or hurt the cause of Negro rights, or would you say they haven't made much difference?				
Helped	37	30	13	14
Hurt	22	24	69	59
Helped and hurt equally	12	11	7	7
Made no difference	21	28	9	17
Don't know	8	7	2	3
What do you think was the main cause of these disturbances?				
Discrimination, unfair treatment	49	48	22	27
Unemployment	23	22	13	13
Inferior jobs	13	10	5	5
Bad housing	23	20	15	15
Poor education	10	9	7	7
Poverty	10	8	11	9
Police brutality	10	4	2	1
Black power, "radicals," communists	4	5	33	26
Looters and other undesirables	11	11	34	34

Table 7–6 *(continued)*

	Negro		White	
	Men	Women	Men	Women
What do you think is the most important thing the city government could do to keep a disturbance like the one in Detroit from breaking out here?				
Better employment	26	24	11	9
End discrimination	14	15	2	3
Better housing	8	8	4	4
Other social and economic improvements	7	5	4	3
Better police treatment	6	1	0	1
Improve communication between Negroes and whites	12	13	10	13
More police control	9	8	51	42
Can't do anything	3	5	8	8
Don't know	15	21	10	17

SOURCE: *Supplemental Studies for the National Advisory Commission on Civil Disorders* (Washington, D.C.: Government Printing Office, 1968).

their rights" (see Table 7–7). On the contrary, most blacks are prepared to put their faith in "laws and persuasion" and "nonviolent protest." When asked the question "If a disturbance like the one in Detroit or Newark last summer broke out here, do you think you would join in, or would you try to stop it, or would you stay away from it?" three out of four urban blacks replied that they would "stay away." Only a tiny percentage said they would join in the disturbance, and an even larger percentage said they would try to stop it. Yet, even though the overwhelming majority of blacks renounced violence, more than half still expressed sympathy for those who do participate in riots. In summary, most urban blacks regard the riots as a form of protest activity. A majority feel sympathetic toward the rioters, but only a small minority are willing to join in the rioting themselves. Most blacks reject violence as a means of securing their rights, but many blacks nonetheless believe that the riots helped rather than hurt their cause.

Table 7–7   Black Attitudes toward Violence
             in Large Cities

	Negro Total
As you see it, what is the best way for Negroes to try to gain their rights— use laws and persuasion, use nonviolent protest, or be ready to use violence?	
Laws and persuasion	39%
Nonviolent protest	38
Be ready to use violence	15
Don't know	8
If a disturbance like the one in Detroit or Newark last summer broke out here, do you think you would join in, or would you try to stop it, or would you stay away from it?	
Join in	8
Try to stop it	9
Stay away	76
Don't know	6
Other	1
Even if you didn't join in, would you feel in sympathy with Negroes who did choose to join in, or would you feel unsympathetic toward them?	
Sympathetic	54
Unsympathetic	24
Inappropriate; willing to join in	8
Other; don't know	14

SOURCE: *Supplemental Studies for the National Advisory Commission on Civil Disorders* (Washington, D.C.: Government Printing Office, 1968).

The reaction of federal officials to the urban riots was mixed. Not until July 1967 did President Johnson publicly acknowledge the wide extent of civil disorder, whereupon he emphatically condemned rioting. His statement typified those of many public officials actively engaged in suppressing a disturbance: "Let there be no mistake about it—the looting, arson, plunder, and pillage which have occurred are not part of the civil rights protest. There is no American right to loot stores, burn buildings, to fire rifles from rooftops. This is a crime. . . . Criminals who have committed these acts of violence against the people deserve to be punished—they must be punished."[33] Later, in 1968, the President cited the riots as an additional reason that Congress should pass various Administration-backed urban programs to alleviate the ills of the cities, including crime control, firearms control, the poverty program, model cities, rent supplements, mass transit, urban renewal, neighborhood facilities, rat extermination, federal aid to education, food stamps, and health programs. But many Congressmen were concerned that large-scale increases in federal expenditures in the ghettos might appear to be rewards for rioting. Thus, Congress reacted by passing overwhelmingly a bipartisan antiriot bill making it a federal crime to cross state lines to incite a riot. The Administration had opposed the bill as repressive and as unlikely to contribute a solution to the underlying causes of riots. No new federal programs were devised by the President or passed by Congress in response to the riots. Nor were already existing federal programs greatly expanded, despite the urgings of the National Advisory Commission on Civil Disorders. Perhaps the financial pressure of the Vietnam war made additional outlays unfeasible at the time, but more likely neither the President nor the Congress had any really new ideas about how to solve the complex problems of the ghettos.

Opinion in Congress regarding the riots and their prevention divided along traditional party and regional lines. A *Congressional Quarterly* poll of Congressmen[34] found that Northern Democrats attributed the riots to (1) joblessness and idleness, especially among young Negroes, (2) the neglect of social and economic problems by state and local governments, and (3) insufficient federal aid in areas such as education, job training, antipoverty programs, and housing.

[33] President Lyndon B. Johnson, in a speech broadcast over national television networks, 27 July 1967.

[34] See Congressional Quarterly Service, "Urban Problems and Civil Disorders," *Special Report,* 8 September 1967.

Southern Democrats blamed the riots on (1) outside Negro agitators, (2) Supreme Court crime decisions, (3) a lack of responsibility among Negroes, and (4) irresponsible news media coverage or bias. The Republicans in Congress most often cited (1) joblessness and idleness, especially among young Negroes, (2) outside Negro agitators, (3) a lack of responsibility among Negroes, and (4) poor administration of existing federal programs in these areas. As future preventative measures to cope with the problem, Northern Democrats most often recommended (1) greater state and local efforts and (2) a massive "Marshall Plan" for the cities using federal funds. Southern Democrats suggested (1) greater emphasis on traditional church and family values and (2) harsher penalties for rioters and persons inciting to rioting. Republican recommendations, in order of preference, were (1) greater emphasis on traditional church and family values, (2) the increased involvement of the private sector through such devices as low income area development corporations, (3) greater state and local efforts, and (4) harsher penalties for rioters and persons inciting to rioting.

What Can Blacks Get Out of Violence?

In assessing what blacks could gain from politics, our discussion at the end of the last chapter centered around legal justice, limited material rewards, the elimination of legal segregation, and marginal changes in public policy. We observed then that political activity is more successful in obtaining *de jure* equality than *de facto* equality. Black political activity is *necessarily* a strategy of limited objectives. The problems of ghetto life—poverty, inadequate education, unemployment, poor health, and substandard housing—are not quickly eliminated by traditional democratic political activity. Absolute inequalities between blacks and whites in incomes, jobs, housing, health, education, and other "life chances" can only be marginally affected by political means. As a consequence of this perception, many blacks have been searching for other alternatives. The question posed here is: What can the black get out of violence?

Stokely Carmichael once remarked that "violence is as American as apple pie." A fact, uncomfortable to many of us is that most important social movements in American history *have* been accompanied by violence. The American nation was created in a violent revolution; the abolition of slavery was effectuated only by a bloody war; the American West was violently seized from the Indians; violence was celebrated as a way of life in the Old West; industrialization and the organization of the labor movement were accompanied by violence; and recent victories in the movement for Negro equality have been anything but nonviolent. Frequently, the American political system is moved by *crisis* when it refuses to be moved by anything else. The civil rights protest movement has sought to create *nonviolent* crises that would impel the system to end direct discrimination. But meanwhile the black militant has arisen to argue that white America will not respond to black demands for true equality until whites feel directly threatened in their own physical well-being. In commenting on the role of violence in the struggle for equality, Louis Masotti and others note:

> Perhaps the black power advocates understand better than most whites that Americans have traditionally paid only lip-service to their notion of consensus when critical issues arose; that, in fact, when critical issues arise, they can no longer be solved through the normal political channels based on common understandings; that, indeed, the only common interest a challenging minority and an unresponsive majority have is violence, with the minority offering peace only when the majority makes the requisite concessions.[35]

Thus, in his struggle for equality the black American faces an agonizing choice: whether to work through the established democratic processes to effect change or instead to resort to violence and threats of violence.

The vast majority of black Americans reject violence. But the violence in our society, and increasing rhetoric of violence, have resulted in a gradual increase in the number of blacks who believe that "blacks will probably have to resort to violence to win rights." Louis Harris reports that this percentage has risen from 21 percent in 1961 to 31 percent in 1970.[36] The percentage of blacks asserting that violence is

[35] Louis H. Masotti, Jeffrey K. Hadden, Kenneth F. Seminatore, Jerome R. Corsi, *A Time to Burn?* (Chicago: Rand McNally, 1969), p. 162.
[36] Reported in *Time,* April 6, 1970, p. 29.

probably necessary is even higher among younger and urban blacks:

Is Violence Necessary

Total	Can win rights without violence	Violence probably necessary
1963	63%	22%
1966	59	21
1970	58	31
Urban	56	34
Rural	64	23
Age 14–21	55	40
22–29	58	31
30–49	55	33
50 and over	65	20

We have deliberately chosen not to comment on the *morality* of violence. Each American—white or black—must answer that question for himself. But social science *can* tell us something about the *efficacy* of violence in achieving equality—and, in fact, the relevant data suggest that violence is counterproductive to success in the struggle for equality.

Violence will not likely produce the type of attitude change among whites that will be necessary for progress in the struggle for equality. The effect of white reaction to violence has been to reinforce old prejudices and to justify new antagonisms toward blacks rather than to prompt any positive changes of attitude. Violence in the urban ghettos in the 1960s failed to shock white Americans into action on behalf of equality, or even to scare them into such action. Instead, the urban violence led to a strong "law and order" movement that was reflected in local, state, and national politics. The available evidence indicates that whites reacted negatively to urban violence. The violence provided an opportunity for some whites to express hostile stereotypes about Negroes (for example, that the riots were "mainly a way of looting and things like that"). The riots also gave whites a political theme—"law and order"—that enabled them to assume an antiblack stance in public affairs without actually appearing racist or bigoted. Of course, not all whites concerned with "law and order" are "racists." But the widespread racial disorders gave the antiblack forces in America an effective political club.

The reaction of most government officials to the riots was also negative. Both the President and Congress pointedly ignored the recommendations of the National Advisory Commission on Civil Disorders for more jobs, housing, and educational programs in the ghettos, probably feeling that new public programs would appear to be "rewarding violence." Little additional money was poured into the ghettos. Instead, Congress became disenchanted with the poverty program and reduced its appropriations. The rhetoric of government officials emphasized "law and order" rather than the improvement of ghetto conditions.

Since 1967 the pattern of ghetto violence and official response seems to have changed significantly. Incidents of widespread rioting and destruction of property have occurred less frequently. City officials and police have learned to react more quickly and firmly to suppress disorder without using unnecessary force. And doubtless many ghetto blacks have come to realize that violence, with its heavy toll in black lives and black property, simply does not bring about sufficient change to justify its costs. However, even though incidents of widespread disorder and property damage have been reduced, a different and perhaps more significant pattern of urban violence is slowly emerging. In a number of cities, black militants have engaged in direct gunfire attacks on police. These attacks, following the pattern of the Cleveland "shoot-out" in 1968, suggest a new pattern of guerilla warfare designed to inflict death or injury on persons representing white authority rather than the former pattern emphasizing indiscriminate disorder and property-oriented violence.

But regardless of which pattern of violence prevails, the impact on black-white relations is bound to be negative. Robert Cipes comments:

> The real danger of the Negro riots is the response they will produce from the forces of "law and order." Repression of riots has already

caused more loss of life than the riots themselves. Historically the worst atrocities have been committed not against but in the name of public security.[37]

While politics may produce only limited gains and gradual change, overall it offers more hope for black America than violence.

[37] Robert M. Cipes, *The Crime War* (New York: New American Library, 1968), p. xii; also cited by Masotti et al., *A Time To Burn?*, p. 176.

chapter 8

Dialogue
in Black and White

Black politics in America is also white politics. No one, save perhaps the most militant black, believes that progress in the struggle for equality can be achieved without the support of a substantial number of whites. The future of the Negro in this nation depends not only on the character of black politics but also on the political response of white leaders and citizens. The lives of blacks and whites in America are inseparably intertwined. For this reason, any analysis of racial politics must deal with the political attitudes and ideologies of whites as well as blacks.

White Perceptions of Black Politics

The attitudes of whites toward blacks in this nation are important for two reasons: (1) the racial issue is more visible to the masses than any other political issue facing the nation, including that of war and peace, and consequently the behavior of elected officials is more circumscribed by public opinion than on most other issues, and (2) blacks constitute less than 12 percent of the total population, and to be effective in democratic politics they must augment their numbers with support from the white community.

215

White attitudes toward blacks in America are ambivalent. Whites agree that blacks are discriminated against. In a recent national opinion survey conducted by Louis Harris, 61 percent of the white respondents believed that Negroes are "discriminated against," with only 28 percent feeling that Negroes are "not discriminated against" (11 percent were "not sure").[1] Even in the South a substantial number of whites (39 percent) agreed that Negroes are discriminated against (47 percent were of the opposite view, and 14 percent were "not sure"). Most whites believe that blacks suffer injustices and that discrimination is wrong. When Lou Harris asked whites what it would be like to be a Negro living in America, he reported these responses as typical:

> A retired woman in California said, "I think it would be terrible to be a Negro. I just couldn't stand it. Suppose I went into a restaurant and they wouldn't serve me. It would be awful." A laborer in Michigan expressed a strong reaction, "If I was colored, I'd feel like I didn't belong. Like a dog. I'd be hurt and bitter against the whites. I'd take revenge." A Pennsylvania housewife, "It would hurt, especially to see your child hurt. I was a foreigner as a child because I'm Polish, and I know how cruel people can be."[2]

Yet, even though most whites will readily admit the injustices of discrimination, an overwhelming majority of whites believe that Negroes are moving "too fast":

> Do you feel Negroes have tried to move too fast, too slow, or at about the right pace?

	Total 1966	Total 1963
Too fast	70%	64%
Too slow	4	6
About the right pace	14	17
Not sure	12	13

[1] Survey results referred to in this section are drawn from the text and Appendix D of William Brink and Louis Harris, *Black and White: A Study of U.S. Racial Attitudes Today* (New York: Simon & Schuster, 1967); with updating from William Brink and Louis Harris, "Report from Black America," *Newsweek,* 30 June 1969. The Brink and Harris data were collected in national surveys conducted in 1963, 1966, and 1969. Copyright 1966, 1967 by Newsweek, Inc. Data reprinted by permission of Simon & Schuster, Inc.

[2] Brink and Harris, *Black and White,* p. 126.

Of course, the figure of 70 percent in 1966 was affected by the urban riots of the mid-1960s. But even in 1963, before the passage of the Civil Rights Act of 1964, two out of every three whites believed that blacks were attempting to move too fast.

The contrast between white and black attitudes on the speed of progress in civil rights is striking. When blacks were asked the same question, the results were as follows:

	Total 1966	Total 1963
Too fast	4%	3%
Too slow	43	51
About the right pace	35	31
Not sure	18	15

A large majority of whites in America support legislation giving blacks equal voting rights (91 percent), the right to a fair jury trial (87 percent), nonsegregated use of buses, planes, and trains (87 percent), and integrated education (72 percent). Yet, whites appear to object to contacts with blacks progressively more as the level of intimacy increases.

	All Whites	Low Income	High Income
Object to sitting next to Negro on bus	16%	25%	9%
Object to sitting next to Negro in movie	21	31	11
Object to using same restroom as Negroes	22	36	14
Object to having Negro child to supper	42	51	29
Object to Negroes living next door	51	54	41
Upset by a close friend or relative marrying a Negro	79	n.a.	n.a.
Object to own teenage child dating a Negro	88	n.a.	n.a.

Interestingly, the cut-off point of blacks' acceptability to whites comes in the area of housing, where whites are almost equally divided on the question of black neighbors.

It is equally interesting to note the wide gaps between the attitudes of low income and high income whites. The most hostile attitudes toward blacks are found among the less privileged, less educated whites. Whether in a public restroom, in a movie or a bus, or across a backyard hedge, low income whites are much less willing to have contact with blacks than high income whites. In fact, Harris found that only 46 percent of low income whites as compared to 78 percent of high income whites believed that Negroes are discriminated against. It is the affluent, well-educated American who is most concerned about discrimination against blacks and who is most willing to have contact with them.

The political implication of this finding is obvious: opposition to civil rights legislation and to the Negro's advancement in education, jobs, income, housing and other areas runs strongest among low income whites. (Later in this chapter we shall examine the social bases of the Wallace movement.) Within the white community, the greatest support for eliminating injustices toward blacks comes from the educated, affluent American.

Most whites in America support *general* statements about freedom and equality; for example, most whites believe that blacks should have an equal opportunity to get ahead. But whites are much less likely to support *specific* proposals intended to implement those very same general propositions. Sociologist Frank Westie, using a national sample of whites, demonstrated their tendency to support general more than specific statements about equality.[3]

General Statement	Percentage Agreeing	Specific Statement	Percentage Agreeing
People should help each other in time of need.	99	If a Negro's home burned down, I would be willing to take his family into my home for the night.	64

[3] Frank Westie, "The American Dilemma: An Empirical Test," *American Sociological Review* 30 (August 1965): 531–32. Reprinted by permission.

General Statement	Percentage Agreeing	Specific Statement	Percentage Agreeing
Everyone in America should have equal opportunities to get ahead.	98	I would be willing to have a Negro as my supervisor in my place of work.	60
I believe in the principle of brotherhood among men.	94	I would be willing to invite Negroes to a dinner party in my home.	29
I believe that all public recreational facilities should be available to all people at all times	63	I don't think I would mind if Negro children were to swim in the same pool as my children.	38
Under our democratic system people should be allowed to live where they please if they can afford it.	60	I would be willing to have a Negro family live next door to me.	35

These results suggest the continuing relevance of that ambivalence in white opinion that Gunnar Myrdal aptly labeled "The American dilemma," namely, the willingness to commit oneself verbally to the principle of equality accompanied by the reluctance to implement this principle in one's personal conduct and affairs.

How do whites respond to various means of achieving redress of black grievances? The evidence from the Harris polls suggests that whites are becoming weary of nonviolent direct action tactics. After the passage of the Civil Rights Act of 1964 more whites came to believe that blacks should abandon direct action tactics in favor of legal redress:

If you were in the same position as Negroes, do you think you would be justified or not to march and protest in demonstrations?

	Total 1966	Total 1963
Justified	35%	53%
Not justified	50	37
Not sure	15	10

In other words, within two years after the passage of the Civil Rights Act of 1964 a clear majority of whites felt that Negro protest demonstrations were unjustified.

In general, whites are willing to support laws eliminating discrimination and guaranteeing equality of opportunity. But what can we discern about white attitudes toward compensatory efforts aimed at overcoming the effects of past discrimination and uplifting the black community? Here the evidence is that most whites are not prepared to make any special effort to change the conditions of blacks. Louis Harris asked a national sample: "Some Negroes have suggested that since Negroes have been discriminated against for 100 years, they should be given special consideration in jobs, that they should actually be given a preference for a job opening, such as the veteran gets today in a government job. Do you agree or disagree with the idea of job preference for Negroes?" Whites responded with a resounding "No!" Fully 90 percent of the respondents opposed special consideration for blacks in jobs, and only 4 percent favored it!

It is interesting to note the change over time in white attitudes toward blacks. In general, white Americans are much more sympathetic to civil rights today than they were a decade or two ago. A national sample of white Americans was asked the question, "Do you think white students and Negro students should go to the same schools or separate schools?" in 1942, 1956, 1963, and 1966 (see Table 8–1). In 1942, not one American white in three approved of integrated schools. Even in the North, a majority was opposed to school integration, while in the South only two whites in a hundred would support integration. In 1956, two years after the historic *Brown* decision, white attitudes had shifted remarkably. Support for integration characterized about half of the nation's white population; in the North it was the majority view, and in the South the proportion supporting integration had risen to one in seven. By 1963, two out of every three whites believed in integrated schools, and, even more noteworthy, one out of three Southern whites believed in integration. Since 1963 the trend has continued upward in the proportion of white Americans favoring school integration. Additional survey information suggests that, over time, whites are becoming increasingly accommodating toward equal rights for blacks in other spheres as well. But we should note emphatically that white opinion generally follows, rather than leads, public policy. White Americans have increasingly come to accept black equality, but certainly they have never pressed for integration.

Table 8–1   Attitude Change among Whites:
             White and Negro Students Should Attend the Same
             Schools, 1942–66

| | Percentage Yes | | | |
	1942	1956	1963	1966
Total whites	30	49	62	67
Northern whites	40	61	73	78
Southern whites	2	15	31	36

SOURCE: Paul B. Sheatsley, "White Attitudes Toward the Negro," in *The Negro American,* eds. Talcott Parsons and Kenneth B. Clark (Boston: Beacon Press, 1967), p. 305. "White Attitudes Toward the Negro" originally appeared in *Daedalus,* Vol. 95, No. 1 (Winter 1966). Reprinted by permission from *Daedalus,* Journal of the American Academy of Arts and Sciences.

White "Backlash"

It is difficult to determine whether civil rights laws, nonviolent protests and demonstrations, or even urban riots have produced any "white backlash" in American politics. What purports to be "backlash" may really be only the surfacing of white racial attitudes that existed all along. For example, white opposition to bussing children to achieve racial balance in schools is not really "backlash" since these proposals were never very popular among whites in the first place. Moreover, white hostility can be expressed subtly in a variety of forms: as opposition to protests and demonstrations; as opposition to welfare assistance, public housing, antipoverty programs, or other activities benefiting the poor; or as support for "law and order" and increased police forces in the ghettos. These are socially more acceptable outlets for racial hostility than the direct castigation of Negroes. Of course, we hasten to add that not all of the individuals and groups that hold these policy positions are thereby necessarily expressing racial hostility or manifesting "white backlash." But this qualification again illustrates the difficulty in identifying "backlash" and distinguishing it from other political attitudes.

Actually, as we have already noted, white attitudes are gradually becoming more accommodating toward the idea of black equality. With the passage of time more whites have come to accept as legitimate such things as integrated schools, equal employment opportunity, equal access to public accommodations, and even integrated housing. We have noted that an overwhelming number of whites are not prepared to give blacks special consideration for jobs, and they are generally unsupportive of other compensatory ideas. But this could hardly be labeled as "backlash." The idea that the Constitution and the laws of the nation should be "color-blind" was once considered a very "liberal" position. However, there is some evidence that white attitudes toward protest demonstrations have hardened in recent years. As already noted, in 1963 Louis Harris found that 53 percent of white Americans felt that "to march and protest in demonstrations" was "justified," while only 37 percent said that it was "not justified"; three years later, he found the percentages reversed. We can conclude that after the passage of the Civil Rights Act of 1964 white tolerance of direct action tactics diminished rapidly. This hypothesis suggests again that whites are sympathetic toward efforts to eliminate *direct discrimination*, but are generally unsympathetic toward public efforts to achieve *absolute equality* between the races in income, employment, education, and the like.

Certainly whites were distressed by urban rioting. Despite the fact that few whites were hurt by the rioting and most of the dead, injured, and arrested were blacks, nonetheless many whites, particularly those in cities, experienced personal fear of racial violence. As early as 1966 national surveys reported large numbers of whites, particularly city dwellers, increasingly distressed over violence.[4]

Compared to a year ago, are you personally more worried about violence and safety on the streets, less worried, or do you feel the same as you did before?

	Total	Metropolitan City	Urban Town	Suburban Town	Rural Area
More worried	49%	62%	39%	57%	40%
Less worried	3	4	3	3	2
Feel the same	44	32	57	36	50
Not sure	4	2	1	4	8

[4] Brink and Harris, *Black and White,* Appendix D, p. 220.

This fear over public safety and a corresponding concern for "law and order" pose the most important political threats to liberal white and black candidates in city politics. The "law and order" theme is not merely a rhetorical device for masking anti-Negro sentiments—though this is doubtless a significant element in it. But even apart from their racial prejudices, city whites *are* fearful about safety in the streets. And crime rates *are* higher in black ghettos.

Thus, where "backlash" occurs, it will likely assume the form of a "law and order" campaign. "Backlash" candidates will not likely castigate blacks directly nor seek to undo any of the substantive civil rights gains of recent years. In this way, "law and order" candidates will also be able to appeal to whites who have no manifest anti-Negro feelings.

The Wallace Movement

One little-recognized aspect of the black revolution in America is the impact it has had on millions of poor whites. While twenty million blacks in America were experiencing a "revolution of rising expectations," many equally underprivileged whites were experiencing a bitter sense of alienation arising from the belief that they were the forgotten backwash of society. Too often the Wallace movement is dismissed as racist, with little attempt made to understand the dilemma of under-privileged, undereducated whites in both the North and the South. Frequently this is the "liberal" response, and understandably it holds great appeal for black students as well. To be sure, the Wallace movement is racist, but that does not excuse students of politics from trying to understand how and why it is racist or what the political consequences of that racism may be.

There is strong reason to believe that black men in America to-day are less alienated, more confident, and more optimistic about the future than poor white men. Blacks correctly believe that the civil rights revolution is one of the great movements in American history. And it is *their* movement. Civil rights and the black revolution is "what it's all about" today. The nation is aware of the black man. But poor whites have no such movement. They believe *their* plight is sorely

neglected. They correctly believe that many of them live in circumstances no different from those of blacks. Of Americans earning less
than $3,000 a year in 1960, only one-third were Negro and two-thirds
were white. Yet the national government has not recognized *their* condition in historic Supreme Court decisions nor in sweeping Congressional acts. They resent seeing Negroes make progress, even if it is
only symbolic progress, while *they* are standing still. They no longer
have even the solace of knowing, as they once did, that despite their
poverty they are at least better off than blacks. The black cushion between themselves and the bottom of the American social structure is
slipping away.

Alienation is far greater among low income whites than among
comparable low income blacks. When a series of items indicating
alienation were read to blacks and low income whites in a national
survey, the results were as follows:[5]

	Total Public	Negroes	Low Income Whites
Sometimes feel that:			
Rich get richer, poor get poorer	48%	49%	68%
What you think doesn't count much	39	40	60
People in power don't care about us	28	32	50
Other people get lucky breaks	19	35	37
Important events in the world don't affect me	18	12	26
Few understand how I live	18	32	36
Nobody understands the problems I have	17	30	40

In brief, though blacks are more alienated than whites in general, low
income whites are even more alienated from society than blacks. Moreover, additional survey data indicate that blacks believe "things are
getting better." Louis Harris, for example, reported that 67 percent of
Negroes believed that things were "better" in 1966 than three years
earlier as compared to only 5 percent who felt that things were "about
the same."[6] Though precisely comparable questions were not asked

[5] *Ibid.,* p. 135.
[6] *Ibid.,* Appendix D, p. 230.

of poor whites, studies of Appalachia and other hard-core poor white areas attest that these people believe just the opposite, namely, that "things" are getting worse rather than better.

The black revolution has deeply divided white America. Though a truly wide gulf separates black and white perceptions of the speed of progress, the tactics of the revolution, and perhaps even its ultimate objectives, an equally wide chasm separates poor and affluent whites in their response to the black struggle. The well-educated, privileged whites are much more sympathetic toward black aspirations than the poorly educated low income whites. Lesser privileged whites do not agree that the condition of Negroes in America is worse than that of whites, nor do they feel that Negroes are discriminated against.[7]

	All Whites	Low Income Whites	High Income Whites
Negro housing is worse than white	65%	46%	69%
Negroes are discriminated against	60	46	78
Negroes laugh a lot	56	66	49
Negroes smell different	52	61	45
Negroes have looser morals	50	56	46
Sympathize with Negro protests	46	24	57
Negroes want to live off handouts	43	53	33
Negro education worse than whites	40	27	58

Low income whites hold very stereotyped views about Negroes, believing that they laugh a lot, smell different, and have looser morals. Their willingness to have contact with Negroes is far less than that among high income whites. As Louis Harris notes: "If there are two races in this country poles apart on the race issue, then it is equally true there are two white societies just as far apart."[8]

The federal government has launched antipoverty programs that presumably benefit low income whites as well as blacks, but the War on Poverty has generally been advertised in terms of its benefits to the Negro—how it will improve black ghettos, thereby relieving the pressures for rioting. Most white Americans are critical of the antipoverty

[7] *Ibid.,* p. 136.
[8] *Ibid.,* p. 137.

program whereas blacks generally favor it. Interestingly, the most bitter reactions *against* the War on Poverty have emanated from the mouths of poor whites. These people believe the program will not benefit them at all. They believe the program is designed to aid Negroes, they feel it will not assist them because their skin is white.

The political consequences of the racial hostility and alienation of poor whites in America are reflected in the Wallace movement. Governor George C. Wallace of Alabama first won national attention on 11 June 1963 when he carried out his 1962 campaign pledge to the people of Alabama to "stand in the doorway" to prevent the integration of their schools. Wallace won the support of many poor whites in both the North and the South when, in defiance of a federal court order, he blocked the entrance of Deputy Attorney General Nicholas Katzenbach and two black students to the University of Alabama at Tuscaloosa. Wallace read Katzenbach a lengthy statement charging the federal officials with "a frightful example of the oppression of the rights, privileges, and sovereignty of this state." Wallace retreated from his stand in the doorway a few hours later when President Kennedy threatened to send troops to Tuscaloosa and signed an order federalizing the Alabama National Guard. But Wallace had succeeded in establishing himself as a symbol of defiance.

Wallace does not base his appeal solely on the racial hostilities of Southern whites. He appeals to "little people" on both sides of the Mason-Dixon line who feel that the national government is ignoring them or who resent the gains made by blacks. In addition to racial hostility the Wallace appeal taps feelings of alienation, anti-intellectualism, and class animosities. Wallace, for example, deplores "theoreticians":

> I think there is a backlash in this country against the theoreticians—some of them in some of our colleges and some of our courts and some of our newspaper editor's offices and some of our pulpits—who look down their noses at the steel worker and the paper worker and the communications worker and beautician and the barber and the policeman and the fireman and the little businessman and the clerk and the farmer and say that you don't have enough intelligence to decide how to get up in the morning and when to go to bed at night, and people are tired of theorists running their country.[9]

9 Quoted in *Life,* 2 August 1969, p. 20.

Regarding the governing "liberal establishment," Wallace promises: "I would take all of those brief-case toting bureaucrats in Washington and throw their briefcases in the Potomac River."

In 1964 Wallace tested his appeal in the North by entering Democratic Presidential primaries in Wisconsin, Indiana, and Maryland. The startling results were that he won 33 percent of the vote in Wisconsin, 30 percent in Indiana, and 43 percent in Maryland. In ethnic, working class wards in East Chicago, Hammond, and Gary, Wallace won two out of every three votes. These were not Southern segregationist votes. They were the votes of hard working, Catholic sons of southern and eastern European immigrants who had labored to pull themselves and their children out of slums and ghettos not much different from those inhabited by blacks today. They had been the objects of ethnic scorn themselves, and they saw no reason for the federal government to come to the assistance of blacks in fighting discrimination when that same government had done nothing to protect them from discrimination.

In 1966 Wallace was thwarted by the Alabama legislature when he attempted to amend the Alabama Constitution to permit his renomination for governor. The opposition was led by State Attorney General Richmond Flowers, who had opposed the growth of Wallace's power in the state and was considered a "moderate" in race relations by Alabama standards. But Wallace was able to bypass the legislature and the state constitution by taking his fight to the (white) "little people" of Alabama in the person of his wife, Lurleen. Alabamans elected her to the governor's chair with the pledge that George would be the de facto executive.

In 1968 George Wallace called upon the nation's voters to "stand up for America." The disaffection of Wallace's supporters extended not only to the federal government but also to the party system, and Wallace was able to organize his movement into the strongest third-party bid for the Presidency in modern times. Wallace electors appeared on the ballot in all fifty states. In winning forty-seven electoral votes, their candidate drew almost ten million voters (13.6 percent of the total) away from the Democratic and Republican parties. During the campaign, opinion polls showed Wallace's strength to be close to 20 percent of the electorate, and both Humphrey and Nixon appeared to shift their campaigns slightly rightward in order to blunt the Wallace appeal. Toward the end of the campaign traditional party loyal-

ties reasserted themselves, and Wallace ended up with fewer votes
than most observers had predicted. Whatever the outcome, the strength
of Wallace's appeal in both the North and the South did reflect substantial disaffection among low income whites with the policies of the
national government.

Wallace supporters were clearly concentrated among the less
affluent, poorly educated segments of the electorate. Typical polls reported support for Wallace as follows:[10]

CHARACTERISTICS OF VOTERS

Education		Occupation	
College	8%	Professional and business	8%
High School	15	Clerical and Sales	18
Grade School	26	Manual labor	20
		Farmer	18

The evidence is strong that Wallace voters were generally alienated from the political process and had little faith in government. For
example, when the Survey Research Center at the University of Michigan asked a national sample of voters whether they thought the government is pretty much run by a few big interests looking out for themselves or run for the benefit of all the people, 63 percent of the Wallace
voters subscribed to the "few big interests" theory as compared to only
38 percent of the Nixon voters and 32 percent of the Humphrey voters. On the issue of race, 38 percent of Wallace voters identified
themselves as segregationists, compared to only 11 percent of the
Nixon voters and 10 percent of the Humphrey voters. Regarding the
war in Vietnam, 35 percent of the Wallace voters favored doing
"everything necessary to win a complete military victory, no matter
what the results," while only 16 percent of the Nixon voters and 14
percent of the Humphrey voters felt this way. Interestingly, on the
question of welfare programs Wallace voters in part reflected their less-
privileged economic status; when asked whether they thought the government in Washington should help people to get medical care at a

[10] Gallup Poll findings, as reported in *Congressional Quarterly Weekly Report*,
19 July 1968, p. 1815.

low cost, 49 percent of the Wallace voters replied affirmatively, as did 35 percent of the Nixon voters and 61 percent of Humphrey voters. (The study found that 45 percent of the Wallace voters considered themselves Democrats, 41 percent independents, and 14 percent Republicans. However, the study also disclosed that Wallace voters generally preferred Nixon to Humphrey. Thus, had Wallace not been in the race most of his supporters would have backed Nixon, and there would have been no change in the outcome of the election.)

It is difficult to predict what will happen to the Wallace voters—to the alienated poor white—in American politics. Numerically they constitute as large a group as blacks. But they lack solidarity; they lack crusading zeal or moral standing; they lack the support of white elites; and they have been consistently defeated in national politics. They may simply drop out of the political system, turning their attention more and more to private needs. Many may be content to express their anger through support of outspoken, if ineffectual, state and local demagogues. A few will resort to sporadic, senseless violence against blacks. But so long as they feel misunderstood and forgotten, their anger, frustration, and bitterness will pose a potential threat to the hard-won gains of blacks in America.

Equality Politics in the Future

The period from the 1954 *Brown* decision to the 1968 Fair Housing Act marked a great era in the struggle for equality. This era saw the legal foundations of segregation collapse and the concept of legal equality become public policy.

But today the meaning of equality is no longer limited to the absence of direct discrimination. Today the problem of equality is one of differences in the "life chances" of blacks and whites. The late President Kennedy stated this problem clearly in 1963:

> The Negro baby born in America today, regardless of the section or the state in which he is born, has about one-half as much chance of completing high school as a white baby, born in the same place, on the same day; one-third as much chance of completing college; one-third as much chance of becoming a professional man; twice as much chance of becoming unemployed; about one-seventh as much chance

of earning $10,000 a year; a life expectancy which is seven years shorter and the prospects of earning only half as much.[11]

The equalization of life chances in America clearly promises to be a much more difficult task than was the elimination of legal discrimination.

Many whites are less sympathetic toward the equalization of life chances than they are toward the elimination of discrimination. Many whites believe (or at least hope) that the problem of life chances will gradually diminish once discrimination has been eliminated. The traditional "melting pot" approach to the problem of life chances admonishes the individual black: "Speak better, dress well, become moderate in your behavior, work harder, save your money, fix up your property, attend concerts, symphonies, and ballets, visit art museums, go to the theater, educate your children, and your problems will eventually be resolved. It's only a matter of time. Haven't the Jews, the Irish, the Italians all solved their problems this way?" Viewed in this light, the problem of equality becomes one of an individual's applying himself over a prolonged period of time.

But many blacks are dissatisfied with this solution to the problem. The "melting pot" approach places responsibility in the hands of individual blacks, and in no way addresses itself to blacks as a group. It perceives the problem of equality as an *individual* rather than a social problem. In contrast, many black leaders believe that inequality is a *societal* problem—one originally created by white society and that must therefore be resolved by white society. This view was echoed in the report of the National Advisory Commission on Civil Disorders: "What white Americans have never fully understood—but what the Negro can never forget—is that white society is deeply implicated in the ghetto. White institutions created it, white institutions maintain it, and white society condones it."[12] Viewed in this light, the problem of inequality becomes one that whites must assume a major responsibility for solving.

---

[11] President John F. Kennedy, in a speech broadcast over national television networks, 11 June 1963; quoted in Henry Steele Commager, ed., *The Struggle for Racial Equality: A Documentary Record* (New York: Harper & Row, 1967), pp. 164–65.

[12] National Advisory Commission on Civil Disorders, *Report* (Washington, D.C.: Government Printing Office, 1968), p. 2.

The melting pot approach raises some other problems. First, since blacks had so little voice in shaping American society, they may not wish to join it on an individual basis. Many blacks feel that the melting pot approach threatens to submerge black culture and identity with its implication that culturally the black man would do well to become white. Yet there are some very unpleasant aspects of white culture that many blacks have no intention of accepting. Second, the melting pot approach may have been successful with immigrant groups whose skins were white and who arrived in America at a time when it was possible to start at the bottom as an unskilled or semi-skilled worker and to move up the ladder acquiring new skills along the way. But racial differences run deeper than nationality differences, and blacks must start up the ladder in the midst of a technological revolution that is destroying unskilled and semi-skilled jobs and is making it difficult for small businesses to compete successfully in a market dominated by giant corporations. Finally, the melting pot approach is very slow. It frequently took two or three generations for immigrant groups to become fully integrated into American society. It is unlikely that blacks would be willing to wait another two or three generations. They feel they've waited long enough. They want to share in America's affluence "NOW!"

Thus it is likely that the movement for equality in America will turn its attention from civil rights, in the narrow sense, to broader social objectives. As Bayard Rustin explains it:

> The civil rights movement is evolving from a protest movement into a full-fledged *social movement*—in an evolution calling its very name into question. It is now concerned not merely with removing the barriers to full *opportunity* but with achieving the fact of *equality*. From sit-ins and freedom rides we've gone into rent strikes, boycotts, community organizations, and political action. As a consequence of this natural evolution, the Negro today finds himself stymied by obstacles of far greater magnitude than the legal barriers he was attacking before: automation, urban decay, de facto school segregation. These are problems which, while conditioned by Jim Crow did not vanish upon its demise. They are of a more deeply rooted socio-economic order; they are the result of the total society's failure to meet not only the Negroes' needs, but human needs generally.[13]

13 Bayard Rustin, "From Protest to Politics: The Future of the Civil Rights Movement" *Commentary* 42 (February 1965): 27.

Public action to eliminate differences in black-white "life chances" requires a public commitment to guaranteeing *absolute* equality, not just equality of *opportunity*. This type of commitment would necessitate a fundamental alteration in the underlying values of American society. Liberal democrats since the days of our Founding Fathers have stressed not absolute equality but always equality of opportunity. Thomas Jefferson himself recognized a "natural aristocracy" of talent, ambition, and industry; and liberal democrats since Jefferson have always accepted inequalities that were the product of individual merit or hard work. Absolute equality, or "leveling," is not a part of the traditional liberal democratic creed.

Some black leaders apprehend the truly revolutionary implications of their demand for *absolute* equality. Rustin writes:

> I believe that the Negro's struggle for equality in America is essentially revolutionary. While most Negroes—in their hearts—unquestionably seek only to enjoy the fruits of American society as it now exists, their quest cannot *objectively* satisfy within the framework of existing political and economic relations. The young Negro, who would demonstrate his way into the labor market may be motivated by a thoroughly bourgeois ambition and thoroughly "capitalist" considerations, but he will end up having to favor a great expansion of the public sector of the economy. . . .

> But the term revolutionary, as I am using it, does not connote violence; it refers to qualitative transformation of fundamental institutions more or less rapidly to the point where the social and economic structure which they comprise can no longer be said to be the same.[14]

Responsible black leaders have called upon blacks to prepare themselves for prolonged struggle to equalize their life chances in America. For example, Whitney M. Young of the Urban League has proposed a long-range, three-pronged strategy for action involving (1) political organization, (2) economic control, and (3) group solidarity.[15] He calls for political power "to elect officials, to pass or veto issues voted upon by the electorate and to procure a reasonable

---

[14] *Ibid.,* p. 28.

[15] John B. Turner and Whitney M. Young, Jr., "Who Has the Revolution or Thoughts on the Second Reconstruction," in *The Negro American,* eds. Talcott Parsons and Kenneth B. Clark (Boston: Beacon Press, 1967), pp. 678–93.

distribution of the rewards of the political system." He sees economic power as "the ability to withhold purchasing power, to influence vital centers of decision regarding the economic allocation of resources, to mobilize capital for interest, to control an equitable share of wealth, to get a fair return on the dollar spent, and to become dispersed throughout the occupational structure." Group solidarity is perceived as "the capacity to mobilize psychological and social resources" for mutual self-help. Young contends that Negro leaders, after mobilizing these resources, "must ask what policies, what programs, what practices at the national, state, and local levels are most crucial in equalizing the life chances of the Negro." Bayard Rustin proposes a similar course of action for the future; he emphasizes the political problems in reshaping the distribution of wealth in America.

> Neither that movement nor the country's twenty million black people can win political power alone. We need allies. The future of the Negro struggle depends on whether the contradictions of this society can be resolved by a coalition of progressive forces which becomes the *effective* political majority in the United States. I speak of the coalition which staged the March on Washington, passed the Civil Rights Act, and laid the basis for the Johnson landslide—Negroes, trade unionists, liberals and religious groups.[16]

Any attack on inequality other than the "melting pot" approach will require a massive public effort to redistribute income, jobs, housing, education, and other resources to blacks. There appears to be little support in the white community for such an effort. The recommendations of the National Advisory Commission on Civil Disorders for a massive attack on ghetto problems have been largely ignored. Moreover, redistribution efforts challenge traditional liberal values that emphasize equality of opportunity rather than absolute equality. It is not yet clear whether the liberal coalition that staged the March on Washington can be held together in support of government programs to redistribute income and other resources in America. The primary black demand is no longer the demand for equal opportunity but rather the demand for "equality of economic results." James Q. Wilson has suggested that this demand may place new strains on the traditional Negro–white liberal coalition:

[16] Bayard Rustin, "From Protest to Politics," p. 29.

American politics has long been accustomed to dealing with ethnic demands for recognition, power, and opportunity; it has never had to face a serious demand for equal economic shares. Thus in the North as well as in the South the principal race issue may become a conflict between liberty and equality. This may be the issue which will distinguish the white liberal from the white radical, the former will work for liberty and equal opportunity, the latter for equal shares.[17]

Perhaps the most realistic expectation for the future of black politics is that blacks increasingly will participate more effectively in the processes of bargaining, accommodation, and compromise, on behalf of limited yet significant objectives. Black leaders and voters can realistically expect to have an increasing influence in traditional brokerage politics. They can reasonably expect to come off better in the bargains, accommodations, and compromises of democratic politics than they have in the past. The new awareness of blackness and the resulting increase in group cohesion, identification, and solidarity assures the Negro of his greater future success in democratic politics; so does his increased voter strength in both the North and the South. Blacks can organize or join coalitions in support of policies and programs designed to alleviate the worst aspects of urban life—poor health, poverty, unemployment, inadequate educational efforts, slum housing, hunger, economic exploitation, official indifference. Blacks can assist in rearranging national priorities so that domestic problems replace military preparedness and foreign adventurism as the focus of national effort and commitment.

But it is unlikely that participation in traditional brokerage politics, however effective, will bring about immediate changes in the conditions of the masses of blacks. Democratic politics does not work that way. At best, change will be incremental. Jim Crow crumbled in a decade, but differences in black-white life chances will unquestionably remain throughout the next few decades, and the ghettos are not likely to disappear in the near future.

Throughout American history, public policy has evolved slowly without seriously calling into question the ideas or values underlying the American political and economic system. The "Negro revolution"

---

[17] James Q. Wilson, "The Negro in Politics," in *The Negro American,* eds. Parsons and Clark, pp. 438–39.

is a misnomer. No truly revolutionary or radical solutions to inequality are likely to result. At best, blacks can expect marginal changes in public policy and the gradual rearrangement of national priorities. But while public policies evolve and national priorities are rearranged, the forces of the "melting pot" will be at work. Black leaders are compelled to denounce the melting pot philosophy: to do otherwise would be to invite inactivity and tokenism. But the forces of assimilation will be at work whether assimilation is denounced or not. Equality of *opportunity* has become a reality in many segments of American life. Individual blacks in increasing numbers and increasing percentages *can* achieve a decent, satisfying way of life. Inevitably they will do so in growing numbers, acquiring in the process middle class values and an interest in preserving American traditions as they have come to know them.

The elimination of legal segregation represented only the first step in an arduous odyssey for both blacks and whites in America. Justice and equality have always been elusive goals for mankind. There is no guarantee that America will attain these goals, no matter how hard Americans strive to do so. Relations between blacks and whites in American society has been the central domestic issue in American politics throughout the history of this nation, and so it is likely to remain for the foreseeable future.

Index